Derek Jarman — painter, theatre designer and film-maker — held his first one-man show at the Lisson Gallery in 1969. He designed sets and costumes for the theatre (JAZZ CALENDAR with Frederick Ashton at Covent Garden and DON GIOVANNI at the Coliseum). He was production designer for Ken Russell's films THE DEVILS and SAVAGE MESSIAH, during which time he worked on his own films in Super 8 before making his features: SEBASTIANE (1975), JUBILEE (1977), and THE TEMPEST (1979). Since 1980 he has returned to painting (a show at the ICA) and design (THE RAKE'S PROGRESS with Ken Russell in Florence), and has been working on scripts for a film about the life and times of Caravaggio. Other recent scripts have included NEUTRON, an hallucinatory futures film, and BOB UP A DOUN, a medieval film.

Dancing Ledge

Dancing Ledge

Derek Jarman

Edited by Shaun Allen

QUARTET BOOKS
LONDON MELBOURNE NEW YORK

First published by Quartet Books Limited 1984
A member of the Namara Group
27/29 Goodge Street London W1P 1FD

Copyright © 1984 by Derek Jarman

Designed by Namara Features Limited
Typeset by MC Typeset, Chatham, Kent
Printed and bound in Great Britain by Mackays of Chatham Ltd

British Library Cataloguing in Publication Data

Jarman, Derek
    Dancing ledge.
    1. Jarman, Derek   2. Moving-pictures——
    England——Production and direction——Biography
    I. Title
    791.43'0233'0924   PN1998   A3J/

    ISBN 0-7043-3461-5

TO THE BRITISH CINEMA

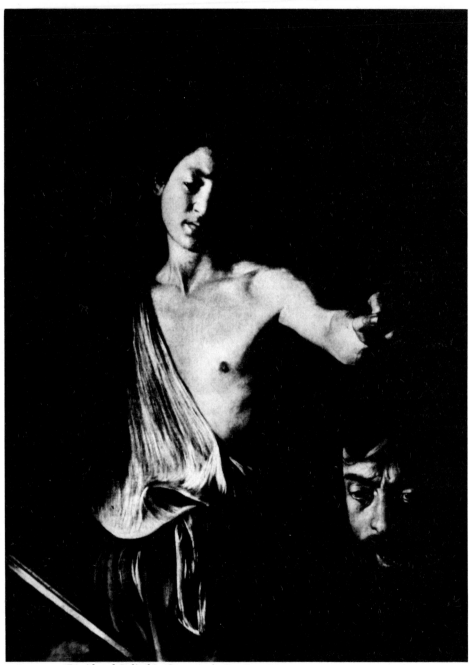

'David and Goliath' – Caravaggio (Borghese, Rome)

I
The Rough Cut

26 DECEMBER 1982. MONTEVERDE, TUSCANIA

All through Christmas, spent in this old farmhouse high on a windy hill in Tuscany, I have told myself I must begin recording the labyrinthine saga of the Caravaggio film – 1·30 and the family has left for a hunters' lunch with the *contadini*, who have been chasing wild boar all morning through the maize fields and woods along the banks of the Ombrone, which glitters below. The first sporadic bursts of gunfire were to be heard at sunrise, and upon coming down for breakfast I found the maid, Zara, in tears: her dog had just died. Shot, I thought, like the butcher last year, by some local cowboy. As she brushed back the tears she told me her 'darling' had had a heart attack at the ripe age of fourteen, over-excited by the traditional Saint Stephen's Day massacre.

Six days ago, when Nicholas Ward Jackson, producer of the Caravaggio film, and I left very early in the morning for Rome, we had hoped to have the contracts signed by the Italian co-producers before the turn of the year. . . Nothing that I've worked on has ever produced such problems as this life of Caravaggio. Everyone is excited by it and everyone is suspicious. Friends find two years of delays perplexing, the lack of funds annoying. Why lose yourself in the chiaroscuro? Films about painters end up pleasing nobody; there is a visionary tug-of-war from which neither artist nor film-maker emerges victorious.

MICHELE C. (PAINTER, 1572–1610)

Had Caravaggio been reincarnated in this century it would have been as a film-maker, Pasolini. It's impossible to have a conversation about the film in Rome without Pier Paolo's name being mentioned. Today Michele C. would toss his brushes into the Tiber and pick up Sony's latest video, as painting has degenerated into an obscure, hermetic practice, performed by initiates behind closed doors. There is a remarkable lack of emotional force in modern painting. Who could shed a tear for it now? But you *can* weep at Pasolini's *Gospel According to Matthew*, and *Ricotta* can make you laugh. In 1600, who knows, painting might have evoked the same immediate response. Of course Pasolini painted very badly.

─┼─

30 DECEMBER. THE 'STAR' OVER BEDLAM
A tabloid, the *Star*, has devoted its front page to an attack on Channel Four for its policy of buying certain 'gay' films, *Nighthawks* and *Sebastiane*, particularly the latter. 'It must not be shown on television.'

When he first met me last March, Jeremy Isaacs, the director of Channel Four, said that although they had bought my films they would probably never show *Sebastiane*. I was surprised when he said it would be too 'controversial'.

Nicholas has not rung from Rome and the article won't make the launching of *Caravaggio* any easier.

─┼─

31 DECEMBER
Today the *Telegraph* printed a statement from Channel Four denying that they intended to show either *Sebastiane* or *Nighthawks*. They explained that they had been bought as part of 'a package'. Times change. Last week they completed the show print for transmission.

─┼─

MARCH 1978. LONDON
I meet Nicholas Ward Jackson at a gallery opening in Covent Garden. He proposes a film on the life of Caravaggio and the next day sends all the available material on the painter's life.

─┼─

MAY 1978. PARIS
I travel to Rome to write the first screenplay of *Caravaggio*, stopping on the way at Cannes where *Jubilee* is opening as part of the Semaine de la Critique. I come down

with two actresses from that film, Jordan and Jenny Runacre. Jordan is at the height of her media fame as 'punk princess', with her ripped Venus T-shirt, Bunsen-burner hair and extrovert make-up. Educated at Miss Angela's 'academy de danse', Jordan has carved a meteoric career as a shop assistant at Sex, now Seditionaries, in the bend of the King's Road, and her style has launched a thousand hairdos. We stop in Paris and I take her to the Louvre to see Caravaggio's 'Death of the Virgin'. As she walks through the gloom of the great galleries whole parties of soporific tourists switch their attention from the Poussins and Rembrandts and illuminate her with a thousand flashbulbs. All this reaches its climax in a momentous confrontation with the 'Mona Lisa'. For the first time in her 470 or so years of existence the Mona is utterly upstaged; for a fleeting moment life triumphs over art. Then the walls open, guards rush out and bundle us into a secret lift; and we descend into a basement office where an embarrassed lady expels us from the gallery for 'disturbing the aesthetic environment'.

At Cannes Jordan was a star. From the moment we arrived on the Carlton Terrace she was besieged by the press. Within seconds of her arrival Miss Nude America, a sun-kissed Martini blonde, was deserted. Businessmen fell about while their starlet protégées sulked in the shadows. In the streets photographers ran backwards through the crowds. I followed discreetly a few steps behind, like a Muslim wife. The whole silly show, which we thoroughly enjoyed, ended at the Five Nation Televised Opening in the gilded casino with its glittering chandeliers and banks of carnations. With Louis Malle we were made the guests of honour, perched on little gilt music chairs, while an audience of punks invited by the TV company staged a riot. The fashion model presenter continued making her announcements, trying to hold back her tears as the Festival President was deluged by champagne, and the vases of carnations flew through the air. We watched the chaos on the video monitor as the cameramen and editors fought desperately to eliminate the unexpected riot from the screen. Within seconds the entire casino dissolved into anarchy, like the climax of René Claire's *A Nous la Liberté*, around the distraught announcer who sat at her table and forced a last tearful smile into the camera. Hefty electricians were chasing punks and shouting *'merde!'* Completely forgotten, Jordan, Jenny and I sat alone and sipped our champagne.

A couple of days later I took the train to Rome, having been shunned by the little clique of British journalists, accused of instigating the disturbances and letting down 'the side'. At the airport Jordan was refused admittance on to the plane until she'd changed. Someone lent her a shabby old mackintosh to cover up the Venus T-shirt.

Jordan with David Bowie at Cannes, 1978

Jean Marc Prouveur, self-portrait 1978

JUNE 1978. ROME

Jean Marc and I booked into a small hotel near the Spanish Steps where each morning for the next eight weeks I tried to unravel a narrative from the jumble of highly partisan and often antagonistic records we have of Caravaggio's life.

Not a victim like Orton or Pasolini but a murderer who happened to be an artist. Caravaggio painted some of the most powerfully religious images of the seventeenth century; and changed the way an entire generation *looked*. Notorious amongst his contemporaries as a dangerous and dangerous-looking young man, the violent trajectory of his life calls assumptions about an artist's relation to society into question . . . casual pickups painted as Saint John, dead prostitutes hauled from the Tiber hung as Virgins over the counter-reformation altars of Rome. Self-portraits of deepening disillusion: himself as Medusa, Saint Francis and Goliath, not merely to represent, but anticipate and instigate the life itself.

There he is as the pretty vain boy of the early genre paintings, painting himself in the mirror as Bacchus, toasting himself with wine, laughter and music; he points at a piece of paper with words written coyly 'you know that I love you', the beginning of the song. Shadows disturb the ambience of enjoyment – the winglike shadows, for instance, that rise behind the boy with a basket of fruit. There is the hungover Sick Bacchus; it is known that the young Caravaggio had suffered from a malarial illness. And the fruit in the still lives is always rotten – the first time it had been painted in that way.

In his late twenties came the first public commission, the Contarelli Chapel, when the task of painting became a struggle: he spent far more time than was thought necessary to produce these paintings of Saint Matthew; and this was used against him by his enemies in Rome to cast doubt on his ability to draw and paint. He always painted from life.

＋

'I, CARAVAGGIO DID THIS'

Through his patron the Medici Cardinal Del Monte he received his first major commission, the 'Martyrdom of Saint Matthew' in the Contarelli Chapel, in which a handsome assassin – he occupies the centre of the canvas – is cruised by the artist gazing guiltily over his shoulder; it is a self-portrait of one in his late twenties whose good looks have been prematurely destroyed. Meanwhile, the martyr lies abject, a cypher of holiness, at the feet of a murderer reminiscent of the triumphant Christ in Michelangelo's 'Last Judgement.'

Caravaggio, the theatrical hard boy, fades into the chiaroscuro, the light and dark of his schizoid vision – gambling in taverns, stones through windows, artichokes thrown at waiters, the endless petty sword fights. Finally he murders Ranuccio Thomasoni (his lover?) after a game of tennis then goes on the run. Safely in Malta, he signs a confession in the blood of John the Baptist, 'I, Caravaggio did this.' In one of the final paintings the hollow eyed severed head of Goliath which the young David holds in his hand is recognizably the artist's own. David is not pretty; he is a rough little number, one of those Roman street boys in whom, like Pasolini, C. continually sought 'perfection.'

+—

When I left Rome in July I had completed the first script which was based on a reading of the paintings rather than the biographies of Baglione or Mancini. The tale was a good one but the characters I had invented were dead on the page. I felt that a great deal more work had to be done. In any case, the sudden funding of *The Tempest* was to defer the project for another two years.

+—

BRIDESHEAD RECIDIVISTS

March 1981: I've started on the third *Caravaggio* script spurred by a meeting with Melvyn Bragg who was interested in the project for LWT. Nicholas thinks it should remain a feature and Melvyn agrees. It might be possible for LWT to make a film of us working when the project is financed. Looking back over the first scripts the narrative seems strong enough but the dialogue is dry and rather pretentious. The tale of Lena and Ranuccio, the prostitute and her pimp, both destroyed by their relationship with Caravaggio, the artist, is excellent and makes very exciting reading. But I dislike the brown varnish which seems to cover it. There is nothing more excruciating than English Historical Drama, the stuff that is so successful in America and is usually introduced by Alistair Cooke as Masterpiece Theatre; in which British stage actors are given free reign to display their artificial style in period settings (*Brideshead*). At all costs this film must avoid that. There are so few examples of films where 'period' is treated with imagination. The Swedish *My Sister, My Love* is one. In this rewrite I'm going to filter in my own life. My Italian childhood in Villa Quessa would make a perfect start, a few miles down the road from Caravaggio.

+—

'Martyrdom of Saint Matthew' – Caravaggio self-portrait
(Christopher Hobbs storyboard, 1981)

First birthday party, 1943

MAY 1946. LAGO MAGGIORE – 'DOLCE FA NIENTE'

Four years old: the sound of swallows, *itys itys itys*. I lie awake in a grand old mahogany bed, staring at the high ceiling of my bedroom, which glows pearl-white in the early morning sunlight. *Itys itys itys*. In the yard Davide, the handsome one, who rows across the lake and throws me high in the air and takes me hunting on the handlebars of his bike is whistling 'Dolce Fa Niente.' A swallow sweeps in through the window along a random sunbeam like a dark meteorite through galaxies of glowing dust clouds. *Itys itys itys*. For a second it becomes a crucifix, flattening itself against the wall, then falls away and out through a foaming tide of lace curtains. The hours pass. The clock in the yard chimes in six, then seven, then eight. Then Cecilia *'Zia di questo bel uomo'* bustles in with a long bamboo feather duster swearing incoherently at the swallows, the mess they've made building their nests. She lies in wait like an evil cat then *shoo shoo shoo* her feather duster waves through the air like a palm tree in a tornado. The swallows are gone, the spell is broken.

—⊦—

NEW YEAR 1971. VENICE

Karl. *More* beautiful than Botticelli's angels. Jet-black curls, grey-blue eyes, and a Texan slouch, he sits with me at the base of one of the columns in the candlelit interior of Saint Mark's. Listening to the hidden choir singing in the New Year with Handel's 'Messiah'. Outside it is raining. To our left at a side altar a little priest bobs up and down like a sleek tourist-fed pigeon. Suddenly he comes over. *'Cattolico? Protestante?'* Taken aback, I say *'Pagano!'* not knowing if this is Italian, but the message goes home. He darts back to the altar, crosses himself and prays for us.

Don Giovanni is the priest of San Servolo, the madhouse of Venice: an island surrounded by a prison wall, with large barred lunettes which open on the lagoon. After a lunch which is served by his maid, a lady who resembles Punch with dark frizzy hair, he asks me in French (the language in which we must communicate) if we would like to take a bath. As we both decline he is satisfied only when we agree to take a siesta in his bed, while he goes below to take a service. The singing of nuns drifts up. Karl is furious with me as we're both stuck here for the afternoon, till the boat returns. Later, Don Giovanni creeps in on tiptoe, hoping to find us entwined in one another's arms.

The madmen, he said, tend the garden between the asylum walls. They shuffle about under the huge funereal cypresses in their grey prison-like garb. We have to dodge them as he thinks the presence of strangers will upset them ; 'Last year one of the madmen picked every last rose on the island and trundled them in a

'Saint John' – **Caravaggio** *(Nelson Art Gallery, Atkins Museum, Kansas City)*.

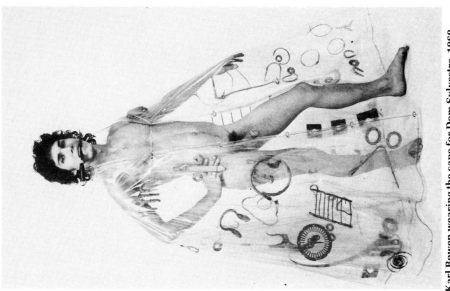

Karl Bowen wearing the cape for Dom Sylvestre, 1969
(Photo: Ray Dean)

wheelbarrow into the church while I was saying mass. He tipped them up right here in front of the altar as I was elevating the host.' Don Giovanni is scandalized; for him this is true madness.

✝

MAY 1982. ROME

We are here to look at costume-houses as there is a possibility *Caravaggio* might take off in the autumn. Yolanda Sonnabend, the designer of *The Tempest*, sits in her bedroom at the hotel surrounded by pills. She swallows so many it's no wonder she doesn't feel well. Everyone gives advice, homeopathic, macro-neurotic, antibiotic. Yolly listens to it all and dispatches Nicholas for more unlikely potions. This afternoon the jumble on her bedside table was so chaotic she took a swig from a bottle of black Indian ink!

✝

NEC SPEC NEC METU

Tom Priestley, who edited *Jubilee* and will be working on *Caravaggio* is providing a sounding-board for the fourth rewrite of the script. In the third version I introduced myself as a protagonist and onlooker, which although it has brought the piece to life has left a certain confusion. Now I'm writing myself out; and using a deathbed sequence which allows the film to progress as a series of flashbacks, cutting through the tedium of a straight A to B narrative. This is a similar to Prospero's sleep in *The Tempest*. After three years, the voices of the main characters and their relationships are much clearer. I find I know them now and can see them through the work in a much freer manner. Caravaggio, when he is sober, sees himself as Saint Francis, his lovers as Saint John the Baptist, Lena as Mary Magdalene or the Blessed Virgin. In the middle of this motley array Caravaggio's patron, the Cardinal Del Monte, is a mephistophelian figure with whom Caravaggio makes a pact when he receives his confiscated dagger, with its motto 'no hope, no fear', in return for a painting.

The one major loss in the new script is at the final moment when I stretch hands across the centuries with Mayakovsky's wonderful final poem – 'Love's boat has smashed against the daily grind now you and I are quits' – but perhaps that is now implicit in the script and doesn't need to be realized as a tangible image.

There are two areas which need attention. Caravaggio's deep religious conviction, which is so difficult to portray in a contemporary film, and the problem of time. At present the confusion between 'now' and 'then' has to be resolved. The script must avoid the baroque. Michele is the most austere classical painter of the Renaissance.

+—

PAH-LAH-REH EE-TAH-LEE-AH-NOH

July 1982. London: Each morning, I walk over to the language school where I'm doing an intensive course in Italian, one-to-one across a table, no English at all. At tea-time, back to Phoenix House where Julian has organized tea with a different actor or actress each day. Since I have no television, hardly ever go to the theatre, and I've asked Julian not to tell me who my guests are – he introduces them as Nigel, Bob, Julie – I am usually unaware, at least for a while, who they are. This worked well until Julie Covington, surprised I hadn't recognized her, rang Julian to say she was taken aback by the meeting. The blind approach does have its drawbacks. Jules and I altered our tactics.

+—

WINTER 1947. ROME

The winter was bitterly cold; it snowed in Rome. No fuel except for cooking. Admiral Ciano's flat, with its marble floors, was icy. The living-room, with its huge copy of Titian's 'Sacred and Profane Love', was unused. The only warm spot was the kitchen where Lena the Italian maid sat me beside her and spoke non-stop. In this way I picked up my first few words of Italian. When I was not in the kitchen, which had the added attraction of Nada Ziganovitch singing rousing Yugoslav partisan songs, I played in the Admiral's box-room: a treasure trove. There were two circular ostrich-feather fans with handles, sown with hummingbirds, a tinsel Christmas tree, and letters to the Admiral from Mussolini scattered across the floor. The flat in the Via Paisiello still exists, and I wonder who lives there now.

Then Rome was empty, closed to everyone except the military. There were very few cars, everyone travelled on bicycles. Limbless soldiers and maimed children begged in the streets and lived in the ruins on the Via Appia, a quiet little lane that wound into the countryside. At every turning there were priests like flocks of crows, scurrying busily about their work. My father called them Grubbies. When the Pope extended his hand for Dad to kiss it, Dad shook it firmly. We would tell this story and then show us the rosary he was given.

By the time we returned to England I was speaking Italian; but at a party my parents asked me to perform and I was so embarrassed I forgot it on the spot. I have never been able to pick up languages since that day.

+—

SEPTEMBER 1981

Caravaggio is shelved again. Winter is setting in and we need the light; although the film could be made in January, we would then have to rewrite Caravaggio's childhood, which takes place in sunlight.

+—

SEPTEMBER 1982

The violence of Caravaggio's paintings is echoed in the work of his contemporaries and followers which are on show at the Royal Academy's exhibition of Neapolitan painting. 'Judith and Holofernes' and 'The Beheading of John the Baptist' occur over and over again. The blood-soaked canvas by Artemisia Gentileschi has Judith revelling in the decapitation: a picture of such sexist violence you have the impression the blood should be dripping on the floor. Although not on show, Caravaggio's work on the same subject and also his 'Sacrifice of Isaac' portray a similar violence. He was obsessively interested in knives and swords. They occur all over his canvases and also in the police records which document his life in Rome. To carry arms legally one had to be a *gentiluomo*, which he became when he was dubbed a knight of Malta in 1606; but by then the habit of violence had led to Ranuccio's murder. 'The Beheading of Saint John', in which he'd signed himself in blood spilled on the floor, was painted in Malta, and hangs in the cathedral in Valetta: 'I, Caravaggio did this.'

+—

Before he fled from Rome he had painted Ranuccio Thomasoni as Saint John (the version in the Kansas City Museum) and carried it with him on the run. Saint John and his lover were synonymous; the iconography of the knife as an instrument of execution is unusual.

Now that I've embarked on the fifth rewrite of this script I have carefully traced the adventures of the knife. 'No hope, no fear' is engraved on its handle, and is given *back* to the young painter by Cardinal Del Monte in exchange for his art.

His first major commission was the violent Martyrdom of Saint Matthew; before that it was wine and roses. Then the violence escalated until the murder was committed. After 1606, when he was on the run, the paintings became more introspective. The violence of 'The Beheading of Saint John' is confessional; in 'David and Goliath' he notes his own destruction. In his last, and only recently discovered painting, 'The Martyrdom of Saint Ursula', there is resignation in death. The saint looks at the arrow which has pierced her without a trace of horror (we must bear in mind the taste, at this time, for dramatic explosions on canvas – a violent deed evoking a violent response). Less in anguish and more in reverie, Ursula is oblivious to her executioners. The arrow is an object of contemplation.

꜡—

To Caravaggio's sexuality there are two references. One to the girl Lena, his girl, in the police records, and the second to his involvement with some schoolboys in Sicily which led to his leaving town rather quickly. Neither is in any way conclusive; so the evidence is to be sought in the paintings. This, as all the work was painted from life, is much easier than might be imagined. With so little documentation on such a taboo subject it's difficult to know how the seventeenth century understood physical homosexuality. How it was viewed obviously depended, as now, on who you were. It was certainly associated with heresy, and was an ingredient of many contemporary witch trials and public burnings – hence the expression 'faggot'.

In the cities, people must have identified in underground groups; leading to rumours of covens, celebrating 'wild' sexual acts. The laws of the Church certainly forbade what it called 'sodomy', and Saint Ambrose linked it with usury as a social sin '*contra naturam*'; in Dante's *Purgatory* the sodomites occupied the same circle as the usurers. The term 'homosexual' which identifies and ostracizes a group because of their desires and inclinations, is a nineteenth-century clinical invention, *c.* 1860.

I suspect that Southern peasant society remained relatively oblivious to the strictures of urban moralists. As late as the latter part of the nineteenth century the Baron von Gloeden's orgies with the boys of Taormina caused no comment.

The revival of the male nude ensured that the civilization of the early Renaissance in Italy was dominated by male images, images of homosexual passion, of varying degrees of refinement. The ideological savagery of the seventeenth century marked the loss of this refinement; and the Church eventually managed to assimilate these trends and turn the sinners into saints. Caravaggio's life illustrates this dramatically.

He identified himself personally with the heathen gods of the Renaissance. For Michelangelo a century earlier, Bacchus was sculpted as an ideal youth, but when Caravaggio raised the wine to his lips as Bacchus it was not as a courtly ideal but as himself. Later, he painted the god with a hangover, 'The Jaundiced Bacchino Malato'.

Caravaggio breathed his life, himself, into old ideals. Bacchus was the androgyne god and this was a reflection of the painter's sexuality. At first Caravaggio was probably bisexual, at eighteen or nineteen growing up with the conventions that surrounded him. Later you hack them away, but the strictures of Church and society leave a cancer, a lingering doubt, which leads to dis-ease in this painter, and to the extraordinary force of his work as he attempted to overcome it. He brought the lofty ideals down to earth, and became the most homosexual of painters, in the way that Pasolini is the most homosexual of film-makers. In a hostile environment this extreme of self-analysis became self-destruction. It's worth noting how many 'gay' artists die young: Murnau, Pasolini, Eisenstein, Fassbinder, Marlowe, Orton, and Caravaggio . . . From the moment he grew up and identified himself with the murderer in 'Saint Matthew' – the murderer imaged as god – he unconsciously took on the Church as his true and deadly enemy – after all, its authority, its over-selective reading of its holy texts, had led to the outlawing of the centre of his life.

Michele gazes wistfully at the hero slaying the saint. It is a look no one can understand unless he has stood till 5 a.m. in a gay bar hoping to be fucked by that hero. The gaze of the passive homosexual at the object of his desire, he waits to be chosen, he cannot make the choice. Later his head will be cut off by a less godlike version of the young assassin; his name is now David and all the weight of society is behind him and he can cut off the head without a trace of pity.

PASSION AND CRUCI-FICTION

At first the painter is unaware. All the boys together chant the latest song, 'You Know that I Love You', and share his bacchic orgies. The boys are beautiful, healthy and young; the worst they can do is play at being Medusa and frighten nobody. Then comes the pent-up violence, and the destruction of his looks with the wine, over-indulgence and success. He hasn't identified the enemy: it's his landlady, some boys in a restaurant. He bolsters up his insecurity with hostility and he numbs the

'The Sick Bacchus' – Caravaggio *(Borghese, Rome)*

La Ricotta, 1962, **Pasolini** *(BFI Archive)*

hurt with *wine*. He paints his lovers as Saint John, the wild one in the wilderness, who will be destroyed by a capricious woman. When he's not gazing at these heroes he paints himself as Saint Francis, contemplating death. He paints with a knife: painting is a revenge; on the knife is written, 'No hope, no fear'. He hacks his way through altar pieces, Isaac and Holofernes, crucifixion, wounds, flagellations. It culminates one morning in the real murder of Ranuccio.

'For each man kills the thing he loves'; following that, shadows envelop his work; but after the confession of 'Saint John' at the end there is complete awareness of self. Even if his head has been cut off, he can contemplate the wound and venerate the arrow in the Saint Ursula. The battle is inevitably lost, but the understanding is gained. He is the most self-conscious of artists, a man who understands the Passion, the most powerful religious painter of the Renaissance.

＋—

SEPTEMBER 1982

I have made a final decision to update the costuming and settings of the film. It has to take place in the present. The paintings will not be seen as an anachronism but in their true perspective. I'm certain they will survive in the hurly burly of the modern world – only by making Caravaggio a contemporary will we see how revolutionary a painter he was. He was the first Italian painter to depict street people on religious canvases. This will be lost if Lena is dressed as a seventeenth century whore – she will seem a sort of romantic gypsy dancer. Only if she is presented sitting by the side of the Via Appia in a white fur coat can it work. Then, when she's painted as a virgin, the sheer bravado of Caravaggio will be appreciated. His life is also very 'contemporary'; he has the self-inflation that has driven many contemporary idols to destruction. His excesses create similar 'scandals' to those of Jim Morrison or Janis Joplin. When he is not hurling insults and writing scandalous poems about his contemporaries, he is uncommunicative and surly. But the film will not be a modernization – the structures of ideology and power will remain emphatically those of Caravaggio's lifetime: in matters temporal and spiritual the Pope shall be supreme. This should give the spectator quite a jolt. The streets of Rome will be ridden with violence as they were in the beginning of the seventeenth century. Not the Red Brigades, but religious factions. The Spanish against the French parties. Suddenly the Swiss guard are in combat gear, and the bankers scheme over Vatican contracts and buy Caravaggio's paintings to hang over the altars of Rome. On them are the publicans and sinners whom Christ preferred to the priests and moneychangers. This should allow us to make a genuine exploration of this painter and his impact on the culture. The film will dig and excavate and make no attempt to hold the mirror up to reality. When Caravaggio paints the reflection of Narcissus it is no true reflection but a comment on all vanity and our film should treat his life in a similar way, penetrate the surface.

This film should be called 'The Murderer who Held the Keys of Heaven'. Nicholas has just phoned from Rome and told me he's away in ten days to meet with Suso d'Amico, who also sent me a letter in a very small hand saying how much she'd enjoyed *The Tempest*. I'm writing back this afternoon and I'm certain that I'll be able to construct a fuller script, something nearer the vision of our extraordinary painter. She will also give me enormous help if we encounter any of those producer problems of the kind that warp your vision for a quick buck!

At Tony Rayns' farewell dinner last night Carole Myer, distributor of *The Draughtsman's Contract*, asked me why I thought the film had been so successful. I said I'm certain it's part of the reaction we find around us – unlike the films that Ron Peck, Chris Petit or I make, it has no shadows, in spite of the murder at the end. It has more than enough elements to appeal to British snobbism – aristocrats, a country house, a pretentious, stagey script, and named actors. It's the upstairs without the downstairs of independent films. . . . On the whole I liked the film; it was over-designed but nicely shot. I didn't care for the acting but this was compensated by the countryside which has all the swirling clouds and sunlight of a beautiful 'English' day. I mentioned that I thought the drawings were atrocious. They certainly were not seventeenth-century and were pretty abysmal art-school stuff. Carole said that they were meant to be like that, which left me decidedly undecided about the whole thing . . .

27 JANUARY 1983

Nicholas is still stuck in Rome with endless discussions with the lawyers during the day and dull evenings at the Collona Palace. I rang him late this afternoon after a sudden decision to rewrite the film in period or an approximation of period. Quite counter to all my last ideas – it's a pingpong game I'm playing to keep the project alive. The decision to update was grounded on the old obsession to modernize texts. It was Russell's idea to update the production of Stravinsky's *The Rake's Progress* that I designed for him in Florence, not mine, and when I returned to London and rewrote Caravaggio, flushed with the opera's success, it naturally spilled over into the new script. A year later, I feel that the modernization would become the *cause célèbre* of the film at the expense of content and would destroy its subtler shades. In period perhaps a gentler, less brash effect and greater depth would result.

✢

4 FEBRUARY 1983

Nicholas rang from Rome last night and managed to string everything on yet again with his open-minded genius. He swore he'd serve writs on the producers through his lawyer Forsyte Kerman if they thought of producing my script of *Bob-up-a-down*, which the British Film Institute might finance, which he added was hardly a film script at all, using Suso Cecchi d'Amico's comment that it was great but only good for sixty minutes. Then he flew into a tantrum about the suburban English film world; and when I said that was all right but I was down to my last suburban £ while the millionaires played with themselves in Italy, he snapped, 'Why don't you get a job on the roads? You're so tiresome, it would do you good.' Ron Peck sat on the chair laughing at this transcontinental battle. Nicholas pronounced that he'd put the Italian investor Dr Giacomo on the line but it's a line that at this end seems to curve like a figure of eight into infinity. Christopher and I talk of the problem for the umpteenth time. *Screen International* announces the film and Carole Myer says she knows of no other British film that has so much pre-publicity, and that perhaps they should all go through this refined torture.

✢

A ROCK AND ROLL SWINDLE

John said, 'It's a bit lopsided, isn't it?' (he asked me if I'd received any money when the *Rock and Roll Swindle* and *Jubilee* played together last Saturday). Alasdair laughed: 'Oh! Oh! The naïve. You've obviously never heard of Publicity' – only insults, I said. Someone got up and left saying, 'Middle-class rubbish' – they couldn't sing along with it and the *Swindle* is much more fun. *Jubilee*'s no 'fun' at all. Did you know that the black and white footage of Paul picking his nose in the *Swindle* is mine, I said. That's the best bit. I filmed it at Andrew's one afternoon when no one else had heard of them. Jordan came down to the studio and said the band's upstairs, come and film us. I had some grainy black and white 4X and dutifully recorded it. During the filming, Christopher came over and yelled, 'My God they're certainly going nowhere.' Paul was stuck at the drums so he couldn't avoid the evil lens, Johnny turned his back on us. Jordan and Vivienne aggravated the audience. I had to hang on to the camera for dear life. Later I gave the Pistols the footage and forgot about it. Lopsided, said John. Oh I got paid for that. That piece of Super 8 made me more than *Sebastiane*. The receivers paid my tax bill of £700 in exchange for my signing the release. Not a bad exchange at all. And the other films? NOTHING. I was told I should be happy with the publicity which apparently cost a fortune.

+—

Nicholas rang commanding me over to Rome with a peremptory NOW having promised forty-eight hours earlier that I was free to take my time. The film is starting off in the worst possible way. He's locked both of us into an iron lung, and the dear Doctor's made certain there's no oxygen till we've won the prize. The film should of course be the film about the film, but those films close even quicker and make less than films about painters. Gaudier-Brzeska lasted two weeks at the height of Ken Russell's notoriety. Michele Caravaggio has to beat that! By the time this film is made, film itself will be out of date. But anyway, who cares? I've seen enough to convince me that film is a very tacky medium. That brushes off on the people who work on it. Even the nice ones are monsters after a few years. Once you believe that there's nothing to lose, that they've lost it for you before you've started, you're OK.

The weather is awful here. Freezing. There's six feet of snow in Rome, said James. Everyone laughs, I hate it there. The hotel is a complete prison.

+—

Mog Johnson, who was taping an interview, said this morning that both Michael Ginsborg and Keith Milow, two painter-friends from the sixties, had been suspicious of my painting – that if it wasn't working I gave up the struggle and tore it up. They thought that unless you showed yourself thrashing all around all over the canvas looking for the right note, you weren't working. For me then the line of least resistance was the line of wisdom. Maybe life has come full circle and I'd agree with them now. Life's more fun when you don't know what the hell you're doing.

10 JANUARY 1983

5.30: the phone rings and I wake with a start and by 8.30 I'm on the plane to Rome. Nicholas looks fitter and has lost weight. At 4 p.m. I catch the bus to Via Paisello to meet Suso Cecchi D'Amico, who was Visconti's and Rosellini's collaborator and scriptwriter, who lives just across the road from the flat we had in 1947 when my father was posted here after the war. On the bus I remember that it is almost four years to the day since we started filming *The Tempest*. Suso meets me at the door wrapped up against the cold. She calls herself a *'pollo freddo'*. We sit in a large living-room. She looks at me quizzically, her face a thousand smiling wrinkles, and speaks rapidly in Italian with a deep bass. You've written a script without characters. Caravaggio has to be more forceful, the script more violent and should concentrate on the murder of Rannuccio. I'm tongue-tied. I can't bring myself to defend what has been written so long ago. I'm certain she must think I'm quite spineless. She asks me which part of the script means anything to me. Nothing, I hear myself say. I don't need to keep anything. The problem is that I've written a self-portrait filtered through the Caravaggio story, which is of course not in any way Caravaggio's life. Perhaps all that should be saved is a certain perception about the content of the paintings, particularly the 'Martyrdom', the 'Profane Love', and the 'Goliath', which provide a key to Michele's character. At one moment I want to save it, enrich it; at another, destroy the whole thing and start again. I'm so bored with it all. I've made this film several times already in my mind.

By the end of the afternoon conversation switches to English – this helps: my ears are attuned to taxi-drivers, not exquisite Tuscan. On the way out my pen falls from my pocket and hits the pavement, smashing the nib. I'm very upset. Maybe this is some awful premonition. Suso is by turns interested and gloomy about the project. I found it very difficult to counter her pessimism. I'm certain I did the best thing by sharing it. At the end we talked briefly about Visconti. I said he looked sad in his pictures, had sad eyes. Not at all, he was very violent, she replied.

+—

ARTISTS STEAL THE WORLD IN ORDER TO RE-PRESENT IT AS ART

One of the chief topics of conversation with Suso yesterday was the idea of art as a form of theft, artists being involved in the theft of the everyday creativity which the entire world should share. Theft in the story of Apollo's lyre – and also murder . . .

APRIL 1964. ROME

Ron and I spent the morning hunting through the market at Porta Portese and I bought two candlesticks in gilded wood. These I had to carry with me for the rest of the day (which we spent sightseeing) much to the amusement of passers-by. In one church we entered there was a side altar which was ablaze with huge candles in candlesticks which were like mine. Ron said, you need a candle – you keep a look-out and I'll take one of them – and before I could stop him he's shinned up the altar and bagged a candle, stuffing it up his jacket sleeve as quick as lightning. We were off and out of the church in a trice. We had gone only about 100 yards when a police car screamed to a halt and a couple of plain-clothes men jumped out and grabbed me, seizing my candlesticks. Both of us were bundled into the car and taken back to the church. Out of the corner of my eye I could see the candle protruding from Ron's jacket – so to distract attention I waved my arms about and protested loudly my innocence. All eyes were on me. In the sacristy the priests who were waiting for us looked at my candlesticks and apologized for their mistake. They had never missed the candle. I could tell they still felt that something was amiss, so as they apologized I backed out covering Ron as much as possible and when we were on the street again we walked rapidly away. Hitch-hiking back to London the candlesticks got us many a lift and for years after the candle burnt in them.

+—

11 FEBRUARY 1983. ROME

The morning started with two thunderclaps and peels of bells, after the sound of heavy rain which was slowly drowned by the noise of the traffic horns. I get up much later and open the window, Nicholas rolls over with a snort. It's about 11 a.m. – so much for bright and early. It's raining, I said. It's been raining like this every day for the last month. Thank God we didn't start the film at this time. No one suggested it, said Nicholas. Dear Nicholas, this film has been started every month for the last two years. Perhaps we should declare a new calendar like Robespierre, and rearrange it to suit ourselves.

+—

I arrived a little early for my meeting with Suso so I walked along the Via Paisello to see if I remembered anything from my childhood. The building has to be No. 47, a thirties' building with large balconies. Across the road was a mimosa tree in full bloom, a cloud of yellow set off against an ochre palazzo.

We drove to Cinecittà and watched a film made for RAI on the life of the Saint Filippo Neri – which as it is in our period exhibits all the problems we will face. There were a thousand DON'Ts and hardly any DOs. I have seen only a handful of historical films that have worked and all these have reinvented period. This film made no attempt to do that. So, a few points:

1.   Design the film so you don't need a set dresser. Props and furniture look disastrous enough but nothing is more awful than the artfully dressed street. The hay waggon standing in a vacuum, or the business one knows can't run. The baker's built into the corner of a church or blacksmith's with a calor gas fire.

2.   I noticed bananas in one of those still lives of fruit which are used in nearly every historical film to denote plenty and fill up a blank space. This was particularly disastrous in a film which made a great point about the introduction of a turkey from Brazil.

3.   Extras pose their own problems. This film was littered with undirected people going about their daily business absent-mindedly. They would stand still for minutes at a time and then suddenly spring into life.

4.   Costumes are also a great problem. Because they never look as if they are worn. The costumes of the poor always look phoney. In this film they were designed like a uniform of rags which was in a style that bore no resemblance to the late sixteenth century. Very often the poorest clothing is made from the most expensive modern rough weaves, lurex is particularly disastrous and rich costumes turn up in hideous modern colours.

5.   All the ragged children were in perfect health and their eyes sparkled – nowhere was that dull glare of starvation to be found.

On the way back we talked of *The Tempest*, how the exterior scenes just don't have the strength of the interiors. This was partly because time and weather did not permit, but Suso had a point. Caravaggio shared this problem with me. We're both nocturnal back-room boys. He avoided landscape as well.

+

17 February 1983
My script meetings with Suso begin at about 4 and last until about 7 p.m. She sits up straight on a high-backed chair and complains about her eyes, putting on her spectacles with slow deliberation, then we begin. She dissects my Caravaggio script

and deftly turns it on its head: 'Derek, you like Marino?'

'Not particularly, it's confusing to have two artists in a film.'

'He go.'

'Derek, you chose "Saint Matthew", why?' It's the key to Caravaggio's character and one of my favourite pictures. 'Nobody understands thees picture' – 'Entombment, thees is right, we begin. We end him.' The maid brings in the tea and Suso pours a saucer for her large white hunting dog. 'Thees dog is jealous, he love me.' The dog laps up his tea and then, pushing his snout between Suso's legs, tries to fuck her. She pays no attention to him as he pants and puffs. She cuddles him without the slightest embarrassment. 'He theenk he is a man.' We carry on. 'We build a house very strong. After we furnish. Then the film will be small masterpiece.' Every now and then she digresses. She tells me of the uneasy relationship between Visconti and Zeffirelli and the disastrous Zeffirelli *Othello* with Gielgud. 'The moment he appear he try to leave. He put his hands on set of Franco and the black come off all over it. Lucino he smile like thees,' and she puts her hands to her high cheek bones, pushing her face into a wicked Florentine grin. After four days the script is transformed from the shambling poetical original with its private connections to a triangular love affair, Roman in its complexity. Into this is woven nearly all the best imagery of the old script, bridged by the 'Entombment' which now starts and ends the film.

+-

SUMMER 1971. PORTO ERCOLE
(The Beach on Which Caravaggio Died)

The beach at Porto Ercole stretches in a wide arc towards the distant mainland which disappears in the shimmering heat haze. I walked at the sea's edge, skirting the foam on the drowsy July waves, and after fifteen minutes or so, started to leave the tourists behind. Half an hour and a good two miles further the beach was deserted – the only object a rowing-boat at the water's edge in the distance. I decided to make it the full stop of my walk. When I drew closer I saw a young man lying in its shadow and as I passed his eyes met mine and sleepily followed me up to the dunes at the top of the beach, where I sat down and gazed into the sun, aware all the time that I was under observation. Far in the distance the family was unwrapping its picnic lunch, no doubt wondering where on earth I'd gone. I decided to leave them at it, and out of the sun-narrowed slits of my eyes watched my fisherboy. After a few minutes of this cat-and-mouse game, he got up and without averting his eyes for a second, walked up the beach and sat down with cool deliberation on the dunes a few yards from me. I smiled. My smile was returned. I got up and walked over to him. He looked up at me, suddenly shy. I sat down next to him and said, 'Hello.' He spoke no English and I, with my few words of Italian, attempted a formal introduction which I knew was useless. Then I put my hand very slowly through his dark hair. He smiled again and without touching me stretched out on the sand and slipped his bathing-trunks off with one movement. After we had made love, we lay together under the sun for an hour, our salty bodies burning in the sand. Then I kissed him and said goodbye for ever and walked slowly back through the frisbees and Ambre Solaire, castles and buckets and spades to find the family. They had almost finished lunch.

'Wherever have you been, Derek?'

'I went for a long walk, almost to the mainland and lost you in the crowds on the way back.'

✛

Later that day – Terme di Saturnia: We were sitting in the beach bar this evening when Tony Fry suddenly suggested a trip to the hot springs at Saturnia on the mainland; so, slightly drunk, we piled into two cars and took off into the hills. After an hour's drive we arrived at midnight at the springs which cascade down a wooded hillside past a massive stone-built millhouse at the water's edge, with the old millstones scattered around like loose change. In the cold night air, in the moonlit valley, steam drifted off the warm water – giving the place a most romantic air, a landscape from Claude, 'The Enchanted Castle', and ourselves, a group of revellers from another age. In the darkness the damp ground was icy underfoot but the springs were the temperature of a hot bath, cascading over smooth worn rocks. I stood under a waterfall bracing myself against the rockface to stop myself being swept away. The water roared in my ears washing the centuries away, till one was back in the golden age, naked under the huge summer moon. The swirling waters swept away all the cares of the world while the dark wrapped a soft blanket round me. The sulphur dried on my skin which glittered like precious rock and set hard in my hair. Later, back home in Porto Ercole, I slipped into a delicious sleep. The waters of Saturnia washed through my life and carried it in whirlpools and eddies into a sea of still dreams.

✛

MONDAY 7 MARCH 1983

I woke up and felt a gauze separated me from life. The whole day washed grey, flapping listlessly. *Caravaggio* weighs like lead. Julian arrives. I make tea. I say that I took two looks at Responsibility, the world of 'grown-ups', and decided I'd have none of it. The infantilism that so upsets Nicholas – 'You meet a heavyweight like Suso and collapse.' Underneath, the ground is no longer firm. We're on the defensive. Britain is a poisoned little stream. The dark satanic mills fold their sails but who walks in a green and pleasant land? Just the ruined factories and unending dreary housing developments with missiles hanging over them, Damocles style.

GROUND ZERO

My dreams are disturbed by ghastly luminous cathedrals that glow with a slight flickering of coals, the scarlet angels sinking into ash drift and ebb away over the darkening landscape.

+–

COMPLETING THE C. SCRIPT

26 March 1983: I completed the script this afternoon and with a rush of relief took off for Heaven. I had walked around the club a couple of times before I spotted James in his studded leathers and working cap sitting in a corner. As I walked over, a young man in a grey sweater and khaki army trousers smiled. He was stocky with a shock of blond hair – I cuffed him on the shoulder as I passed, chatted with James for a few minutes then walked back and sat down beside him as decisively as possible, and waited for a conversation to develop. I fancy both you and your friend, he said, but since you're here – we spent some time from our vantage-point on the staging spotting likely lads. One we called Alexander after the emperor – he looked Greek, I suppose – no, the technique he said. He had a very fine neck. What was your name? Mine's Derek. I told you I was from Finland – it should be quite obvious – Tom. He smiled; made no reply. Tom said he liked necks, they were the link between mind and body. Sight is situated just behind your ears; if you think of that it gives things perspective. He bought me a drink and refused to allow me to buy one in return. 'What do you do?'

    'Paint.'

    'Oh I hope it's ceilings.'

    'That as well,' I said.

    'Artists are prostitutes,' he said.

    For a moment I thought that was a leading reply. I asked what he did –

no, he wasn't a prostitute – Compostion, he said, which left me wondering. Where do you live – Hackney – Charing X. We walked downstairs to meet James and then he suddenly said let's go. I was in two minds but said OK, yes. I'm not walking – he said – we'll get a taxi. The first one refused us – 'Look it's just round the corner! I'm going East.' The second one took us with slight disbelief. He pointed out the dossers' cinema and the cafe across the road – he obviously knew the area. Who was this 'Tom of Finland' I was taking home? At home he glanced at the books, declared Thomas Mann was 'for kids', pulling out *The Holy Sinner*. He pulled out *The Art of Memory* and said he spoke four languages. After some guesses, Spanish and German – I never got the last one – I suggested Greek. He laughed and said Ancient Greek. Then back to *The Art of Memory*: I was explaining how Yates deduced the seven tiers of the *Inferno* were based on the ancient memory system, which directly visualized abstract ideas as buildings and statues. And what's Nijinsky's Diary like? I made a joint and some tea and we carried on talking.

Caravaggio – well, if it's a matter of murder where's the Gesualdo? I found a tape of Moro Lasso and he complained of the women's voices on the recording. I undressed him and climbed into the freezing bed with my clothes. It's freezing, said Tom. A blackthorn winter. He was a master of accents; earlier he had asked around for a light in perfect Somerset. He had a firm, well-muscled body with broad shoulders. Trace of a love-bite on his neck. He asked me if I ever got anything together in bed – sometimes. I undressed and held him close, he seemed to sob a little. Surely you brought me back for only one thing. We fucked – no amyl but baby oil's OK.

Thank God that's over he said and we laughed. But he carried on talking half to himself, half to me. I slept fitfully and dreamed that I was sold four fake tickets at an Underground station. Eventually travelling into London from the South along an arterial dirt-track on the top of a bus. Red brick houses and Victorian town halls; at one stop I saw the Swedish tenor Gosta Winberg.

We woke early and he said he must be going. I put on Rossini's *An Italian Girl in Algiers*; 'What music do you play first thing in the morning?' He'd asked the night before. Opera arrests time, a minute becomes an hour. Rossini must have been very confident to allow himself so many repeats. Self-satisfied, he said. Strange to think this music was written twenty years or more after the Revolution, after Europe had gone metric. He was out of date, they all complained; but we've lost the ability to repeat. We exchanged phone numbers – is this a formality?

+–

28 MARCH 1983

The script for *Caravaggio* is typed up. Francesca and I celebrated at the dance gala for the Riverside at Sadler's Wells last night; and this morning I took it to Jill at Scripts. We talked about it for a few minutes; then I breakfasted at Valerie's. The sun shone all morning and I felt elated as I can get on with other work again. And try to clear my debts, which after a year of no income threaten to swamp me. The struggle with Caravaggio is resolved – all the personal elements still in it, and the work is structured around the paintings, which form a firm armature. But I also have characters and a narrative which is clear and straightforward as well. If this film can be realized, the right actors and locations found, it could be very beautiful and very unusual.

+—

1970. AMSTERDAM

A sailor boy with an earring danced through the crowd on the floor of the DOK, chained to the sea by a loop of gold – a gold tooth in his smile and a blue tattoo on a pale shoulder. At the jeweller's the next morning, I asked nervously where I could get my ears pierced – sit right there – said the old man and before I could change my mind it was done. He said he'd not pierced a man's ear since the twenties when many of the Dutch sailors wore gold earrings. At home in Northwood there was a moment of shock – what would the neighbours think? But since I knew that my parents couldn't care less what the neighbours thought I took this as a ploy.

> On the top of Vesuvius the man who cooked the eggs in the volcanic stream stared up and called his mates – Zingaro? Zingaro?

+—

APRIL 1983

I've always preferred the painters of the North to those of the Italian Renaissance. The latter has an artificiality – is an exotic graft on stronger roots – *quattrocento* saints look like fashion plates from *L'Uomo Vogue*; everyone seems in an indecent hurry to strip off his clothes and swagger around self-confidently in the neoplatonic sauna.

> Now it's over, and our millennialist century has revived the crusaders and flagellants – embalmed its saints – and turned its back on the Enlightenment and overthrown reason. We are closer to Bruegel than Titian; the former's brooding, stormy skies and studies of work and play should have been the seed corn of social realism.

For two years now the *Caravaggio* project has held me a prisoner. I've played the willing host as it has slowly sapped all will to action. For the last few months I've known I must shake it off as it's proving spiritually and economically debilitating. In the last year it has swamped the present with the past and has led me inexorably backwards to painting and designing. Last week I completed the rewrite which has taken the project as far as I'm capable – if this is not funded then the film will never go forward.

+—

II
Painting It Out

A SHORT FAMILY MYTHOLOGY
Great-Uncle Tommy, who worked with my grandfather in India, had a secretary called Merle Oberon. When she later became a film star she never failed to invite him to her premieres, until one day he unwittingly mentioned their shared past.

At seventeen my mother, Elizabeth, went to the Viceroy's ball. The Vicereine of India had an obsession with imperial purple. The tablecloths and every detail down to the purple sweet-wrappers reflected this megalomaniac vision.

In the early twenties there was a slump in rubber consumption which followed the boom in the Great War; the slump devastated the plantations in Malaya. George V announced an Imperial Rubber Drive and my great-Aunt Doris, who made a bouquet of pink rubber roses scented with the most expensive perfume from Paris, became the symbol of the campaign when she presented them to Queen Mary.

Then Mimosa, my grandmother, and Doris fell out over the following affair: one Christmas Eve Doris decided to go to dinner at the Dorchester with her two teenage sons Harreton and Ian. The Dorchester told her that at such short notice a table was impossible. Maybe she'd like to come next year. Doris, who was a determined lady, was undeterred. She told Harreton to ring up saying he was the secretary of the Maharanee of Jaipur and HRH would like a table for three. A table was immediately organized and Doris, donning a sari, arrived with both her sons blacked up. My grandfather was scandalized when he read this in the gossip columns, and a family rift was born.

Later, when the first Sputnik was launched, Doris was in the papers again. Now in her eighties, she congratulated the Russians and presented herself at the Embassy as a possible first woman in space. She was quoted as saying that she'd had a good life and at her age she wasn't too worried if they didn't resolve the problem of re-entry. As a footnote the article said she was the first woman who played polo in India, side-saddle.

Both my mother and my father, Lance, had an artistic bent. Dad's father, Hedley, was the first violin and a founder member of the first symphony orchestra in Christchurch, New Zealand. Father played the piano and sculpted beautiful Deco candlesticks for Syrie Maugham in Duralamum. My father often flew up to Syrie's house for weekends. When, at the opening of *Jubilee*, he met Jordan, he said, 'You young things might think you're daring, but I remember Vivienne Leigh wearing a leopard-skin bikini at Syrie's before the war.'

My mother went to Harrow Art School against her parents' wishes and afterwards Norman Hartnell employed her with four other girls as a personal assistant. She helped get the clothes ready for the royal tour of Paris and would talk to the customers while they waited – the most important job being to keep Bebe Daniels from meeting Jessie Matthews as they'd swapped husbands or something of that ilk. She left this job as an excellent designer of clothes, and went on to make all her own clothes from the *Vogue* patterns for the rest of her life.

My parents met at a dance at Northholt airfield and were married at Holy Trinity, Northwood, on 31 March 1940. Their marriage photo, taken under a daffodil bell hanging from the lychgate, was published in nearly every national newspaper. They were a most glamorous couple. My father in his RAF uniform, my mother, her veil caught by the wind, holding some lily of the valley. The photo is full of joy and spring sunlight – a photo of hope at this dark moment. Many years later my mother said, looking at it, 'It's a pity neither you nor your sister inherited our good looks.'

✠

OTHER PEOPLE'S MYTHOLOGIES

When he was six Anthony Harwood decided to test a theory that he had heard at school. Seizing the family's white Persian cat, Alex, he climbed gingerly to the top of the house and threw him out of the highest attic window. Then he rushed downstairs to retrieve the shaken and angry tom. Before it could escape his clutches Anthony had whisked it away, breathless with excitement and fear that he might be caught; he hurled himself back upstairs before hurling Alex through the window a second time. This time he crept downstairs feeling slightly guilty, but he needn't have as Alex was sitting on the lawn, still alive and kicking and very angry. Employing all the arts of cat-seduction, Anthony managed to grab him again and up and away they went and Alex flew through the window a third time. On the way down again Anthony collided with his mother on the stairs who asked him what on

The Wizard of Oz, 1939, Victor Fleming *(BFI Archive)*

Anthony Harwood, 1967 *(Photo: Ray Dean)*

earth he was doing. 'An experiment,' was the reply – 'I'm testing Alex for his nine lives.'

✛

THE WIZARD OF OZ

Rome 1947: a matinée for Forces' children. I think my parents had difficulty in getting me out of the flat since I'd never been to the movies before, and the lettuce for my tortoise's lunch seemed more important. I can't remember anything about the cinema itself but the film that I was about to see was to fill my childhood with dreams and nightmares, with witches and wizards and the emerald city itself. The lights were dimmed and we were transported to Kansas. It started happily enough with Dorothy singing 'Somewhere Over the Rainbow'. She was magical and I wished the other kids in the cinema – my schoolfriends – could have sung like her. But then it began to go wrong. A terrible storm blew up. I hung on to my seat, desperately, as the menacing dust devil bore down on us. No one else in the cinema seemed to be taking the danger seriously, and then, pure horror, we were blown into the sky. I ducked under my seat with a terrified wail to emerge wide-eyed a few moments later in Munchkin land with my mother trying to stem the floods of tears. The Munchkins calmed me down and all went well till Dorothy, Tinman, Lion and Scarecrow were set upon by the wicked witch and her creepy-crawly minions. This time I bolted and was captured by the usherette and handed back along the row to my embarrassed parents. I took part in the rest of *The Wizard of Oz*, rather than merely watched it, and am grateful to this day that it had a happy ending.

Since that day I have always loved the film, a love tinged with a little apprehension of the power of movies to move. If it plays anywhere I take my friends to see it. There is nothing in it that isn't perfect, the ideal escape film, where 'Over the Rainbow' is drenched in gorgeous technicolor unlike our black and white reality. Tinman, Scarecrow and Lion have a simple, delicious human 'frailty' – how nice to have a scared lion, a scatter-brained scarecrow and a tin soldier constantly beset by rust as three avuncular heroes. And how wonderful it would be if we could all sing like Dorothy as I wished so long ago; and our problems could be righted by a wizard who frankly admits his incompetence.

In my work I have often thought of Oz. When I worked with Russell on *The Devils* the glistening white floor I'd designed for the huge index library went all blotchy in the damp English weather and caused a Monday-morning crisis. Oh for the emerald floor at Oz, that shone with a Hollywood lustre. Then later, when I was filming *The Tempest*, Stephano, Trinculo and Caliban danced along the Bamburgh sands and I realized I'd directed them as if they too were on the road to the wicked witch's castle.

And the wicked old witch herself, well, I often thought of her secretly, and after my initial fright grew to love her. One day I told my Oz story to Frank Dunlop, the theatre director, who said he could easily arrange for me to see her. As it was Christmas she would be entertaining children in one of the big New York department stores. I never took up the offer, too worried a cherished childhood memory might evaporate. Then one morning I caught the Second Avenue bus – the bus was crowded and I was strap-hanging. The bus stopped and a little old lady climbed on next to me. I was vaguely aware that all eyes in the bus were trained in our direction. I looked without looking, and my God I was standing next to the witch! I thought maybe I'd speak to her about Rome and then thought better of breaking into her privacy. So stop after stop we travelled together with my heart thumping so loudly I was certain she must have heard it; until finally she got off and disappeared into the crowds.

+—

MIMOSA

Grandmother Mimosa lived on the fourth floor of a flat block in Northwood, which, as we constantly moved from Nissen hut to Nissen hut, seemed the permanent home of my childhood. The hours were chimed in by the Greek Temple clock in the dark hall. Pale grey walls and peach mirrors, lace antimacassars on the sofas. Mahogany furniture that had been bought at Maples, shipped to India and back again. The table set for lunch, with a peach satin tablecloth and cut-glass salt and pepper pots like pineapples.

I play with my chemistry set in the bathroom, constructing crystal gardens, or handle the delicate ivory Mah Jong set. At night I dream I'm holding on to the balcony for dear life, the flat tilting at a crazy angle while down below the Metroland trains thunder past.

In the morning, Mrs Peachy dusts the ornaments and methodically breaks them. Granny scolds her and glues them together with sticky brown secotine. 'See no evil, hear no evil, speak no evil' – the dread monkeys glower at you. In Mimosa's bedroom there are amber beads, which pick up tissue paper when you rub them, scattered over her dressing-room table; over which a blue bird flies.

She arrives in triumph: 'This, Derek, is a banana. We haven't seen them

My grandmother Mimosa

Mother and myself, Northwood, 1945

since before the war.'

Mrs Peachy dusts the radio, which often plays Grandma's favourite songs from *Oklahoma!* On top of it are silver-framed photos of Harry Lytton, her late husband with the sweet smile. There are others, of my mother. They have mimosa pressed behind the glass. Mimosa, Grandma's flower. So evanescent, like a morning mist it dissolves in the sunlight – smell of the Côte d'Azur before the war. Before the war. You won't remember.

POLTERGEISTS

Christmas, 1951. Northwood: Aunt Moyra, my mother's younger sister, newly married to her doctor-husband, moved into a small house round the corner from my grandmother, Mimosa. Here she invited the whole family for Christmas dinner. The large turkey required for this event wouldn't fit into her small oven, so an elaborate plan was hatched. My mother cooked the turkey in Grandmother's larger oven; and when Moyra telephoned, the turkey, placed on Grandmother's huge willow charger, was driven over by my father and put into the oven so that its legs stuck out. Meanwhile, preparations for the feast were finalized. I stood by watching while my mother and aunt removed the great bird from the oven, heaving it on to the small collapsible table. They missed the centre of balance and the table tilted under the weight and the turkey, on Gran's beloved charger, came rumbling towards me as I stood at the end. 'Catch!' shouted Mother and Aunt Moyra, waving their hands in the air hysterically. I stood with my arms outstretched and my eyes closed as the huge fowl sped towards me in horrid slow motion. When we collided it knocked me flat. The willow charger hit the floor and shattered into a thousand pieces while the turkey burst at both ends under the impact, sending a salvo of stuffing across the room. The meal never recovered. My father shouted at me, Gran lost her temper, came to my rescue and nagged her two daughters for the loss of a plate that had survived Hitler's bombs.

After the dinner a television set, the first I'd ever seen, was switched on and a greyish, crackly image misted its tiny screen.

Christmas 1952: At the end of the Christmas lunch we are waiting for the Queen's speech from Australia. There is great excitement because it is being broadcast live, an immense technical feat of radio. My father, a New Zealander, listens intently as messages are relayed from Auckland and Sydney. There are vivid, on-the-spot descriptions from all over the Commonwealth that cackle on and off. Then, silence. The silence is long, and my father remarks on the distance: 'They'll get it right for the speech.' He gets up to fiddle with the knobs on Granny Mimosa's mammoth walnut wireless. And then we notice – the set's on fire! Smoke is pouring out of it. My mother gives a startled cry: 'A hot-water bottle; don't touch it, Lance.' But my father seizes it with both hands, staggering under the weight, and shoulders it over the edge of the balcony into the yard where it smashes far below. My mother stands holding a hot-water bottle in the middle of the room. 'I thought it might be live,' she says.

––

AUGUST 1953. SOMERSET

When my father was posted to RAF Merryfield in Somerset we moved into the most beautiful house of my childhood. The ancient, stone-built manor of Curry Mallet, rented from owners who lived in Australia, was one of the oldest in Somerset. It was built around a central courtyard with high, ornate Tudor chimney stacks. There was a great medieval A-frame hall – panelled rooms with vast fireplaces and a circular stone staircase. The huge garden, divided by tall yew hedges, was bordered by a high stone wall and the remains of a moat, now the village duck pond. In the middle of the lawn stood an ancient yew which, the villagers maintained, was recorded in Domesday.

The house was haunted. The ghost, a young girl, appeared frequently. The lady who lived there before us had stayed only three days. One evening, as she was gazing into a dressing-mirror, the wraith appeared over her shoulder and joined in the gaze while she sat frozen on the stool. Apparently in the 1680s a daughter of the Mallet family – who had come over with the Conqueror and established this as the first manor on the site – fell in love with a lad from Cathanger, who had joined the Monmouth rebellion against James II. He fell victim to Judge Jeffreys' assize at Taunton; and ever since she had stalked through the house, heartbroken.

None of the villagers would come near to the manor after dark, except old Mrs Pilkington who lived next door, who would sometimes babysit for my parents. Deaf, and in her eighties, she had never gone further afield than Taunton, eleven miles down the road, and that infrequently. She would insist we stay up with her in the living-room with the wireless up to full volume until they returned, listening to spine-chilling episodes of 'Dick Barton'.

My father takes his picture, 1930s

Karachi, my parents at a reception, 1954

In the summer my father left for Pakistan, leaving my mother to pack up the house alone. In the evenings she went to bed early. After several days she noticed that after Big Ben had chimed in the nine o'clock news, a door would swing open and then close with a crash. So every evening she would walk through the old house closing the great oak doors, and each evening at nine, though there was not the slightest breath of wind, she would hear the heavy iron latches open and the doors swing, as the ghost walked.

—+—

THE HIMALAYAS

On Boxing Day 1953, my mother, my sister and I caught the boat train to Liverpool and boarded one of the last liners to do the run to India, the SS *Circassia*. The voyage was uneventful until we reached Port Said; except for a terrible gale in the Bay of Biscay, during which we were all battened down, and the dining-rooms were empty with everyone suffering from sea sickness. Our arrival at Port Said, however, changed all this. Suddenly the ship was a-bustle. As we steamed past the statue of De Lesseps on the quay, conjuring guly-guly men appeared as if out of thin air – produced live chicks out of eggs, tore pound notes in half, threw them overboard, and miraculously restored them. Then we prepared to go ashore and visit the department store – Simon Artz – which sold all manner of things, tooled with hieroglyphs. There were Eighteenth Dynasty handbags, wallets from the Old Kingdom, Fifth Dynasty cigarette cases for the Egyptian cigarettes in their gilded and bemedalled packaging. Also, gaudy silken carpets with camels and pyramids and of course scarlet fezes with black tassels.

We passed through the customs and were given a body-search by some zealous young Egyptian guards. Everybody grumbled but went along with it until two English dowagers, who had been doing the trip to India since the death of Queen Victoria, put a stop to it. 'What do you think you are doing? This is an outrage. Where is your commanding officer?' They barked like drill sergeants, their petticoats rustling like machine-gun fire. The young soldiers blanched and fell back under this onslaught. There was obviously no quarter going to be given, and blood was about to be spilt. 'Out of my way. You should be ashamed of yourselves. Come along Doris, we're not having any of this. It's perfectly disgusting.' And the two of them, styled like the Himalayas, pushed their way past.

—+—

As we sailed through the Suez Canal the gang of kids who'd formed themselves into a lethal pack during the long voyage fell to debating whether the Red Sea would be red or not. We sailed out of the canal into a beautiful rosy sunset mirrored in the calmest sea I have ever seen. The Red Sea was indeed red, and all sorts of wagers were unexpectedly won and lost. I had pillaged the Christmas tree for silver balls when it was taken down. I tied one on a piece of cotton and gently lowered it over the side of the liner where it bounced along in the wake. A tiny, glittering spark in the sunset.

+−

231B SOMERSET STREET, KARACHI

Pakistan, 1954: swarms of locusts drifted like grey veils across the evening sky. In the wasteland at the end of the garden the wild dogs barked. My mother 'turned a blind eye' as the cook – the most irascible of our battalion of servants – grilled the toast on a prong, his feet propped up on the charcoal range, using his toes as a toast rack. Later, he fell asleep in the warm afternoon with his feet in the huge old refrigerator which chugged and hummed away while the punkahs turned listlessly above.

+−

SUBCONTINENTAL SUBURBIA

The last stragglers of the Raj were cut off in their enclaves with their endless social round, the cocktail faces sweating it out over the gin and tonics; life ordered by a routine of exquisite boredom within well defined parameters. As a child of eleven one's curiosity neatly offset any sense of alienation. Small things preoccupied me: butterflies, my fish tank. I hardly noticed the anomalous situation around me. Here you woke up in the morning to find your clothes neatly folded, the toothpaste already on the toothbrush, and breakfast laid.

You had 'to behave' under the watchful eye of Yacoub or Nikka Khan, with their white and gold uniforms, hold your nose and swallow the glass of salty water which my mother ordered to begin the day. The salt pills she had discovered were so strong they made me sick. Then the tutor arrived and attempted to teach me maths, a kindly soul who had adopted local dress – it always looked slightly soiled and somehow out of place in the blank, rather antiseptic rooms.

The afternoons were spent swimming, or in one of the old fishing-boats;

the evenings, with luck, were spent on the beach at Bilagi, where the turtles lumbered out of the phosphorescent surf to lay improbable numbers of ping-pong eggs in the sand. Their young, tiny perfect replicas, dodged the ghostly spider crabs which ambushed them, sideways along the dunes.

The flimsy copy of *The Times* arrived to announce new riots in Karachi – which we, living there, never saw. Instead, there were military parades with kilts, bagpipes and camels; and once, Pandit Nehru a few feet away taking the salute.

One afternoon I threw a tantrum after a tea-party of obnoxious, precocious eleven-year-olds, on the lawns of the Beach luxury hotel – given by the sons of the prime minister and the grandsons of Jinnah, the founder of Pakistan. A bearer stood behind every second spoilt child. I refused to attend any more of these social events.

Once Yacoub went north and brought back a stuffed peacock which an army of ants then removed, with military precision, to the last feather, from the table beside my bed deep in the night.

+—

GONE WITH THE WIND

The woods around the hillside station near Muree (Pakistan) were a riot of wild flowers – the azaleas and rhododendrons were over, but in the sunlit clearings the garden flowers of England bloomed in their wild state.

Back home, at school in Hampshire, the rose pergola through which we walked in a crocodile to Chapel bisected an old walled garden – scattered with gnarled fruit trees. On either side, deep wine-coloured peonies bowed, heavy with raindrops, and scattered their petals like the crinolines in *Gone with the Wind* (Mimosa had forbidden my mother to call me Ashley). Lupins bloomed, blue and magenta. There was one which, when I was eleven, produced as many flower spikes. There were shirley poppies, jet-black and silky scarlet, which I helped burst out of their hairy green casings – when no one was looking – unravelling their petals like butterflies emerging into the sunlight from their chrysalis. The roses on the pergola were pink and heavy; their petals fell like confetti along the gravel path. On Sundays the crocodile wound under them twice and we sang 'Abide with Me/Fast Falls the Eventide' to the rickety harmonium, and then walked back in twos and threes, the formality broken. The scent from the lime trees mixed with the sharp smell of the creamy privet flowers, as we stopped and searched for the caterpillars of the privet hawk, which no one ever found. Along one of the hedgerows which bordered the grounds were violets. I kept their whereabouts to myself, and used to press them between the pages of Caesar's *Gallic Wars*.

Along the paths that bisected the scrub – clinging to the sandy cliffs which tumbled on to the shingle of the Milford beach – there were oak eggers and puss moths, and the drinkers that sent secret signals to each other. At night, I crept into the bathroom, turned on the light and opened the window to capture the emerald and downy white ermine moths for my collection. And once a year we were driven to the New Forest for a picnic – after lunch I hunted among the beech trees for white admirals, but never caught sight of the elusive emperor, whose capture would have made me a king. In the cornfield we hollowed out a nest, and ate the green ears, pretending to be field mice; and sharpened lethal pea-shooters from the stalks of wild cow parsley, using the verdigris ivy berries as ammunition. Up above, in the trees which were bent and stunted by the wind sweeping up the Solent, we created a secret walkway to cross the school grounds in the air from where high above the ground you could see the foam-flecked waves dashing themselves against the Needles.

+—

SWANS

My first 'conscious' painting was copied from the top of a biscuit tin, a watercolour of swans flying in the sunset by Peter Scott. Up until that time I was unaware that painting and writing were set apart as disciplines. In the art class more copies were undertaken, but in a hidden recess I kept my own first sketch-pad, a lined HMSO notebook in which I carefully copied dinosaurs, fought airy battles over Tudor townscapes, and made meticulous watercolours of flowers.

+—

HORDLE HOUSE, MILFORD, 1951

At nine I discovered that sleeping with someone was more fun than sleeping alone and climbed into my mate Gavin's bed. Cuddling each other alleviated some of the isolation of boarding school. This wholly innocent affair was destroyed by a jealous dormitory captain who crept out one morning and informed the headmaster's wife. She descended on us like a harpy and, in her fury, pulled the mattress right off the bed, turning us on to the floor. The headmaster whipped us both, and afterwards commended the sneak and threatened to tell our parents of this horrible crime; before calling us out of the class and denouncing us in front of the other boys with,

'This sort of behaviour will make you blind,' and the like.

From then sexual encounters at school became furtive and unsuccessful, in the lavatories and bushes, fearful they might be discovered. Masturbation and exhibitionism, which only involved yourself, and was therefore somehow less reprehensible, became the way. To have an orgasm with ejaculation was the dream of every boy in the dormitory, as it meant you were on the way to growing up; and when this happened the whole gang would cluster around the bed of the lucky individual to have a look.

+—

NASCENT SEXUALITY

Growing up on RAF stations and at boarding school in the 1950s, one was extremely isolated. By sixteen I was fully aware of my sexual orientation but imagined, and probably even hoped, that I'd grow out of it. I became increasingly reclusive – something all my friends noticed. I went to parties with dread and made every excuse to stay at home, where I painted in our neighbours' attic or spent my time gardening, staring at the plants for hours at a time. I developed an aversion to physical contact and found sports and changing-rooms a nightmare. The destruction first wrought at Hordle, my prep school, grew like a poison vine.

Since then I have talked to scores of young men about their own first sexual experiences and have made love to many of them. One fact emerges quite clearly. Boys who've had the good fortune, at fourteen or fifteen or even earlier, to meet older men are nearly always more at ease with themselves sexually and are much better lovers. The old Greek way of men and women initiating adolescents of their own sex, helping them to discover their own sexuality in an atmosphere of responsibility, contained much humane and practical wisdom. I'm unconvinced that any boy's 'natural' inclinations are ever altered by contacts of this kind – the only damage that can be inflicted is the threat of exposure by a 'morality' which outlaws innocent and uncomplicated desires, uproots affections at least as valuable as family ties, and affronts the basic freedoms of everyone. The bigotry of centuries has left a mass of dead wood, which honest people should now hack away and burn.

+—

PAINTING IT OUT – CANFORD SCHOOL, 1956

At fourteen I paint in self-defence. The school is bleak and soulless, dominated by bells, prayers, bullying, and everything that brings a chill; a huge shadow cast over life, distilled into a distressing muscular Christianity. We dress in grey suits with stiff starched collars which cut into your neck; we polish our black shoes, and polish them again and parade past the prefects twice a day. On Wednesdays we change into prickly khaki uniforms and march up and down and on the spot. A subtle terror rules, thoughtfully preparing us for the outside world. I feel threatened, isolated, and friendless – I'm hopeless at all the communal activities, particularly ball games. And so I take refuge in the art house, where there is an old coke stove, broken and comfortable furniture, books and drawers full of postcards. Every free moment is spent there.

Here there is blossom by Van Gogh, empty wine bottles for cubist still lives and mirrors to stare at yourself. These are my weapons against the other order.

Once in a while we escape into the outside world in 'Percy', my art master's drop-head Rolls-Royce circa 1928, made of aluminium riveted by brass; although it's seen better days you can still do seventy down the Dorset lanes with your hand on the klaxon to warn the world you're coming. 'Percy' is perfect for scavenging old doors and other treasures from the demolition sites around Poole. Once he takes us north, to Stanley Spencer's Burghclere Chapel. The paintings image the sacrifice of an entire generation. At sixteen I am convinced that together they form the greatest masterpiece in the history of painting.

My art master, Robin Noscoe, ran his art school with a delightful absent-minded shrewdness. It was from Robin that I learned that an artist was practical, whatever his outward eccentricity. Robin was mentor rather than teacher, he ignored the gulf that separated master and pupil and embraced you as a collaborator and equal. His interest in his own painting was minimal; in fact he'd probably have agreed that you were as good a painter as himself, if you had dared suggest so. This situation would have been impossible in a history or maths class where the individual is of no consequence. Robin's prime concern wasn't painting – he was an excellent silversmith who stamped his spoons and rose bowls with his own hallmark. He built his own house with help from the boys, who learned bricklaying and carpentry, while Phyl, his wife, brewed cups of tea. The house was up to date, but its design incorporated medieval doors, old mirrors, cobbles from the beach, and fine antique floors from a demolished country house. Later he incorporated a door which I had carved and painted with quotations from Chaucer. He also built his own furniture, constructing a fine dining-table from an acacia tree that was brought down in a storm. In the art school he was a potter and every two weeks or so the great brick kiln we had built would be fired with wood scavenged from the grounds, and the pottery with its fine ash glazes would be scattered through the building and used as brush pots and crockery. As the kiln was unpacked Robin would stand by, stroking his grey goatee beard, his face wreathed in a delightful boyish enthusiasm. For a fourteen-year-old it was remarkable to see a grown-up so openly enthusiastic and in love with his work. For the boys he taught, Robin was an inspiration. Art was never mentioned in any academic context, but was a part of living in which anyone, whatever their natural ability or talent, could share.

+—

The bell chimes like a raw tooth, the spell is broken. I walk back unwillingly to Montacute House, with its echoes of John of Gaunt, feudal power and the ideals of chivalry – antecedent to the vicious fraudulent gentility that in this school masks a system of bullying and repression, coupled with a deliberate philistine aggression towards learning and intelligence, which are only acceptable if saturated with the muddied values of the rugger pitch. Canford epitomizes an English education and distils in miniature the most (truly) distressing aspects of the society that maintains and underlies it. The aggression carries over into many aspects of the teaching, which serves not to enlighten but to repress. A systematic destruction of the creative mind, called 'education', is under way. This has one aim: to awe you into impotence under the guise of teaching you judgement. Painting escapes, as for a word-bound culture the image is not so important, but the word used creatively could endanger the system. Thus expression, not just political expression, is frowned upon. At Kings my tutor, Eric Mottram, asked, 'Why are you here? The only place where you can receive a genuine education in England is the Royal College of Art.'

+—

I was always academically backward; I learned to read late, could just add and subtract – and no more. I failed exams with dismal regularity, a backward boy who when given an IQ test on my arrival at Canford came out with ninety-five subnormal. However, what I lacked in the disciplines I made up with a sharp eye. In the Senior Common Room at Montacute there was an oak cupboard, under which prayers were said both morning and night, which held the silver cups the House had won. Mr Shorland Ball, our housemaster, was up jogging before dawn, his pipe thrust into his face with its fixed smile, encouraging the lads – without success. The cupboard remained bare, except for the huge silver pot for art. It was a constant reproach, and for winning it I, with a small gang of friends, was treated mercilessly and bullied constantly, while at each year's 'promotion' that might have cut down the amount of fagging and given me a few hours' more freedom, I was passed by. I reacted predictably – I deliberately missed my tackles on the rugger pitch, was bowled out for nought, and crossed the line last. Even now, as I write this, images of a flame-thrower and cans of petrol cross my mind and I see Barry's ugly barren building wreathed in purifying flames.

—+—

At seventeen my reports said 'Fair' and 'Average' and 'Could do better', when Andrew Davis, an English master who was conspicuous amongst the staff for his stand for the 'mind' – he collected antiquarian books and first editions, was a Rhodes scholar, and had an easy ironic humour – took me into a private class that he held in his study for the brightest sixth-form pupils. He was interested in painting, my 'daubs' as he called them, and sensed the difficulties I was having. I joined the class nervously. It was May, and outside Andrew's window a chestnut tree bloomed with deep-red flowers shimmering in a sea of green. Andrew caught me daydreaming, laughed, and set an essay on *Antony and Cleopatra*. I came back the following week with a short essay on Cleopatra as Isis and received glowing As. Perhaps Andrew deliberately rigged this, but the effect was electric. Here I was, a fifth-former with six of the brightest boys in the school, receiving the best results for an essay. The same week my housemaster had told me that to try for university would bring disappointment; he mentioned the dreaded IQ test with its near-moron results. Quietly I decided to beat them at their own game. What had been done once could be repeated.

That summer holiday my father told me I could leave the school if I wished. I realized that this was a considerable concession on his part as he took immense pride in the fact that he was seeing me through a public school. But his attitude was strangely mixed; as a New Zealander who had worked his passage to England he could at times scarcely conceal his dislike for a system in which he was an outsider, and his correspondence with my housemaster was to say the least edgy. But I had already made my decision in the English class, and declared I would soldier on. The question of university came up. He was determined I should go, and we made a pact. If I got a university place and also got into the Slade where I dreamed of going, I would go to the university and in return he promised he would see me through art school afterwards; a promise he meticulously fulfilled, even though I knew he would have preferred otherwise.

At eighteen I climbed the stairs to Mr Shorland Ball's study, still not a prefect, as the system of preference had rigorously passed me by, clutching a piece of paper. Down below the art pot glowed in the cupboard. 'I know what you've come to tell me,' he said. 'You've failed to get into Kings like the others.' I smiled and said, 'No, they've accepted me.'

BEARINGS – LONDON UNIVERSITY

In 1960 I left school and came to London where I read a general degree in English history and art at Kings College in the Strand. For the first two years I commuted daily from my parents' home in Northwood, a tight middle-class suburb where my father built a house after leaving the RAF. By the time I had made the two-way journey, ploughed through my reading schedule and done some painting, there wasn't much room for a social life.

At Kings I was not much nearer solving my problems. There was no gay society in those days, and I had no idea of the existence or whereabouts of pubs or clubs – even had I known, I was much too shy or inhibited to make a first move. So at Kings I bought any books that had a gay subject-matter: Cocteau and Genet; and through my tutor, Eric Mottram, I discovered the existence of Allen Ginsberg and William Burroughs.

My life at Kings was uneventful. I ploughed through the work schedule diligently, and came away with a 2.1 at the end of three years. The college remained firmly in the 'background'. Out of the gates in the Strand you had London with its theatres and exhibitions; the university could hardly be said to exist and the parochial hothouse atmosphere of Oxbridge was absent. Every now and then I would spend a morning at the Slade, life drawing. I painted scenery for Miller's *The Crucible* and designed the covers for the college magazine, *Lucifer*. Apart from that I belonged to none of the college societies, and kept myself very much to myself.

BEARINGS – EUROPE, SUMMER 1962

Colmar: My lift stopped at Colmar for twenty minutes. In the main square a postcard of the Isenheim altar piece caught my eye. I stopped and discovered that it was in the museum – only twenty minutes. So I ran. I couldn't stop off because my lift was going to take me, via Lâon, all the way to the coast. In five minutes I was at the museum door. Breathless, I asked where the altar piece was. Then I ran through the gallery past startled visitors, reaching the hall with four minutes to view the picture. The others looked at me curiously, probably thinking I was on a five-countries-in-five-days marathon. There are some paintings which diminish when you finally see them after years of reproductions in art books. They shrink away, pale ghosts of your imaginings, and others are overwhelming. When I hurled myself into the hall where the great panels were mounted, I was thrown into a terrible state of agitation. Breathless from the run I was surprised by the scale of the work – unlike many jewel-like paintings of the North, it was enormous. The colours blazed forth in great flaming haloes with shimmering rainbow edges, and the participants in the drama were transfigured by an assurance of their place in the late-medieval world.

+

August 1962, Amfissa: Last night we hitched to Delphi on the back of a truck. We were dropped off several miles down the mountain road and began walking through the darkness. Before reaching the village we heard a stream, which flowed from the rocks at the roadside. We were all very tired, so we stopped and set up camp, resolving to carry on in the morning. At about 5 a.m. the sky began to brighten up, and we got up. After several weeks on the road, we are used to getting up with the sun. The nights were cold and rather uncomfortable, we hadn't any proper camping equipment, so there's no reason to stay abed if you're sleeping on bare ground with a rucksack as a pillow.

    We found ourselves in a grove of fig trees, in a cleft in the rocks with cliffs towering above. High above, eagles were circling in the updraught over Mount Parnassos, glinting in the sunlight that caught on their wings. Below us, the valley was a sea of smoky-grey olive trees. We built a fire and cooked breakfast on a large flat rock, and afterwards washed ourselves and our clothes in the icy water, hanging them up to dry on the fig trees. At 6.30 a couple arrived, looked at us strangely and retreated. Then Peter and I cleared up the breakfast and sat on the rock in the sunlight, while David, with his usual bravado, ignored some barbed wire and started to climb the rockface for a better view. He'd climbed about a hundred feet when our idyll was destroyed. Two police vans tore round the corner and screeched to a halt. All hell broke loose as a group of very angry men spilled out. Shouting abuse, they tore our clothes off the trees and kicked them in the dust, while we stared uncomprehendingly. In the excitement David lost his footing, and came

Byron's signature at Sounion, 1961

crashing down the rockface to land, semi-conscious, on the barbed wire. There was a sudden uncomfortable silence, while everyone assessed the situation. Then we were bundled into the vans.

Expelled from Delphi, we've set up camp on the ancient acropolis above Amfissa. David is in hospital with concussion and a lot of stitches. It turns out that, quite innocently, we spent the night in the grove of Apollo, bathed in the water of the Sacred Well, and cooked our breakfast on an altar stone.

At Sounion, where we went to view the sunset, we crept round the barbed wire that ended at the cliff face, and spent the night in the temple to watch the dawn alone, before slipping away.

August 1962 – Crete: We arrived in Ayios-Nikolaos at lunch-time, after a gruelling ride over the mountains from Heraklion. Sitting on the beach recovering, we were plagued by kids demanding cigarettes. Tourists are a rarity here, so we are the object of curiosity and expectation. Expectation was crushed when I explained we did not smoke. One of the kids lobbed a stone, half in play but with a hint of resentment; but it hit a tired and irritable David, who grabbed the culprit and ducked him in the sea. He emerged tearful, and picking up another stone, this time threw it in earnest. Then his friends started to do the same and we were forced to retreat as the stones were accurate and dangerous, and we were protected only by our rucksacks. We fled over the bluff into a small sandy cove where an old man was sitting at a table in front of his hut at the top of the beach. He sensed something was up, and as we approached, out of breath and panting, he stood up and shouted, waving his stick in the air. The kids stopped in their tracks, crouched in the rocks and shouted abuse.

We stayed with the old man for over a week, sleeping on the roof of his hut. We bought him new crockery and ouzo, and helped water his small orchard of pomegranates and olive trees from a brackish well. Each morning at sunrise, I climbed the thyme-scented hill above the orchard and watched the sun come flaming out of a glassy blue sea. One morning, as I clambered up the rocks, a huge boulder detached itself and sped past me, almost knocking me flat, before clattering down the mountain. For a few seconds I could hear it echoing in the silence. When I reached the top I sat down. David and Peter were still asleep far below. I wondered which god had hurled that boulder.

＋

Ayios-Nikolaos: the old man is nearly blind, and has charming, old-fashioned manners. He's the wicked old man of the town – he sits in his chair on the beach and tells wartime stories like a comic hero. His speech is punctuated by machine-gun fire, and great explosions which he traces in the air with his stick. Each day he walks into town and refills a couple of old lemonade bottles with marbles in their necks, and sits with them as the bubbles rise in the warmth. He has never asked us what we are doing here, courtesy forbids. He has made us welcome like medieval pilgrims en route to the Holy Land or some great shrine. And we have been made welcome like this in every village in Greece. Grapes, rough bread, ouzo and wine are given and exchanged – everyone refuses money, and although we brought so little we seem to have spent barely any. It is four weeks now since we started to hitch here from London.

＋

September 1962, Switzerland: Last night I spent at the youth hostel at the end of the St Gothard pass. I had no money left, so I had to beg them to let me in. They agreed, on condition I did some housework. I also had my first meal for nearly two days. It is very cold, after the warm nights in Greece. At eight in the morning I started hitching, shivering at the roadside in my jeans, with a filthy rucksack, and so brown I must have looked like a gypsy. I expected it to be as difficult as the day before – Switzerland was the hitch-hiker's nightmare. After only ten minutes a car ground to a halt, with a tough-looking middle-aged man inside. I asked him if he was going in the direction of Basel, and he said OK. He got out, locked my dirty rucksack in the boot, as he thought it might mark his upholstery – and then we were off. After about fifteen minutes he announced he had to make a phone call – and when he returned he said he could take me all the way to Basel, but that as it was early, and he was in no hurry, we'd go over the mountains. Although I wanted to press on, because of my money situation, I agreed: I'd reach the border, and the day was pleasant and sunny.

    The car left the main road and began to climb along a country lane, and then up into the pine forests until suddenly, without warning, my lift drove off the road and ground to a halt in the trees. Without a moment's hesitation, he grasped me around the shoulder and tried to kiss me, while with the other hand he unzipped his flies. Before I took in what was happening, he had my hand in an armlock and was trying to make me suck his cock. We struggled for a moment, with him threatening that if I didn't do what I was told he'd leave me where I was and report me to the police for assault. The whole business was so sudden and unexpected, and he seemed totally crazy. I managed to struggle free and get out of the car – then realized that my rucksack, with my passport, was locked in the back. By now I was on the point of breaking down. He seemed to soften up a little. But when I climbed back into the car he grabbed my cock so hard I gasped with pain. Then he slammed the door and reversed out of the wood, and for the next half-hour drove like a maniac along the narrow roads in silence glowering at me. Suddenly, at a junction, he slammed on the brakes, jumped out and, opening the boot, hurled the rucksack on the roadside. He bellowed at me in Suisse-Deutsch, and finally drove off, leaving me so distressed that I must have cried for nearly an hour, sitting on the kerb. Then a truck pulled up, and a boy shouted out, asking me where I was going. He was another hiker, by the name of Hans Dieter Hengstenberg, and to my relief took me home to his house in Basel.

+—

NORTHWOOD, 1962

At the first opportunity I shut up the books on Anglo-Saxon and imperial history and was off over the garden wall to our neighbour's, Güta, where I would quietly let myself in and tiptoe up to the attic she had given me. Here I painted a series of landscapes from tins of cheap Brodie and Middleton oil paint. I was hardly aware of American painting – the influences were English: William Scott and Paul Nash who had succeeded Stanley Spencer in my affections. 'The inspiration of the megaliths' spawned charcoal drawings of Kilve in Somerset which were pinned to the walls.

Sometimes Güta would hear me open the door and intercept me, and we would sit in the kitchen and talk for hours of gardens over a cup of tea. Gardens and flowers were a mutual obsession, and then I'd bring down the canvases for her inspection: the deep-red fields of the Quantocks with clumps of trees brooding under grey skies, and the slate-grey seashore at Kilve with its muddy rock pools.

+—

A FIRST NEWS CLIP

5 May 1961: from the *Express*. 350 works by students in art show opened by Lord Birket at the University of London Union.

Professional Class – students studying art and planning to make it their career:

First Prize of £25 to David Hockney (Royal College of Art).

Amateur Class – students whose first subject is not art:

First Prize of £20 to Michael Derek Jarman (Kings College).

MOVING OUT

In my last year at Kings – 1963 – I left my parents' home in Northwood and moved up to London, to an unfurnished flat in Marchmont Street near Russell Square, which I shared with Michael Ginsborg and an old schoolfriend, Dougal Campbell. Through Michael, who was studying medicine at Kings, I became friendly with a very handsome, dark-haired theologian, Roger Jones, who had flunked a drama course to study theology. Roger lived at the mission in Bethnal Green – almost every Sunday I would take off without an *A–Z* into the unknown – and like a homing pigeon arrive by instinct some two hours later at his door.

After weeks of self-debate, I sat with him one evening and told him I thought I was homosexual. I was terrified that this revelation might destroy our friendship. He was very sympathetic, but had no real solution. I told him about my Swiss experience, and he said we must approach the whole thing with caution. The telling helped, but the whole subject seemed as obscure and remote as my Anglo-Saxon studies. So I returned home and while my flatmates went out to the pub, played myself to sleep with Gregorian chant.

+—

AMERICAN ACTION AND FINE ART – THE SLADE, 1963

Growing up in the 1950s we dreamed the American dream. England was grey and sober. The war had retrenched all the virtues – Sobriety and Thrift came with the Beveridge plan, utility furniture, and rationing, which lasted about a decade after the end of hostilities. Over the Atlantic lay the land of cockaigne; they had fridges and cars, TV and supermarkets. All bigger and better than ours. Food parcels arrived with unheard-of luxuries: bubble-gum and chocolate, fruit cakes wrapped in comics – all virtually unobtainable here. Then, as the decade wore on, we were sent Presley and Buddy Holly, and long-playing records of *West Side Story*, and our own *Pygmalion* transformed. The whole daydream was wrapped up in celluloid, and presented nightly at the 'Odious' at the end of every high street in the land. How we yearned for America! And longed to go west.

In 1960 every young English artist had an eye across the Atlantic. Four years before, Richard Hamilton, one of those Ur figures of English art, whom the glossies announced as 'seminal' in 'Just what makes today's home so different, so appealing', realized the dream with the cunning of an ad-man, and invented Pop.

Here we have a dream room, narcotically Hollywood, where even the light which lit the bodies-beautiful was emblazoned with FORD. A little later the

'Just what is it that makes today's homes so different, so appealing',
1956 – Richard Hamilton

Americans themselves got in on their own act – Jasper Johns covered the walls of every gallery in the 'free' world with the stars and stripes, J. Edgar Hoover slept more soundly in his imperial bed, for the last great binge of Capital was on.

Now everything had to be new. Modernism became mass-production. We eagerly accepted it. There were new designs for houses, clothes and cars. A new world with a bright young President and his glamorous lady in the White House.

The English art world quickly decided the canvas ad was bigger, brighter and therefore better in the USA. 'Go west young man!' and David Hockney did, trail-blazing for a whole generation. What price Typhoo tea or the Bradford Public Baths when you could sit in the sun by a pool in Los Angeles? What price all this? Later, we would find out that you were invited to admire, not to partake . . . The real prizes were for the home-grown product, washed around the world on an ocean of tax-deductible dollars. In the meantime, every young English artist kept a suitcase half-packed. I myself waited for the BUNAC charter that in June 1964 would take me along the same great highway.

MARCH 1964. CAMDEN

After I switched the lights off I lay in the dark with my heart pounding. Then Ron said, 'Why don't you come over to my bed, it's really cold in here.' I nearly fell over in the haste with which I crossed the room – in case he changed his mind. I leapt into his bed. Each time I touched him it was like an electric shock. He had beautiful hair, blond, like silk, and really smooth skin. He was about the same height as me, but better built. He worked as a lifeguard at the swimming pool at Calgary University, where he was doing his degree. We stared at each other for ever in the darkness and every time I touched him he laughed.

In the morning, when I was half-asleep, Ron slipped out of the house: later when I got up I asked Roger and Brenda for the number of the house where Ron was staying. When they said they didn't have it the roof of the world caved in.

All day at the Slade I paid no attention to what I was doing, and at the first moment rushed back to Camden. There was no news from Ron. By six o'clock some dark force overwhelmed me. I seized Brenda's dressmaking scissors and in a blank frenzy hacked my paintings which hung on the living-room wall into shreds. Roger, who was also in tears by now, took hold of the scissors, imagining I was about to turn them on myself.

The canvas hung in limp tatters off the stretchers, and I sat motionless on the sofa as the great tide, the years of repression and self-hatred rolled away, leaving me like an empty shell from which a dark death's-head moth had escaped. We stared at each other in the silence, and Roger and Brenda vowed they would find Ron.

+–

JUNE 1964. NEW YORK

My charter to the States cost £54 return, and the unlimited ninety-nine days for $99 Greyhound ticket, another £20. I'm here until late September, for nearly three months. And today I'm going off to Calgary, where I'm meeting Ron. We are going to get a job together, as I've very little money.

My first night in New York was spent in a stifling hot room in the Knickerbocker Hotel, which came free with the air ticket. We were crammed eight to a small room.

In the morning I phoned Roger's friend John, an Episcopalian priest who said he'd put me up at the Henry Street mission in Greenwich Village. And so, I met up with him at the Episcopalian headquarters near the United Nations building, and he piled me into a cab. We'd hardly gone a block before his hand was on my crotch. I decided the best course was to pretend it wasn't happening, and stared resolutely at the architecture whizzing by, hoping that the taxi-driver wouldn't notice. At the mission in Henry Street I found all the priests were after me, all of them unbelievably forward. I felt as though I were a lottery ticket.

They all wear blue jeans, T-shirts and look just like garage mechanics – if it weren't for the black wooden crosses worn over the T-shirts. Not at all like the dear old C of E reverends. I tried to act as if I were used to all of this. Two of them insisted that I sleep between them, and didn't allow me to get a wink. On Sunday we went to an Episcopalian church which they called 'Mary on the Verge', where the altar boys were all strikingly good-looking, and spent the entire service cruising the all-male congregation, winking at them through clouds of incense and lace.

+–

July, Calgary: As we climbed in the Rockies this morning, Ron disturbed me with grizzly bear stories – so that when we saw a white mountain goat which stared at us before clattering off over the moraine, I convinced myself it was only a matter of moments before a ravenous grizzly poked its face through the scrub. Apparently, they attack on sight and are carnivorous. Last year one attacked some campers, and a boy who failed to get out of his sleeping-bag quick enough had his head bitten off!

It was a brilliant sunny day, and after a couple of hours climbing we reached the top of a ridge between two snow-covered mountains. The ridge itself was capped with snow and over the edge was a sheer precipice. We were looking into a vast bowl in the mountains, with cliffs on all sides from which waterfalls plunged for hundreds of feet, sparkling in the sunlight, before disappearing in the dark forest below. In the distance, mountain after snow-capped mountain as far as the eye could see. An Altdorfer vision which murmured like the sea in a shell. Around us it was unutterably quiet. We made snowballs and threw them into the void.

Later, we sat eating the picnic lunch we'd brought with us from Calgary on the side of a deep cutting in the pine forests, through which the Canadian Pacific runs. You could hear the train far below, hooting like an owl in the night – *Wooooo wooooo*. We'd drunk rather a lot of wine and Ron suggested making love right there, as the train went past. After a moment's hesitation we both climbed out of our clothes and sat looking at each other in the sunlight. Ron looks radiant, a beautiful brown from sun-bathing while looking after the pool. Then the train – *Wooooo wooooo*. I started to put my pants back on when Ron grabbed me to prevent me and we fell wrestling on top of our clothes while the train passed, very slowly, by. *Wooooo wooooo*. Neither of us dared look up as the glass observation carriages, packed with trippers, passed within a few feet of where we lay in each other's arms, breathless and still.

＋

I'd arrived in Calgary in time for the stampede. At the bus station Ron was waiting for me, and for an idyllic few weeks we shared the basement rumpus room at 20 Ave NE. During the days I worked on the city land survey, making nearly $100 a week. After work I'd join Ron at his swimming-pool. We spent nearly all our spare time in the countryside, sitting sunning ourselves on huge flat glacial rocks, spread along the icy sparkling rivers which rushed down from the Rockies, or climbed the mountains. Outside our windows Ron's Russian neighbours cultivated opium poppies which they picked every morning to make their opium tea. In the bookshop I bought all the City Lights poetry books that had been so difficult to buy in London. Corso and Ferlinghetti, Ginsberg and Kerouac, including Henry Miller's *Big Sur* and *The Oranges of Hieronymous Bosch*: and when it was time to go, took off to the south after Ron had promised to return to England early next year:

In the common silence
of the world the white
Poppies of my love are dancing.

+—

NOVEMBER 1982. BERKELEY

California. The sweet dream of capitalism curdles – where the seasons are scrambled. Minds seep away at the boundaries, snowdrops bloom with mesembryanthemums. There's a camelia and apples hanging on the tree. Palm trees and daffodils. In the land of institutionalized insecurity: Pat says guns are a feminist issue, and the boy on the plane with the tattoos and flared jeans complains he's defenceless – they've packed his rifle in the hold.

While Kenneth and I curl up on the futon it just rains outside . . . Breakfast is our only meal – all else is soggy mayonnaise-soaked sandwiches. Kenneth has been mugged because he wandered over the boundary of the ghettos. Off we go to Nepenthe, down the highway to Big Sur, Nepenthe the drug of forgetfulness.

+—

August 1964: My Beatles hat which cost me a fortune – £8 – in Herbert Johnson's has paid dividends, as everywhere I've travelled it's made me instantly recognizable as the most desirable of foreigners – an inhabitant of swinging London. Hitching up the coast from San Simeon to San Francisco, with the hat, has been easy, the people extraordinarily friendly. Some girls asked me if we had chocolate in England, offering me a Hershey bar! When I told them that in my childhood I lived in a house parts of which were seven hundred years old they looked sad. 'You must be very poor,' they said. This puzzled me, until I remembered everything has to be brand-new in California.

I picked up a stoned boy on a bike called Michael, and we drove for a couple of hours up the coast. We booked into a cabin at the motel at Big Sur!! It was set in the Redwoods alongside a stream, and here we carried on smoking his grass. The oranges of Hieronymous Bosch. Tomorrow we're off to Monterey, where Joan Baez and Dylan sing.

+—

September 1964, NYC: When I got into the Greyhound terminal I was exhausted after the non-stop ride from San Francisco. I tossed a coin for which of the

Reverends I'd ring – the least obnoxious, as Ron would say – and decided on Tom, who without hesitating invited me round. When I got to his place, he told me there was no time to unpack as we were going to a party. All I wanted to do was to go to sleep, but he wouldn't leave me behind. So we arrived at a small flat which was so packed that people were hanging out of the windows. In the centre of the room a gang of black drag queens were swishing around announcing they were the most 'glamorous', and when some weedy-looking white drag queen took them on in the beauty stakes the room divided, and it nearly started a fight in which someone pulled a knife. I took refuge in a bedroom with a black boy, Marshall Hill, who was at art college – painting. We curled up on the floor and made love.

Afterwards, I was so drunk and exhausted, deprived of food and sleep, he offered to drive me back as Tom had disappeared, leaving me stranded. Tom hadn't arrived home, so we lay on the carpet outside the front door and fell asleep in each other's arms. When Tom arrived back at 4.30 I asked him if Marshall could come in and stay. He began shouting, telling us we were a disgrace and threw me and my luggage into the hallway and slammed the door. So much for Christian charity – Marshall and I spent the rest of the day sightseeing, then he took me out to the airport in the evening more dead than alive.

+–

III
The Thaw

Life was to change for ever after my return from America in the autumn of 1964. By October I had discovered my first gay pub – the William IV in Hampstead; and shortly after, the La Douce in Poland Street and the Gigolo in the King's Road. These were two of a handful of gay bars which were the only haven in a city of eight million souls. From our flat in Priory Road I could walk to the William IV, but on several occasions went to the Gigolo, quite prepared to do the two-hour walk back to West Hampstead late at night.

At the Slade things had not stuck still. By the end of the year I had met Patrick Procktor and Ossie Clarke, two artists who were establishing reputations. The Gregorian chant was put back into its sleeve and replaced by the Who and the Stones. On the literary front, too, old loves faded. From America, like a smuggler, I brought back Burroughs' *The Naked Lunch* and my own City Lights copy of Ginsberg's *Howl*, which displaced *The Waves* and *The Years* of Virginia Woolf. At the Slade I resorted more frequently to the Theatre Design room where there were sympathetic spirits. I'd brought some muscle mags, and I collaged them into the set for Stravinsky's *Orpheus* which I was designing that winter. This caused a minor contretemps with the Slade professor Bill Coldstream, who talked about the acceptable limits of art, citing his role at the British Board of Film Censors, while standing with his back to my set.

In the theatre room homosexuality was accepted quite openly, while upstairs the atmosphere of the painting studios was fairly equivocal. 'Straight' painters were envious of connections made quickly through 'the gay mafia' with painters and gallery-owners. Also, many of them were affronted by our insouciant, happy-go-lucky lifestyle – a reaction against the deadening world around us. But who could blame me if after years of repression I found that homosexuality, far from being a disability as I'd been brought up to believe, led to an easy social mobility and with it incredible advantages? The homophobia of the art schools was mixed with a lot of plain jealousy.

In the garden at Priory Road, 1965 *(Photo: Ray Dean)*

For the first time I could view myself in the mirror – I became aware of how I looked and how I dressed. I discovered that I was handsome enough and with new confidence and sympathetic friends, I made some first faltering steps into the 'art world'. And as my own repressed past broke up like ice in a spring thaw, so did the old England which had produced it.

+—

BUILDING FOR PLEASURE

January 1965, Priory Road: Peter Cook was here to look at Dougal's work, and we fell into a row about modern architecture. It started off with some remarks I made about NYC, that once you're out of the lobbies of those skyscrapers you could be anywhere. The upper storeys are all the same, whether or not the architect is a Philip Johnson. I said I thought functionalism was totally crazy, unless you saw architecture as disposable. The function of any modern building is bound to alter after a few years from the original intention. And then you're left with something that's not only obsolete, but also probably ugly. Buildings should be designed for purely aesthetic reasons: form should respond to the demands of pleasure, the inward function. More often than not you'll find that an 'aesthetic' building is an adaptable one.

During the course of the evening Peter Cook came up with the horrific notion of cities on stilts, which are to roam the world like vast praying mantises. I said I thought most people wanted to put roots down. Who wants to wake up in a location that someone else has decided for them? Presumably, someone drives the awful thing. Dougal was rather cross with me as Mr Cook is a current architectural hero.

+—

Architecture was as much a daily topic of conversation as painting. Perhaps more so, as nearly all my friends were either at the AA in Bedford Square or at the Poly. For weeks on end the basement flat at Priory Road, which I moved to in September, was taken over by students working through the night for crits. I was glad to have avoided this fate. It all seemed infinitely tedious, dry and academic. My own interest in architecture was historical; and as I had had Niklaus Pevsner as a tutor at Kings for three years, every Wednesday evening at the annex of Birkbeck College, my knowledge of architectural history was usually greater than my friends'.

With Pevsner, architecture became a passion. We would travel to the cathedrals – Lincoln, Winchester, Canterbury – and spend the entire day leaving no stone unturned. At Lincoln we clambered through the roofs; the timbered forest above the crazy vaults was spectacular, with great beams radiating in every direction like the spokes of a wheel. Hitch-hiking to Greece or Italy my route would be planned by way of the cathedrals, Laôn, Rheims, Strasbourg or Aachen, Cologne, Ulm. The Renaissance architecture interested me less – though Brunelleschi's Pazzi Chapel in Florence I believed to be the most exquisite building in Europe, with an oriental calm and clarity of proportion that was unequalled in any other work, even Michelangelo's stupendous lobby in the Laurentian library. But neither of these buildings, or indeed any of the French or German cathedrals, gave me as much pleasure as Ely.

+–

ELY

A sudden decision: we drove to Ely in the gathering dark. I am eagle-eyed for cathedrals, and the first to spot the building looming up, caught in the mesh of gaunt winter trees. A gale was whipping across the fens, and the towers almost touched the heavy rain-laden clouds that flew past and reeled as you looked up at them. Jackdaws, falling in gusts of wind, encircled the great lantern. Inside, our footsteps died away in the deep shadows which enveloped the vast emptiness of the unlit nave. The wind outside came faster, battering the silence. We walked through the massive stony piers like trespassers, our hearts beating loudly, absolutely alone in the building.

Far at the end, hidden by the choir screen, the sound of the boys singing evensong mingled and dispersed with the rushing wind, and filled the building with its stillness. The octagon, suspended as if by magic over the crossing, disappeared into a dark, dizzying vortex. With my eyes fixed high above I began to turn in a circle, and gradually the whole building spiralled with me to the sound of the boys' singing and that roaring winter wind.

+–

WE TWO BOYS TOGETHER CLINGING

David Hockney was the first English painter to declare his homosexuality in public. By example, he was a great liberating force, reaching far beyond the confines of the 'art world': his work paved the way for the gay liberation movement at the end of

Ely Cathedral *(British Tourist Authority)*

'Cool Waters', 1965 – at The Young Contemporaries, Tate Gallery 1967
(Photo: Ray Dean)

the decade. From the beginning, with his 'Rake's Progress', his 'shower paintings' including 'We Two Boys Together Clinging', and finally the exhibition of his etchings for the Cavafy poems, he produced vital new images that pulled away the veil behind which the work of older painters had had to hide. The Cavafy etchings were particularly powerful. With his fine line he produced images of boys in bed that resembled Cocteau – but without a trace of the sentimentality which so often bedevils gay art.

When I met him, his golden hair signalled a new dawn. Gentle, with a wry northern wit, his unassuming presence confounded all criticism. With his Bradford brogue, and wholehearted love affair with the American dream, he was the spirit of the age. His presence in a room blew away cobwebs. In thanks a whole generation called at Powis Terrace with flowers – tulips, if possible, for our man of all seasons.

+—

TRAVELLING LIGHT

Ossie Clarke and I went to the Picasso sculpture show. On the whole, I greatly prefer the sculpture to the paintings which were shown here in 1960. I particularly admired the cubist constructions, and the (late) metal cut-outs, which were painted over quite roughly.

At the show we met David, who'd just arrived from California. He invited us back to Powis Terrace, which had been left unoccupied and was freezing. Ossie and I climbed fully clothed into the bed in the living-room while David made tea. David put on the TV and joined us. Ossie asked what he'd brought back with him, and David produced two suitcases, one full of physique mags featuring hunky American boys, and the other packed with fluorescent socks and brightly coloured underwear. I asked him if this was all he'd brought. He said he used to travel with luggage, but realized his mistake. One should travel as light as possible. Now he went in what he was wearing, and bought razors and even toothbrushes at the other end. This to me seemed the height of modernity.

+—

A GARDEN AT LUXOR

Patrick Procktor asked me one bitterly cold March day where I would most like to be. Off the top of my head I replied, 'Sitting on top of the pyramids.'

'Go and get your passport. Come straight back and we'll go. David's in

Alexandria doing some etchings. We can meet up with him.'

Taken aback by this sudden gesture I demurred, making some excuse about work.

Patrick: 'You really are silly. Nicholas Ferguson went round the world twice while he was at the Slade. You're so unadventurous.'

I said that we'd go when I could afford to pay my way.

'What a perfectly middle-class attitude,' said Patrick. 'Now you'll never go.'

I felt awful.

'Can you play chess?'

I said, 'No,' and went home to Priory Road feeling very foolish.

+—

THE ANTIQUE ROOM

The Slade has just witnessed the passing of an epoch. The old antique room has fallen victim to the huge canvases everyone is now painting – American gigantism has pushed aside the academy. Skeletons, gnarled branches, shells, stones and classical plaster casts are thrown out. In the yard the copy of the head of Mausolus (the original is in the British Museum, and once crowned a tomb which was one of the seven wonders of the ancient world) stands in the rain. Clement Greenberg has spoken. Henry Moore and the English megaliths are out. Instead, American Popism and the fluorescent spaghetti trails of the Cohen brothers ensnare us.

+—

AND OTHER LANDSCAPES WENT AS WELL

I was brought up to loathe the Victorians – one thrilled as the ball and chain demolished their work. Down came Josiah Doll's Imperial Hotel in Russell Square, with its mosaic maps in the imperial pink of school atlases. Down came the Euston Arch, the Coal Exchange, Birkbeck's Penny Bank, whose great rotunda exploded as I watched in showers of multi-coloured faience. Off came the grey suits, the starched white collars, the pullovers and sensible shoes. Down came the tiled Lyons Corner Houses, the grocers' shop which weighed your orders, and packed them in blue bags; and the row houses, with their little back yards. In their place, curtain walling, Carnaby Street, supermarkets and finally, American hamburger joints – aptly known as The Great American Disaster.

+—

1966 – the Slade: I'm working more and more in the theatre room. I like working on shared projects. It breaks down the isolation of working as a painter. There is much greater aesthetic freedom. The theatre is not subject to the same strict rules we surround ourselves with as individual producers: I can employ imagery I would not dare or wish to use in my painting. So I'm definitely working as a theatre designer, not as a painter imposing an individual vision. The designs for Stravinsky's *Orpheus* are a direct response to Rauschenberg's 'Dante Suite', which were shown at the Whitechapel and made a great impression on me. The set is black and white, and made up from xeroxes of physique magazines and a variety of fragmented classical motifs. The backdrop contains a haunting portrait of 'A Boy in an Asylum' by Avedon collaged against an Inferno whose gates are the Brooklyn Bridge.

I've also designed Sartre's *Huis Clos*, in a set made entirely of red-hot velvet, with three velvet-covered armchairs, yellow, blue and black; and a set for *Volpone*, which has his bed high up on a pyramid of treasure. The atmosphere in the theatre room is friendly, and the tutors, Peter Shaw and Niko Georgiadis, give me enough freedom to hang myself.

+—

LOOKING BACK TO 1967
I can see clearly the division that was opening in my work between the painter and the designer, that was to be confirmed in two events that year. In May I opened the Lisson Gallery with Keith Milow, in a joint show. Nicholas Logsdale, the owner, was a fellow student at the Slade, who converted his small house in Bell Street with a junk shop underneath into a gallery. During the early part of the year we helped him with the painting, and by mid-May were ready to open to the sounds of *Sergeant Pepper*.

Keith's work was architectural, mine landscape. We were both figurative painters, but where was the figure? Keith was a fine draughtsman, perhaps the finest of his generation. At Camberwell, he produced beautiful life drawings. I also drew from the model at the Slade, but when the show opened there was no evidence of this.

During the previous years both of us had 'come out', and spent most of our spare time with the small band of gay artists around Patrick Procktor and David Hockney. David was the star – although other artists in the group were equally adventurous painters. But David fullfilled all the rules of the classic sixties' success. He passed for a working-class hero, had a sure grasp of publicity: his dyed blond hair, sharp American dress sense, coupled with his identification with the stars and stripes of Pop singled him out. By 1967, with the Cavafy etchings, David had made the gay vision his own. The drawings were matter-of-fact, the simplicity of their content a revolution. Any treatment of the homosexual figure was precluded, unless you wished to be labelled a follower. Patrick Procktor stopped painting the boys at La Douce.

The 'new generation' show three years earlier had established the painters of the sixties. Those of us who came right behind had a great struggle ahead. Success was the order of the day, and it had to be instant and heady. We all believed in it. Fifteen years later and the figure has at last surfaced in my work, and also in Keith's. For the moment we were the interregnum before Nicholas Logsdale provided a final solution when he turned the Lisson Gallery into the Temple of Conceptualism.

Meanwhile, that autumn, I exhibited theatrical designs at the Biennale des Jeunes in Paris. My entry was Prokofiev's *Prodigal Son*, which sent me on a different path to share for a brief moment the 1960s razzmatazz – not, as you might expect, at the Round House, but the wrong end, at the Opera House. The beginning of my career was to resemble the end of anyone else's.

─┼─

MANCHESTER STREET

Patrick looks down his long nose at me quizzically. Sitting down, we can talk to each other eye to eye; otherwise he towers over me, his voice booming around high above. Every now and then he peers down to take stock of the situation, like a delicate wader sizing its prey. He's painting a watercolour – 'Derek Telling Me about Orpheus' – with his butterfly washes, in the tiny room he sometimes uses as a studio. The sun streams through the zebra blinds, falls across the floor in bars. The sun is always shining in this room. Watercolours of Peter Hinewood lying in the sofa. Watercolours of Ossie, and new oils in washed pastel shades with Peter, Keith and myself; and a strange pink gymnasium filled with disembodied leather boys, with a drawn venetian blind . . . Patrick's speech is full of sudden enthusiasm, enquiries left suspended in the air. He seems taller than ever this afternoon.

─┼─

August 1966, Liverpool Road, Islington: The new house is in a permanent state of decoration . . . Michael's tropical fish bubble away in the gloom of the basement.

Stacked between the tanks are a thousand bottles of home-made wine. In the room above Michael plays piano selections from his musicals, which you never quite remember. Then he stops, and begins to type out one of his manuscripts. Brenda comes in from Chapel Market with volumes of the Arden Shakespeare sandwiched between cauliflowers, and trips over Keith Milow's pair of elephant-grey velvet pants, that lie in a hopeful and permanent heap of laundry outside her door. Roger is patiently stripping the wooden casements of the windows in their room. Upstairs on the top floor the record-player plays the Who, while the sun streams in through the window over my green landscape paintings and the rolls of used masking tape which cling to the floor.

+—

BLOW UP

Michael Ginsborg rang to say they needed extras for Antonioni's *Blow Up*. Would I alert the Slade, as the film extras provided by the industry for Swinging London are all middle-aged antique dealers and their molls – Antonioni had a fit when he saw them. So Ron (who arrived from Canada) and I took off for the Porchester Hall to be auditioned. When Antonioni arrived the hall was packed with students. He took one brief look at us and said, 'You're lovely' through an interpreter; and took the lot of us at £8 a day, which is a fortune.

The following week, dressed to the nines, we presented ourselves at the Elstree studios. I stood in the queue till the wardrobe mistress looked me up and down and said 'T-shirt!' – meaning I had to strip and put on a hideous Swinging London T-shirt to dance to the Yardbirds. Ron, who'd made no effort, got by. No way was I going to appear in this film in that T-shirt, even in the background. So I sacrificed riches and failed to turn up for the shooting. Each night Ron faithfully collected his £8 and danced. In the film he appears as a shadow for two seconds.

+—

SATURDAY NIGHT AND SUNDAY MORNING

Last night, after the pub closed, I found myself among a gang of Saturday-night revellers at a bottle party in Earl's Court. I'd already had one too many when we arrived at the flat, and I lost my friends in the crush. The living-room floor vibrated to the Stones, and in the centre a dark-haired boy was throwing himself about, attracting a lot of attention. He smiled at me; and dancing through the crowd asked me my name and what I was doing. Before I knew what was happening I was seated in a car speeding out along the Westway.

We arrived at one of those small suburban row houses, and he deposited me in the uncomfortable lounge while he went to fetch some coffee. I lay back on the sofa and glared drunkenly at the ceiling which billowed above. This reverie was interrupted by the arrival of a small bald man with two mugs of coffee. I shifted on the sofa to be out of reach, as he seemed rather too friendly. It was only when he opened his mouth that I realized my Beatle friend was nothing but a wig. Illusions had evaporated, and no amount of coaxing could rescue the situation. Then he disappeared to return with the wig back on, and a pack of amyl nitrate capsules which he crushed in my face. This made matters considerably worse, for combined with the alcohol it caused the room to blur and fuzz at the edges. I crawled upstairs and hit the bed in a stupor. My Beatle, realizing that nothing would rouse me, gave up the struggle with resignation and went to sleep.

In the morning I woke with a splitting headache. When the Beatle had restored himself in the bathroom, he told me that Aunty was making breakfast for us. I made to put on my trousers but he said they never dressed for breakfast. So feeling utterly miserable I followed him downstairs to the back parlour where 'Aunty', bald, with rolls of cherubic pink fat round his middle, was crouched in front of a gas fire, toasting bread on a metal prong like a devil in the bottom corner of some Last Judgement scene. He paused briefly to look me up and down, and then told me to sit on the bed. The bed was occupied by a large lady with an ample hennaed bouffant and a tough-looking lad of about eighteen, who was obviously also a guest and seemed to be even more embarrassed than I was by this unexpected turn of events. The large lady had picked him up the night before at the local, and now he was trapped in the back parlour while she explained in intimate detail his physical attributes and stamina as a lover. 'He fucks like an angel,' she announced. The boy turned a terrified scarlet and slid further beneath the blankets in protest as she attempted to pull them away to reveal his tattoos for Aunty, whose eyes glistened in anticipation. In the corner was a small Hammond organ at which my Beatle friend sat and played selections from Rodgers and Hammerstein with ostentatious trills. Aunty munched his toast and stared at my cock in appreciation. I managed one slice before making an excuse about feeling cold; then rushed upstairs, pulled on my clothes and came down again.

After breakfast they offered to drive me into the centre as they were going to the Pig and Whistle, a gay pub in Belgravia. Aunty, dressed in a smart suit, led us round the corner to the garage at the back of the little house. The doors opened to reveal a Rolls – in which we drove back to town. At Sloane Square, I made an excuse and got out, and hammered breathlessly at Anthony's door.

+–

ANTHONY HARWOOD

I met Anthony Harwood in 1966 through the Danish sculptor Olaf Gravsen, who stayed with his during part of that year. Anthony lived an itinerant gypsy life with his Georgian wife, Princess Nina – travelling across Europe from one hotel to another. In London, which he considered home, he kept a flat in the block above Sloane Square tube station, where he retired in the daytime to write his plays, before cooking Nina supper, which he would take to her hotel in a plastic carrier bag. During the day you would find him sitting cross-legged on a silver cushion in front of his typewriter, with his work scattered across the floor. He always dressed immaculately, if eccentrically, in silver wind jackets, black polo-necks, velvet breeches and court shoes with diamond buckles. His belt clasp was a snake in gun-metal with a diamond set in its head. There were coats in strange modern fabrics, gold, black and silver. He said that he wished to live in a diamond – hard, glittering and pure. If you arrived hungry there was strong black coffee, fresh orange juice laced with rose water, and scrambled eggs which were scented.

During the year we became firm friends. His life seemed rich and glamorous. He sent postcards with extravagant messages signed 'A' and books dedicated: 'It's better with no shoes on, no shoes at all' – this in the two volumes of Genji, but there were others – Ouspensky, *The Gothic Tales* of Karen Blixen (this was a particular favourite as he had known her and was writing a play based on *The Dreamers*). The music on the hi-fi was Callas, or Stravinsky, if not the Beatles or the Loving Spoonful. I was given the keys to Sloane Square the following year, and it became a vital extension to my life, an escape from my room in Islington – and later, when I moved into my first warehouse at Upper Ground, a place to have a bath. Also, since the King's Road was the 'centre' of London for a few brief years at the end of the sixties, it was the ideal place to start an evening which might drift from the Colville to the Casserole, and on to the Gigolo. In Sloane Square the furniture was kept to a minimum – a bed, a glass table with three clear perspex cubes for seats, and one silver lustre vase with iris or scented narcissus. The flat was on the top floor of the block, and had views right across London. Its walls were clad in grey mirror.

+–

In 1960 the local antique shop in Newport on the Isle of Wight burned all post-Regency furniture. The middle class wanted the eighteenth-century Chippendale in original or reproduction, and everyone else wanted the New. A bright new world came into being – but as the decade wore on nostalgia crept in by the back door and drove out the New like a rampant weed. Teenagers, invented in the fifties, became the pampered trend-setters of the sixties. Success came early – earlier here than in the US – and with it John Stevens' Carnaby Street clothes. Mini-skirts and mini-cars, Beatles haircuts, the whole adrenalin rush of the New. Housing was cheap and plentiful, and the decaying Georgian and Victorian terrace houses of central London were covered with 'Unfurnished flat to let' signs. You could rent a three-roomed flat plus ballroom for a fiver in Notting Hill – many places were half that price. Like an exotic flower that has bloomed and died in one night, by 1970 all this was over; and the Past, which in the eighties is our present, had come to stay – in a thousand shops with names like 'Retro' – and fashions had looped the loop.

Long ago, when things were New, and the Beatles were singing 'It's getting better all the time', Ossie Clarke bought a small Art Deco clip in chrome and glass, and pinned it to his shirt. By 1967 they'd spread like a rash; and the Deco revival, the first revival of our own dear modern twentieth century, was on – (Teddy boys didn't count, as the Edwardian period was a nineteenth-century hangover). Only we knew this. And the great Pop machine, in all its idiocy, was plundering art nouveau and the awful Beardsley's etiolated line in sinuous acid parody. This was most definitely out. Instead, the hunt was on for chrome and glass, and silver lacquer. My own great Deco prize – a Rowley gallery suite, split between our home in Liverpool Road and the Lisson Gallery.

+

May 1967, Liverpool Road: Anthony rings up and asks if I'd please take him and his wife to Camden Passage antique market that Saturday. Although she is quite small, Nina sails through the market, giving the impression that Russian 'royalty' must have dwarfed everything around them. Sailing into Chiu's Art Deco shop she resembles a stately silver barrage balloon, hung with huge gold bangles and strings of enormous pearls which Anthony says belonged to the Dowager Empress of China. At a recent opening of Warhol's in NYC Nina was gliding down the aisle in a white lace mini-skirt, turning all the heads, when a young man said 'Unreal' in a voice loud enough for the whole theatre to hear. It was like a gunshot across the bows of a galleon; for Nina heard too; and looking him straight in the eye, stretched herself so that the diamonds glittered like a Christmas tree and said 'All Real' in RRRussian, very loudly . . .

So, at Camden Passage we walk into Chiu's Deco shop and Nina sits down while Anthony discovers treasures and brings them over for her inspection. She is very short-sighted and holds these prizes within an inch of her eyes. Chiu flutters around amongst his Lalique like a doll in the Peking Opera – his eyes alight with the myriad reflections from the Dowager Empress's phosphorescent pearls.

At this point I must explain that Madame la Princesse (her French maid always makes you wait outside the door while she announces you with true protocol) never *buys* anything. This, I believe, is a prerogative of royalty. Chiu doesn't know this, of course, and allows his cabinets to be ransacked by Anthony, who looks like 'Death of Chatterton' in his silver boots and velvet breeches. 'Thees ees remarkable,' Nina says, peering at a vase. 'Vat ees?'

Lalique, says Chiu.

'Oh, Laleeque, very eenteresting Anthony! Vee buy – Meester Chiu, you deeleever to Hotel Vestbury, vee haf tea.' Then she stretches out her hand and picks up a box of Swan Vesta matches (which Chiu used to light his black Sobranie cigarettes) and slowly, ever so slowly and deliberately, holds it up to her myopic eye, so that it touches her eyelashes. 'Eenteresting, Anthony!! Most eenteresting. Vat ees?'

There is a pause. 'A box of Swan Vesta matches, Nina dear.'

'Oh.' An even longer pause. 'Zo clever, Zo clever. Most remarkable vat zee do zees days. Now vee go Meester Chiu. I keep zees as momento.' And she opens her handbag and pops them in, staring like a basilisk. Needless to say the vase, once delivered, was never paid for.

＋

Anthony walked with a slight limp. He told me that after he met Nina in Paris in the early fifties, she took him to India as her secretary with her husband Denis. While they were travelling Anthony bathed in the Ganges at Benares and caught poliomyelitis, which completely paralysed him. Meanwhile, Nina's husband died.

After exhausting the Western-style doctors, Nina brought Anthony to a holy man in the Himalayan foothills who cured him. Telling this story, Anthony insisted the man could fly.

Nina and he were married, and thereafter he led a jewel-encrusted life. She combed her long grey hair with a gold and ivory comb, sitting on the edge of the bed in her black dress. Besides the Dowager Empress's pearls, she wore Marie de' Medici's wedding ring; on her ankles there were gold bangles. For years she waged a battle for her sister's jewels, emeralds and rubies, with Chanel, who was said to have arrived at the sister's deathbed where she was left alone for a few minutes. When the family returned Chanel was sitting at the bedside brazenly wearing the jewels, saying that the dying woman had gained consciousness for a moment to insist she take them from the dressing-table. Still wearing them, she walked out of the room and drove back to Paris.

When the Arno flooded Florence, Anthony muttered darkly to himself and was off. He arrived back some days later carrying a Clarks' shoe-box, which he tipped out on to the glass-topped table at Sloane Square. It was full of gaudy-looking gew-gaws, among which were three strands of beautiful blue glass beads. I was off down the King's Road and asked him if I could wear them. He said yes, if I really wanted to, but I'd have to be very careful as they were all sapphires.

Anthony kept the whereabouts of his flat a secret from Nina. It was his hideaway. So when one day he decided to 'disappear' she had no idea where he'd gone. Within hours I received a phone call – 'Derek, come to tea at Vestbury.' She allowed no time for an excuse – I was the unwilling rope in a tug-of-war, for Anthony had made me promise I would deny all knowledge of his whereabouts. Arriving at the Westbury I found Nina, tearful, sitting on a sofa in the lobby surrounded by forbidding young Russian aristocrats in dark suits, who stood like a guard of honour. I sat opposite her and nervously sipped my tea while all around I could feel the eyes boring into me.

'Derek, Darleeng, Ver is Anthony – I lov him very much.'

'I'm not certain, Nina.' White lies for White Russians. 'He said he was going away for a few days. He'll be back, I promise.'

'Derek, you know thees flat.'

The rat trap was sprung – 'No,' I said, with a guilt which rattled my tea-cup.

Nina took out a handkerchief and wiped her eyes. I felt truly awful. The next morning there was a knock at the door and a grey uniformed chauffeur handed me a parcel with an 'Are you Mr Jarman?' I opened it nervously – no note, but it contained the painting I had given Nina the previous month.

Anthony fared no better. After tea a quick phone call to the Commissioner of the Metropolitan Police, who assured Nina they could trace a missing person in a few hours. So by lunch-time the next day, along with photos of Anthony coming out of Sloane Square underground, she had the address – 19 Sloane

Square House. She sent a telegram – 'Impossible, yes. Invisible, never.' And for the next month had private detectives follow Anthony and his friends.

—+—

1968 – THE LISSON GALLERY

I have been painting landscapes fairly consistently since I left school, and during that time they've changed a great deal. At first they were sparked off by holidays with Aunt Isobel at Kilve in North Somerset. I painted the red brown earth and dark green of the Quantock Hills, which are at their brightest under the stormy grey skies which blow up over the Bristol Channel. In these paintings there are megaliths and standing stones and clumps of beech trees. By 1965 this has all changed. Oil paint is out. Aquatec, the new acrylic paint, in. The canvas is no longer rough brown flax, but smooth white cotton duck. The use of rulers and masking tape produces a metrical precision, and 'replaces' improvisation.

I began a series of landscapes which were larger – you have to paint large at the Slade or nobody notices. They have flat red grounds, blue skies, above eye-tricking imagery: *Trompe l'oeil* water, real taps, classical statues. The largest of these canvases, nine feet by seven, wins the Peter Stuyvesant award for painting at the Young Contemporaries show at the Tate in May 1967.

Since then things have changed again, and at my one-man show, my first one-man show at the Lisson, the canvases have become linear and perfectly balanced. There are no longer any figures or objects, and definitely no jokes. The canvases which are left raw resemble marble through which a grid of lines has been scored.

I am in love with de Chirico, and the two rooms of paintings which form the show are secretly dedicated to him. I hope they will be seen as 'Enigmatic'. Dom Sylvester Houedard has given me a present of one of his 'typestracts'. He's upstairs, thundering away at the typewriter. He hands me another paper on which is written, 'Mrs God invites you to her opening.' An invitation to my own show.

—+—

THE ROUNDHOUSE

Queuing for returned tickets for the Living Theatre at the Roundhouse, I bumped into Keith Milow with one of his millionaire friends. Keith has a passion for bankers, particularly if they are young and play squash. This latterday Maecenas had bought a dozen tickets which he was giving away at Keith's prompting to the young and promising with much ostentation. I managed to lay my hands on one. As we waited for the performance he managed to drop names like bricks – Andy, Jasper, Don, Dan, Claes – art bricks.

Then Julian Beck and his theatre commenced their performance with a dirge of 'can'ts' – you can't strip in public, smoke dope, etc. They'd hardly begun when, immediately in front of us, Michael Chapman from the Exploding Galaxy, all six foot four of him, started to heckle in a loud voice. First he stripped, giving a loud commentary on the process and apologizing for his spotty torso, and then lit a joint, all the while shouting 'You can if you want to!' In this way the beginning of the performance was reduced to a shambles and the Living Theatre suddenly became the outraged guardians of their own negativity. 'Great – great – great,' said Keith's banker.

Later, when Michael passed by him in the interval he rushed up to him and said, 'You must have dinner with us.' But Michael, looking down from his great height, said, 'What the fuck do I need dinner for?' and spat at him right between the eyes.

+—

THE EXPLODING GALAXY, 1967

From the top of a 19 bus – Michael Chapman walking down Charing X Road, swathed in sheets of white lining-paper, trailing a number of empty cans which bumped along the pavement making a terrible noise.

+—

At 99 Balls Pond Road the Exploding Galaxy is alive with Experiment. David Medalla hops about like a wide-eyed genie, initiating this and that. This evening Richard and I spent the time attempting a dance exercise which became gradually more chaotic as we grew more tired.

+—

I went with the Exploding Galaxy to Artaud's *Spurt of Blood* this evening at the Royal College. There were explosions in which great polystyrene rocks fell on the audience, who ducked and almost panicked. Then a whole troop of Lolita nymphets danced, Isadora-like, in very skimpy Greek dresses through the audience with spray cans of lavender scent, singing as they slid off the knees of the oldest men in the audience. In the row in front of me a woman in an expensive fur sat unaware of the blood dripping all over her from the cow's head and hooves suspended above the audience and hidden by the lighting grid. We were repeatedly informed, like Candide, that we lived in the best of all possible worlds. Everything went wrong. Finally the nanny lifted up her skirts and a red balloon inflated between her legs until it burst. This was the best piece of experimental theatre that I've ever seen.

╼

1968, Paris: Michael Chapman was in the Coupole this evening. We were all exchanging stories of French hospitality. I'd spent last night in a prison cell. Having hitch-hiked from Boulogne and been dumped at 2 a.m. in a strange part of Paris I was foolish enough to ask a jumpy *flic* where I was. I was marched down the streets at machine-gun point, and deposited for the night in a thruppenny-bit cell next door to a cage full of girls who had been plying their trade without the correct permits. They sang all night and made jokes about the *flics'* limp dicks.

In the cafe Michael drew out a scruffy sheet of poems from his bag and proclaimed in a stentorian voice – 'Paris, City of Art' – then proceeded to read aloud a sound poem he'd written. Within seconds a hush had fallen over the cafe, the waiters stopped in their tracks, and a table of gross-looking burghers nearby, who were tucking into a large meal, started to make bleating noises. Michael, undeterred, raised his voice to a howl, rose, and walked over waving his poems in the air, glowering at them, clucking like a chicken. Then he walked slowly and deliberately round the table, grunting like a pig. The waiters, instead of reacting with anger, fell about laughing and brought us more drinks. *Vive la France!*

╼

JAZZ CALENDAR
9 January 1968: The opening of *Jazz Calendar* was a Christmas Day. Anthony gave me a garland of silver bells held by a cascade of bows; Michael Fish, a velvet suit in a soft dark brown, which I wore instead of a black tie. Ma made me a silk shirt and jabot in cream, and gave me a pearl tie-pin, and Robert Medley threw a party for the whole gang. Patrick, David, Anthony *et al. Jazz Calendar* itself looked like a packet of Licorice Allsorts dancing; and the audience, who loved it, gave us curtain call after curtain call. Seventeen in all, I think. This morning the reviews were all favourable.

Studio, Liverpool Road, 1967

***Jazz Calendar*, 1968 – 'Friday's Child', Nureyev and Sibley** (Photo: *Jennie Watton*)

When I drew the designs for the costumes of *Jazz* last November, Sir Frederick Ashton said that if I had any problems with the dancers he'd take care of them; but Nureyev was a law unto himself and I'd have to cope as best I could. I hadn't realized that this was a warning! The design for 'Friday's Child' is a red and blue love-knot, which is reflected in the costumes which are split from top to bottom, half vermilion, half cobalt-blue. When I arrived at the ballet rehearsal-rooms just before lunch one morning, for my first fitting with Nureyev, I found Sir Fred talking to Margot Fonteyn in the dressing-rooms. After Fred had introduced us she asked me to show her the costume, which an assistant from the wardrobe had packed in a box. When she saw it she said, 'You can't cut a dancer like Nureyev in half like that.' I was tongue-tied; and Sir Fred, sensing danger, said, 'I think it's time for lunch.'

I waited nervously for the summons into Nureyev's dressing-room. The whole business of theatres and design was completely new to me and I found costume fittings unnerving – taking in a bulge here and there, and attempting to reassure insecure dancers that they looked good, knowing nothing of *how* they should look in any case. When Nureyev announced he was ready we walked into the room to find him naked, drying himself from a shower. I was even more unprepared for this and didn't know which way to turn my eyes. Blushing, I introduced myself and hesitantly showed him the costume. My hesitation was like a red flag to a bull. He picked up the costume and pinched the material nonchalantly between his finger, before dropping it with disdain. He looked at me mockingly, and said the material was awful. Then rubbing himself suggestively with the towel he lectured me on tights, and said that it would be wasting his time trying them on. He had a perfect pair which he'd brought back from Switzerland. Then looking me slowly up and down he said – 'Well.' From that moment our relationship became one of cat and defenceless mouse. I'd suggested a wig, and he arrived at the next rehearsal with an awful black plastic number from Woolworths. Wearing it back to front, he danced in front of the company and as they fell about laughing declared he always looked ridiculous in wigs.

And so it went on, right up till the last moment. At the premiere on 9 January I had no idea if he would wear the costume or not. When at the beginning of the evening it was announced that he had flu and would not be performing, the whole audience went 'Oh . . . ' Then, just before the curtain went up on my front cloth, the announcer said that in spite of the flu he was going to give it a go. 'Ah . . .' went the audience. Everything was played for maximum effect. I sat on the edge of my seat in terror, half-expecting him to appear in practice clothes and a Beatles wig, but he was wearing my costume. During the curtain calls he said he didn't like the colours, but by then this game of Russian roulette was played out. And after all, I had witnessed one of the seven wonders of the Swinging Decade – I had seen Nureyev naked.

+–

Marie Rambert arrived during the lighting rehearsals this morning and sat quizzically in a box. She made little comment about the sets. Unlit, the Naples yellow cloths looked grey and the stage rather empty. All during the lighting rehearsal there'd been a battle with Bill Bundy, a belligerent and unfriendly man who has given my inexperience no quarter. He is involved in a feud with the manager of the Opera House, John Sullivan. They don't speak to each other, and communicate (I'm told) with acid little notes. When I first arrived in the theatre, I made the mistake of listening to John's advice about the perspex globes for 'Tuesday's Child', while Bill stood in the background. This afternoon when we were lighting the Nureyev scene – 'Friday' – I asked him to light the stage half blue, half red. He threw a tantrum and said it was quite impossible. I rashly suggested he put blue lights on one side and red lights on the other and see what happened – 'Are you telling me how to do my job?' – and throwing his notes down with a crash, he went into a sulk. Fred, who I could see was getting more and more impatient, suddenly said loudly from the stage, 'Stop behaving like Maria Callas, Bill. This is only a little ballet.'

+–

Sloane Square: Anthony sits cross-legged on the white carpets with his 'maxims', postcards, and the playscript of *The Dreamers* lying scattered around him. He hunches over the electric typewriter, knocking at the keys with three fingers. A gnarled windblown tree in a pot rises up behind him, its branches hung with crystal icicles which reflect in the grey mirror walls. Anthony sips his tea from a grey Japanese bowl. The Ting Ling bowl. *Clack. Click. Clack.* – 'Rome's trouble was too few Lions.'

    He gets up with difficulty and walks to the kitchen, where the Princess's dinner is cooking. As he walks, he limps slightly; and an impish smile crosses over the carefully constructed face. Abbé Liszt of the King's Road. He returns carrying Nina's *gigot* in a carrier bag, gives me the door keys and leaves for the Westbury.

+–

DESIGNING FOR MOZART — THE INVASION OF PRAGUE

23 August 1968: When the curtain came down on *Don Giovanni* last night John Gielgud and I faced a barrage of hissing. The opera establishment was out in force for the opening of the Coliseum. And the next day, being the 'outsider' in this production, I copped it in a series of savage reviews. Not one kind word. In self-defence I decided that opera-goers were a race of hysterics, fanatic worshippers at a necropolis, who would go through the most extreme contortions to convince themselves that the corpse is animate.

As we walked off the stage, John Gielgud said that like much modern art my designs had been misunderstood. Today a letter arrived from him saying much the same thing. Even though he has been outwardly encouraging I know that in his heart he dislikes my designs. In the publicity photograph taken last May, when we began all this, he seems puzzled by my enthusiasm as we look at them. Today, everyone avoids me in the theatre: a lesson has been learned – on both sides. First and foremost, that the living and the dead don't mix. The music of the *Don* might seem as alive as ever, yet the sexual politic is obsolete. And since that is the core of the opera . . . I made simple decisions for the design, I set it roughly contemporary with Mozart, in Goya's Spain – but like Tricorne reinterpreted the historical past in a contemporary manner. My original intention was a single all-purpose set, and colour, masses of it, to combat the usual browns and greys of the theatre.

From the moment I began work there had been opposition, and I wasn't old enough or experienced enough to handle it. Drop cloths were ordered and sets were changed; up until the last moment the theatre was being converted – an ugly false proscenium was introduced, and the stagehands changed the sets, so they thundered through the arias, unaccustomed to the new space. Sir John was quite out of his depth as well, and prey to every bit of 'sound' advice. Meanwhile, Sir Fred had warned me that I did the opera at my own peril – adding, of course, that I had no choice. The lesson had to be learned. A career that started in reverse has been brought to an abrupt halt, not a moment too soon.

+—

GIBRALTAR — TANGIERS

Robin and I arrived on the Rock with its schizo culture of Tudor-bethan pubs and Spanish taverns a few days after the ill-fated *Don Giovanni* opened and nearly closed the London Coliseum. We were both wearing long hair, and at the Moroccan checkpoint we were informed that our appearance was degenerate. So, in spite of a

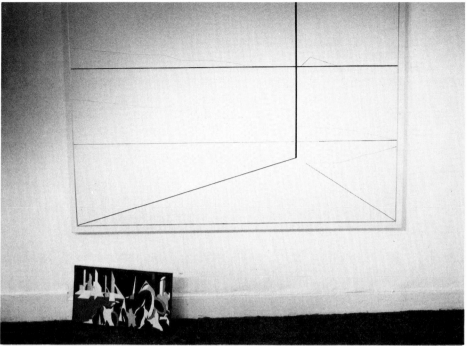

Don Giovanni, **1968 – landscape painting and sketch for the front cloth**
(Photo: Ray Dean)

Don Giovanni, **1968 – final act drop cloth** (Photo: Ray Dean)

request for scissors, we were posted back to Gibraltar where we had military short-back-and-sides from a mess barber. To our chagrin, when we arrived in Tangiers all the Moroccan boys had long hair, except for a few who had no hair at all. We discovered that this was the local police punishment for lads who were too friendly with the foreigners. We spent our time swimming and sightseeing. With our youth, lack of money and deplorable haircuts, we were not attractive propositions. For the boys.

The Hotel Colon was owned by one Andy Flack. At breakfast he entertained couples from Wimbledon and Clapham with risqué stories, his up-swept diamante glasses perched on the end of his nose, his blue-rinsed hair immaculately coiffed. He slept with his Moroccan boyfriend Mohammed behind a curtain near the stairs. This lair was lined with yellowing paperbacks – lives of Heliogabalus – and dog-eared photos from his former life as a drag queen. There was a particularly startling one, taken circa 1940, of him as Carol Lombard in the arms of an immense muscle-bound gladiator. Lads, he told Robin and me, were definitely not allowed in at night – even if you tiptoed, he'd hear.

We went to the old theatre, which was now a cinema. High above, plaster images of Cervantes, Shakespeare, and other great worthies of European literature stared sightlessly down on a mob of Moroccan revellers who treated the Italian B movie – Hercules versus Atlas, Medusa and hosts of busty Italian ladies – like a football match. At times it seemed a fight would break out as the tension mounted. Except for *The Wizard of Oz*, it was probably the most exciting film I've ever watched.

In the evening we used to get stoned in the Dancing Boy Cafe, where the old men played dominoes, smoked kief and drank mint tea, all the while entertained by twelve-year-old boys who danced in diaphanous sequined dresses.

When we left Tangier I nagged Robin lest he try to take any of the nefarious weed home, and he swore he was clean. The Gib customs turned us upside down, tipping out Robin's cigarettes and finding two joints that had been placed there as a parting gift from a crony at the bar.

The cells resembled a zoo, and behind the bars Rob looked like a dejected monkey. I stared at him uncomfortably and slipped a copy of *The Times* through as a parting gesture. He showed up five days later, saying he'd met a sailor in the cells.

+—

MAY 1969 – LE NID

Patrick Procktor asked me to spend a few days with him at Tony Richardson's house in the South of France. We flew to Nice and drove to the old house, which is deep in a pine forest. We arrived as Mick Jagger left, and Patrick, who knew the place, rushed ahead. I discovered him in the guest-room lying on Mick's unmade bed. 'This is mine,' he said, 'and there's no need to change the sheets.'

+—

1969 – MARLBOROUGH FINE ART

Anthony Harwood and I arrived at the Marlborough Gallery to see the Henry Moore show – in that plush environment, the work looked like the perfect foil for the tacky entrance hall of a bank. Visitors were walking around the place in silent reverential awe. Anthony went up to the desk and whispered confidentially to the girl sitting there. A door opened and a dapper young man in a Savile Row suit appeared. He motioned Anthony into the back room, but Anthony said in a loud voice that everyone could hear, 'Could you tell me a little about these sculptures? This one over here in pink marble, for instance.'

'That's Soraya marble from Persia,' said the young man.

'And this one?' said Anthony.

'Oh, that's Carrara.'

Anthony prodded it. 'How much is it?' Art-lovers hovered and strained their ears. Something in Anthony's look allowed no quarter. The young man was about to ask him back, but instead suddenly said '£40,000.'

'£40,000,' said Anthony, 'quite reasonable.' He prodded the next sculpture; 'And what's this one made of?'

By now the whole gallery was ears and eyes for Anthony. While he limped around, his well manicured hands fluttering over the marble, the exhibition was reduced to inflated price-tags and the quality of the material. Round the corner, at the end, was a huge reclining figure in elm. Anthony stopped in front of it and said, 'I like marble but wood's a much finer material. I'll buy that one.'

These words were like stones flying in a glass house. 'That's already taken, sir.'

'What a pity. I'll leave you my card. Do ring me when he does another.'

+—

A ROSE IS A ROSE IS A . . .

Sir Francis Rose, premier Baron of Scotland and Grandee of Spain, descended from the Inquisitor Torquemada, crept like a black beetle with uncertain steps through Soho. A gremlin fallen from the battlements of Nightmare Alley, with his whirly corkscrew walking-stick and black bohemian hat crushed over his silver hair.

At the beginning of the century Francis had crossed all seven tiers of the Inferno to be born as an elegant golden boy in a painting by John Singer Sargent. From that moment legend stuck to him like hoarfrost on a blasted oak. A cardinal dressed in the scarlet silks of the Whore of Babylon, he built an altar in his Rolls-Royce and toured the world. In Paris he was a painter whom Gertrude Stein mistook for a genius in a fit of Moderne amnesia. 'A Rose is a Rose is a Rose,' she wrote, and then announced the advent of the heavenly twins of modern art – Pablo and Francis. Jean Cocteau, impressed and never missing a trick, brought twenty-one sailor boys as a gift to Francis on his twenty-first birthday.

—+—

May 1967, Sloane Square: Anthony Harwood told me this evening that he and Nina were invited early in the fifties to a dinner-party Francis gave in Paris for Anna de Noialles and other celebrities. They were waited on by a young Spanish boy, dressed in scarlet, who changed the courses with an engaging, absent-minded insolence – thumping the plates down – he muddled his way through the dinner. When Anthony asked Francis who the boy was (he was, by the by, very attractive) the latter announced to his guests' surprise, 'My son.'

Later this story emerged: some time in the early thirties Francis was travelling through Spain in his fabled Rolls when it broke down in some fairly remote village. He was forced to stay a few days while spare parts were brought from Madrid, and during this time he seduced the girl who was his chambermaid. Months later all she knew of her son's father was that he was an Englishman called Rose. The war made further contact impossible. Then a month or so before the dinner-party, Francis had been sought out by a priest who broke the secrecy of the confessional to tell him he had a son – a peasant boy in Spain. Francis brought him to Paris, and had him wait at his table.

—+—

June 1969, Belgravia : Karl Bowen and I were invited to tea this afternoon by Francis Rose. He has a small basement flat that Cecil Beaton is paying for. When we arrived, Francis appeared out of the gloom, carrying his cat with a diamond collar. In the hall he pointed out Sargent's dazzling portrait of him as a boy, before ushering us into a gloomy little studio smelling heavily of incense. He shuffled about to get 'tea' together in between snorting snuff.

The studio was crowded by the new paintings which he's been working on. These were all crudely painted in comic-strip Pop about which there was nothing remarkable. But their subject-matter threw both of us. Hitler and Goebbels were most prominent. Francis obviously expected us to say something; and when Karl muttered 'interesting' Francis said sharply, 'I've been painting old friends. Old friends are always INTERESTING.' He then served us with glasses of sickly crème de menthe and enlarged on his holidays in Germany, and Hitler's exquisite good manners. Karl quietly poured his drink into one of the brush pots when Francis wasn't looking as he was certain it was poisoned.

-+-

1971. POWIS TERRACE

The Art Deco blight has taken over David's home. Lemonade is served in precious Lalique glasses. There's a dining-table that would seat the boardroom of the Chase Manhattan, and David has the food brought in from Mr Chow's. The flat now parodies his painting. There are huge bunches of tulips in yet more Lalique vases dotted around like wreaths. The place is antiseptic, a waiting-room for the good life. The same blight has overtaken Warhol's Factory. The room of silver dreams has gone, to be replaced by the lobby of a bank with huge brass Deco desks from the *France*. When I first came to Powis Terrace you could lounge around, but now the decoration dwarfs and depresses. It's the house of any millionaire art-collector. The good taste shrieks: there is the original Mackintosh hall chair, the ample sofas, and a fine twenties' neoclassical decorator's picture of a godlike boy which hangs like Peter over it all. Conversation is forced and very difficult. Henry Geldzahler sits like a Buddha round every corner. Tonight, over dinner, his conversation pours out, an unending eulogy. At the other side of the table Stephen Buckley, a camp-follower, nods his assent.

After dinner I make excuses and leave early. How sad all this is, life illustrating the art so remorselessly. David, who seems the same on the surface, has become a tortoise within a decorator's shell. He let the dollar dowagers take over.

-+-

SWINGING DECAYED

In Liverpool Road you met Joe Orton passing Chapel Market. The bus to the Slade from Priory Road passed over the world-famous crossing at Abbey Road. But life seemed to touch lightly on the decade – an Edwardian yachting hat from Herbert Johnson to hike around America. Listening to *Sergeant Pepper* in Anthony's all glass and mirror flat. Sitting in Patrick Proctor's studio nearer the hub, sun streaming through venetian blinds as he painted 'Derek Telling Me about Orpheus'. Or appearing as one of the characters in the painting 'Shades' of the Coffee Bar La Douce in D'Arblay Street with Ossie and Keith Milow. Sitting in a silver convertible with Peter Hinewood wearing a sky-blue metallic leather jacket Ossie had designed for him . . . Kennedy's assassination announced at my friend Caroline's twenty-first. The march on the American Embassy during the Cuban crisis. The march in Fleet Street to protest against Mick Jagger's arrest, blocking the paper vans by filing across the crossing in front of the law courts. Pauline Fordham's jacket, glittering like Liberty at the barricades. The sun still filtering through the blinds in Patrick's flat as we sipped his favourite Vouvray. Wayne Sleep dancing in the King's Road with a T-shirt: 'To live is to dance – to dance is to live.' Beads and chiffon scarves: clothes seemed so important, they were a means of broadcasting a philosophy . . . The theatre, which in those days seemed alive, even at the Aldwych – *The Comedy of Errors* which I saw seven times – *The Wars of the Roses* – Patrick's designs for *Saint's Day* and the Rimbaud play . . . David Medalla and Paul Keiler's 99 Balls Pond Road. The first showing of Kenneth Anger's *Scorpio Rising* and the *Magick Lantern Cycle* at Camberwell and the endless hours of SLEEP – Satie and Mahler. The Who singing as I painted my landscapes at Liverpool Road – Liquatec acrylic paint and white cotton duck – Ferlinghetti – Corso – Ginsberg – Burroughs – Kerouac's *Book of Dreams*.

Catalogues like manna from the Museum of Modern Art – the Machine – Ouspensky – and the *Tales of Genji* which Anthony gave me, and I never opened, 'It's better with no shoes, no shoes at all.' Peter de Rome in a grey mac showing movies at David Hockney's (one in particular: two boys naked in front of a fire talk of Garbo, and crossing over to the window discover that she's passing far below in the street, dark glasses and woolly hat). The smell of Gallener paint and polish, Kasmin and Cavafy. Robert Fraser's 'Memorial' show – the opening of the Lisson, Nicholas Logsdale obsessed with white paint . . . and painters' lofts, Mark Lancaster at Dick Smith's, 'real' American painting on the walls in Old Street – Ken Noland's vast bales of canvas and his brother painting the Stripes like gigantic awnings. New York City, before the hangover. Cheap housing, Notting Hill and Soho – Anthony Harwood's 'plans' – a mirror Rolls-Royce, dinner at the Dorchester ('You have to see it all, Derek, it's most important') and his *grandes dames*, Nina, Mrs Fraser, Lady M-----, Mrs I-----, ON DUTY.

Shyness. I was immensely shy and gauche – at dinner would sit in silence, a bad table companion who could only talk to those I knew, and usually on home ground – parties were an agony and I found myself at a lot of them; the newly rich and sophisticated gave them with abandon – Tony Richardson, his toucans and metallic rooms – usually after a suitable time I ducked and ran, disappeared without saying goodbye. Often I ate in restaurants alone and nearly always went out alone – preferred to prop up bars with anonymity, talk to strangers in the Gigolo and the Hustler, and walk home early in the morning from Chelsea to West Hampstead.

Painting at Liverpool Road: I was impatient, wanted quick immaculate results, hated 'the struggle', the time that it took physically to complete an idea – I envied Keith Milow's concentration. Felt guilty. Thought the results had come too easily. Thought that facility bought shallowness. Nevertheless, still refused to struggle. I was obsessed with environments and objects, but discarded them with ease. Out of sight was out of mind. I understood Anthony when he shrugged his shoulders after he'd lost a decade's work.

I became obsessed by the beauty of young men – the obsession alternated elation with paranoia. I failed to declare my passions lest they cause embarrassment. Then rushed headlong into the back room for public sex. I created my own delight in exhibitionism. In the sixties the effect seemed all – I took Diaghilev's commandment, *ETONNEZ NOUS*, to heart; but shunned success in myself and others, or wherever I encountered it. At that time wordly success seemed the easiest of prizes, and a deadly trap. I never built on it, always destroyed it. I guarded against it by always being broke; and if the bank balance ever hit the blue, I gave it away in a series of magnanimous gestures which amounted to distress signals . . . All this passes through my mind as I think of London then.

Relationships in the gay art world switched like musical chairs: ABC CAB ACB. Although the world in which they occurred was fairly small, the variety of combinations seemed infinite – and every five years another generation invaded 'the scene'. There are always experienced mentors prepared to spend time with you, give advice, spice up the evening with delicious gossip – who had fallen into which bed – and relate tales of chance and magical encounters. It was easy to have a good time. You felt that to be part of this world was an immense privilege, that the lifestyle was more affirmative than any other available. As the decade wore on the 'straight' world, I realized, was a giant vegetable nightmare from which I'd miraculously escaped. Like everything mundane, it made every effort to keep young men and women in its muddy waters.

IV
The Most Beautiful Room
in London

UPPER GROUND

In August 1969 I moved into the first of a series of warehouses on the river front. Upper Ground was at the end of Blackfriars Bridge. It was a large, airy L-shaped room. After seven years in cramped Georgian terrace houses and basements the change was exhilarating. There was space to spread out – to entertain – for friends to stay without falling over each other. Life could be a bit Spartan in winter, but the summers were an idyll; and the old brick buildings – all of which have now disappeared under improvements – a delight.

The area was deserted since the docks had been moved further down river. Returning home late at night down these empty streets you felt the city belonged to you. In the mornings you would be woken up by the tug *Elegance* towing the barges down river. The seagulls would desert them for a moment and come to catch the bread from your hand. The riverside was my world for another nine years, before the invasion I pioneered with Peter turned the few remaining buildings into DES. RES.

Back in 1969 the warehouse allowed me to slip quietly away from the 'scene' which for five years had been the centre of my life – and had now exhausted itself – and establish my own idiosyncratic mode of living.

✢

January 1970, Upper Ground: I was dreading coming back to London as by Christmas I had very little money and no way of heating the warehouse at Upper Ground, with the exception of the small office I've made of my bedroom. I can just afford to keep the 'pither' stove going, but it does nothing except keep the water from freezing in the lavatory. The old coke water-heater swallows up fuel, and you have to lay in at least half a ton at a time.

The holiday in Excelmans in Paris solved the problem for a couple of weeks as the fridge was well stocked and the building centrally heated. On the train waiting to return home, I noticed a girl carrying two heavy suitcases. Something about the way she was dressed and her long hair told me she was English, so I shouted out of the window that there was a spare seat in our carriage, and she clambered in. Throughout the eight-hour journey we chatted about the theatre and painting. Janet Deuter was teaching at Hornsey in the experimental light and sound department. She was a friend of Ken and Shirley Russell so she told me of their new film project, *The Devils*. When we parted company she told me that she'd tell Ken about me, as she was convinced we would get along.

I soon forgot about this. But a day later the phone rang and Ken asked me if he could come over – 'tomorrow'. OK I said. 'I'll be there at eight in the morning,' and at eight he arrived in the freezing empty warehouse at Upper Ground. He was bowled over by the building and while we huddled over mugs of tea I pulled out the odd drawing from *Jazz Calendar* and the *Don*, plus various other projects I had worked on. After looking at them briefly he asked me to design *The Devils*. I was quite taken aback by the suddenness of this offer, as I'd promised myself that after *Don Giovanni* I would never design again. I asked him if I could think it over, and he gave me twenty-four hours. 'In the meantime can Shirley come to tea to meet you?' In the evening I rushed out to see *Women In Love*. On the strength of that, and conversations with a few friends, I decided to plunge in . . .

+–

DESIGNING THE DEVILS

February 1970, Ladbroke Grove: I sit upstairs on the living-room floor among the bric-à-brac which invades every corner of Ken's home. His latest addition is a portrait of Hedy Lamarr – which I spotted in Camden Passage. Shirley makes coffee while Ken and I thrash out ideas. My architectural history, the years with Pevsner, stand me in good stead.

The town of Loudun is an enormous task. There's the exterior as well as all the interiors to consider, and also a large number of sets for Louis XIII's court in Paris. I've brought a bottle of sepia ink and the finest rapidograph, which I use to make meticulous drawings of the sets, stone by stone, after initial (very rough) sketches. An art director, George Lack, is drawing these up into proper plans and elevations, and the students at the Central are building a scale model of the exterior.

The Devils, 1970 – lot under construction *(Photo: Ray Dean)*

The whole lot is to be built at Pinewood. My source books are Ledoux, Boulée, and Piranesi's prison series. All detail is sacrificed to scale as I want the sets as large as possible, and as forceful as the sets from an old silent.

+−

May 1970, Pinewood: The journey out to Pinewood Studio is a nightmare. I'm usually up by 5.30 to get there by 8.30. So much of the time is spent waiting for trains – and in the evening it's worse unless I manage to hitch a lift. Yesterday I came out with Ken in the white Rolls for a meeting with the American investors – a gang of Hollywood mafia, who took the model of Loudun up to the lot where it was dismembered with a breadknife while they argued about its size. They posted studio assistants to mark its limits on the ground. They spent half an hour dissecting three months' work, and at one point attempted to jettison the cathedral. The set is apparently going to be the largest since the ill-fated *Cleopatra*.

Later, Ken called to say he'd been battling with them all day. Although he's saved Loudun, we've lost the sets for Louis XIII's palace, except for the theatre and perhaps the library; so the original design will never be realized – a historical film shot entirely in sets.

+−

17 August 1970, Pinewood: We started filming after months of preparation. The great white city is nearly complete on the lot and has become a tourist attraction. You could almost pay for it with visitors' fees. It cost £97,000. The finish of the white machine bricks (rather than the stone of the drawings) was decided upon in the plaster-rooms where they have brick and stone moulds of every description. I had various sections painted with more usual brick colours – yellows and reds – but they looked dowdy on the glittering surfaces. Today we take up the catafalque with its shrouded figures; the whole of the studios are devoted to us as we're making most of the props and furniture here as well. A few special pieces, amongst them the life-size crucifix for the nuns' chapel, are being sculpted by Christopher Hobbs; the crucifix is from the Isenheim altar (in polystyrene with a gesso finish). We found an authentic sixteenth-century brank, a skull mask made in limewood. It's in fragments, but we are going to restore it for the burning sequence, for which Christopher is making a half-burnt Oliver Reed out of latex.

+−

The bald nuns have caused quite a stir. At first, they refused to have their hair cut off, but the producer bribed them with an offer of £150 and two wigs each.

Niki, quicker off the mark than the others, made a sensational entrance in the dining-room (which is constructed so that you can keep an eye on who's arriving). She walked very slowly down the stairs at lunch-time before turning and sashaying back again, making sure no one had missed her. The restaurant at Pinewood is a meat market.

+−

September 1970, Northwood: I just picked up the tail-end of a conversation between my parents, who are washing up in the kitchen having insisted on me leaving it to them. Whatever Dad had said, Ma replied, 'I'm so glad our children haven't grown up normal, they're so much more interesting than their friends.'

+−

September, Pinewood: Lunch with Max Adrian, which brightens up the day no end. I found him in bed with the lady who is covered with the most revolting plague sores, eating a sandwich lunch on set. He said why didn't I join them, as she couldn't go to the restaurant looking like that: it would put everyone quite off their food.

Max sat at lunch today eating cherry pie surrounded by empty plates. When I asked him what the plates were for he said, 'For the bones.' He recalled that at his twenty-first birthday party his mother looked him up and down and said, 'Max, you are really quite ugly but at least you're clean.'

+−

Work is a minefield: the courtiers came down to the set this morning with horrible plastic roses in their hair. I told them to take them out, which most of them did quite willingly – but alas I didn't know that the designer's powers do not stretch to hair, and a dispute began which came within a hair's breadth of stopping the film. The whole thing was conducted with the utmost pettiness. The extras can be as stubborn as mules. They insist on wearing watches, never take off their rings, carry newspapers around with them which come out the moment Ken shouts 'Cut!', along with the knitting and the crosswords.

+−

Rushes are like bingo. Each of us votes for his favourite – one, three, four or whatever. Ken sits at the back with the lighting cameraman, Watkins, who usually gets his way. Watkins, who always wears plimsolls, reminds me of a bad-tempered sportsmaster. One expects him to take out a whistle and blow it. He doesn't like me very much, probably because everyone calls me 'the artist' and the sets, rather than his lighting, are the continual topic of conversation.

Today, Charlton Heston was sitting in the projection-room – he has a hide like tanned leather.

+–

Revolting afternoon at the plague pit: it is composed of dummies and extras made up as corpses. Ian laid in gallons of real blood from the abattoir – splashed all over the place, it attracted clouds of wasps which made it almost impossible to act dead. Ken, as usual, stormed around, the bodies shifting as a wasp flew too close even when the cameras were turning. Nothing was right; the blood was a disaster. In the end he made me bring bottles of ketchup from the kitchens, which made everything worse as the wasps preferred it to the real thing.

+–

There was a huge row this morning about the houses on the lot. I'd taken down some shutters without consulting Ken. He'd seen them at an early stage of the design, and was expecting them on the buildings. 'I can't trust you, I can't trust you. In future you're going to bring me everything to be signed.' He looked like the mad empress from some B movie – waving his cane, his long hair flowing, wearing a smock and enormous rings on every finger. He left the set shouting to the air, everyone looking at each other rather embarrassed. I quietly carried on and tried to ignore the whole affair.

+–

October 1970, Pinewood: The wilder scenes in the film are fuelled with champagne, which sometimes arrives with breakfast. In the cathedral Ken has a drum-kit brought in and drums away loudly to whip up fervour. The set is closed, and there are wild rumours all over the studio about 'orgies'.

+–

***The Devils*, 1970 – lot set** *(Photo: Ray Dean)*

***The Devils*, 1970 – the Prioress (Vanessa Redgrave)** *(BFI Archive)*

I'm back at Bankside every night, exhausted, often as late as ten. I'm up at 5.30 to reach the set by 7.30. Ian Whittaker picks me up in his car, on Southwark Bridge, bleary-eyed at about six. I work most Saturdays and often Sundays. Life as I knew it has ceased to exist.

＋

May–September 1970, Ladbroke Grove: Ken asked me what would most upset an English audience. Louis XIII dining al fresco, carelessly shooting peacocks on the lawn between courses. 'Impossible,' said Ken. 'How would you do that?'

'Make some dummies, stand them on the lawn and detonate them.'

'No, you'd have to shoot real peacocks. It wouldn't work otherwise.'

Later, this scene crept into the film in the garden at Pinewood. Ken dressed his Huguenot extras as blackbirds, which the king shot while nonchalantly talking to Richelieu. At one moment our Louis said camply, 'Bye, bye blackbird.'

'Marvellous,' said Ken. 'What do you think of that, Derek?'

'Oh I suppose it's OK,' I said half-heartedly. I didn't want to be the kill-joy. The idea had transformed from the steely, vicious concentration of a scene from *The White Devil* to a farce.

'Do it again,' said Ken, and into the film it went. My sensibilities about what was appropriate were violated. A flip joke in a nasty little garden at Pinewood, instead of a great abstract topiary set with strutting peacocks. In a very dark mood I returned to Bankside.

＋

December 1970, Pinewood: Ken and his camera crew were tempers frayed come the end of filming in December. When the day for the great detonation of the walls of Loudun arrived, when all the charges were laid and we were ready to go, Ken, who had been very moody, said, 'I'm not having this fucked up,' and climbed on to the camera to film it himself. The signals that had been organized to let the explosives experts know we were rolling were primitive; and Ken, waving his arms in the argument around the camera, set the whole lot off. The camera stood idle, and as the dust and debris descended from the massive explosion everyone stood around dumbfounded. The next ten days were spent restoring the walls to get the shot.

＋

Almost every waking moment of 1970 was spent working on *The Devils*. When I began in January I had no idea that a film of this size completely usurps your life. And by the time I emerged from Pinewood in December, the easy life of the sixties – designing and painting – had gone for ever. It was now impossible to pick up all the threads. Painting was the major victim: I continued it over the next ten years very sporadically. After the intense pressure under which a film is made, it seemed undemanding – and the isolation in which it was pursued, enervating.

However, in the autumn the first of my own films took off with the help of Malcolm Leigh; to be followed by a whole series of Super 8s which gradually, without my realizing it, relocated my work. Although much of my time at Pinewood was spent in the constructions of sets, every now and then my presence on the set *was* necessary. In fact, Ken attempted to keep me there full-time; and I discovered (imperceptibly) how a feature film ran. There was no better director to learn from, as he would always take the adventurous path even at the expense of coherence. In December 1971 he asked me to design *The Savage Messiah*, almost a year to the day after I had finished work on *The Devils*.

—+—

1971. THE OASIS

The intervening year was spent painting a series of blue capes, which hung on the walls at Bankside. They were simple sky pieces to mirror the calm that returned after the frenzied year of *The Devils*. That summer was an idyll, spent sitting lazily on the balcony watching the sun sparkle on the Thames. When I wasn't painting I worked on the room and slowly transformed it into paradise. I built the greenhouse bedroom, and a flower bed which blossomed with blue Morning Glories and ornamental gourds with big yellow flowers. On Saturdays we gave film shows, where we scrambled Hollywood with the films John du Can brought from the Film Co-op – *The Wizard of Oz* and *A Midsummer Night's Dream* crossed with Structuralism. There were open poetry readings organized by Michael Pinney and his Bettiscombe Press. Peter Logan perfected his mechanical ballet, and Michael Ginsborg painted large and complicated geometrical abstracts. Keith Milow came down and worked for a month, discovering a plasterer's comb which he drew through his thick paint in spirals.

A continuous flow of people stayed or lived in the studio. Below, in Horseshoe Alley, small groups of earnest American tourists would look up at the building while a guide-lecturer told them about the Globe Theatre that had once

The greenhouse bedroom at Bankside, 1970 *(Photo: Ray Dean)*

occupied this site.

In late summer, we opened the studio for two weeks. This brought a steady invasion of people interested as much in the rooms as in the work. The studio was photographed for Italian *Vogue*, and also featured in a book on modern interiors – where it was sandwiched, barnlike, between uncomfortable-looking rooms furnished in Milanese moderne.

+–

PONTORMO ANGELS

June 1971, Bankside: Late at night Alasdair and I take off from the Yours and Mine where we've been dancing. In the taxi he produces a tab of acid. His drug habit got him sent down from Oxford, where he also enjoyed brief notoriety for his 'scandalous' dancing with April Ashley at a May ball. Now he's gone wild, dyed his hair with henna, and done it in a thousand springy curls. He wears his clothes, even the Blues blazer, like old rags. He broke his nose boxing for the university, and has carelessly failed to have it reset.

We lie in the dark and watch the river swirling below. I put on *Daphnis et Chloe* and the music runs through our heads in riverlets. Alasdair takes off his T-shirt and we lie in each other's arms as the sun comes up. The light dances across the river and streams through the mighty black Doric columns of Cannon Street Bridge. The sooty towers materialize out of the darkness, and the sun, catching the golden cross at the summit of St Paul's, gradually puts out the lights of the City. A fleet of barges is afloat on the Thames, seagulls screeching and diving around them. The clouds turn a dull pink of faded roses, then all the colours of Pontormo angels; finally they become emerald shadows floating away to sea.

Now the city is silhouetted: the sun is spreading flaming bands over the rooftops, and splashing scarlet into the eddies left by the barges. A train crosses the bridge, and the light falls through its windows, transforming it into the richest of ruby necklaces. Tides of Ravel's music swell through the rafters and Alasdair floats in a rainbow geometry of carpets and cushions . . .

+–

AN UNEXPECTED GUEST

August 1971, Bankside: At three o'clock this morning I was woken up by the telephone. 'Southwark Police Station, sir. We have a friend of yours who's lost his way trying to find your home. He says he's called Sir Francis Rose . . .' – this last said with slight disbelief. The sergeant caught the hesitation in my reply and said, 'He's very eccentric, isn't he, sir?' Alarm bells ring – I am suddenly awake. I asked the sergeant if he could find a hotel for my unexpected guest, as I knew that once Francis had climbed the stairs at Bankside he would never climb down them again. The sergeant to my surprise said yes. I pulled on my clothes quickly and sat on the riverbank waiting for him to arrive. A black Maria drew up with two highly amused young policemen in it, and Francis in the back looking like the scarecrow from *Oz* and obviously delighted by the mode of transport. As we were driven to Victoria, out of a plastic carrier bag he produced some exercise books filled with scrawled biro drawings of boys fucking. 'I've been showing the officers my drawings,' he croaked.

When we arrived at the hotel, he insisted I pay for a double room as he had come to London in search of his 'son' Bob. I booked him in for one week, and was then driven back to the studio.

Later that morning, the phone rang again and an agitated Francis asked me to meet him at 11 a.m. in a pub in Old Compton Street: we were going to find Bob, who is an addict. Bob's story is not dissimilar to that of his Spanish half-brother, but is complicated by the fact that when he met his father they fell in love with each other.

In the pub, Francis' inquiries into Bob's whereabouts were conducted as though we were in a forties' crime thriller. He whispered to old cronies in one pub after another, most of them looked like ex-boxers. Eventually, after calling in at a snuff shop, we tracked Bob down at the White Bear pub in the Piccadilly underground, a rendezvous for junkies and hustlers. The two of them fell into each other's arms. The old man silently wept into his beer as his destitute son broke down, every now and then kissing his father with passion.

Later, when Francis had collected himself, he said, 'We'll go to the gallery.' When we arrived at the Grosvenor Gallery, I could hear the alarm bells going again, and quietly slipped away.

—

SAVAGE MESSIAH

Savage Messiah was low budget. Ken put his savings into it. He asked me to design it as he knew I was keen on the painters of the period, particularly Vanessa Bell (who has the finesse of Matisse) and Bomberg's great abstracts. On the other hand, I found Gaudier an equivocal character, and still do. He might have boasted that there

Savage Messiah, 1972 – the polystyrene
Easter Island head *(Photo: Ray Dean)*

Savage Messiah, 1972 – Gaudier (Scott Anthony) carving *(BFI Archive)*

were no artists except himself, Brancusi, Modigliani, 'we the moderns', – but his life, cut short at twenty-three by a bullet in the trenches, hardly gave him time to prove it. He left a small body of stylistically uneven work, much of which decorated his biographer Ede's home at Kettles Yard in Cambridge. When I arrived there I felt like an intruder. Ede told me he saw Gaudier as the god Apollo in a golden sunset. 'The film would be like that, wouldn't it?' Bill Weedon, now in his nineties, saw something different. He told me of the poverty and chaos of the studio, and trips with Henri to prize fights. Sophie Brzeska's breath, he said, would have knocked out a trooper. He should know because he was in the trenches.

Both men retained images of Gaudier as a wild boy. But Gaudier knew Sert and the sophisticated set of Diaghilev, so perhaps they remembered only part of it. When I wrote to Karsavina, she replied that she hardly remembered Gaudier but had met him once or twice at the Serts' – strange company for Ede's rebel.

＋

December 1971, Bankside: The studio has been turned into the Omega workshops, and it's crammed with the furniture that we are painting. There are chairs, tables, trays, screens, crockery. Bill Woodrow and Paul Dufficey are helping to paint the more difficult pieces, which have been made in the studio workshops or bought from Junk City. The pottery is being fired at Wimbledon and looks indistinguishable from the originals. Paul has developed a facility for forging Gaudier drawings: he began by copying them; then introduced variations; and can now turn any goose into a Gaudier swan. Scott Anthony, who is playing Gaudier, comes for drawing lessons, and even he is now quite a dab hand at them. They're very easy to forge. Nicholas tells me that he dumped a whole wad of them that he drew at the Slade into a sale at Polperro. There were no signatures on them, and he made no claims to their identity. They were snapped up by a beady-eyed London dealer, and later no doubt some appeared in London catalogues 'in the style of . . .' Now they are in private collections as originals? The next step will be the museums.

＋

March 1972, Lee Studios: Down in the yard they're filming *Steptoe and Son*. Up here Christopher Hobbs and I are chipping away at the marble torso in relays to get it finished for tomorrow. Since we started filming the sculptures have overshadowed all our other problems. Christopher has carved several of them in soft stone, as well as a huge seventeen-feet-high Easter Island head out of blocks of polystyrene, which filled the whole building with snow as we hacked away at it with kitchen knives. All this was easy compared with our present problem:

Sequence. Megalomanic film director in a fit of creative frenzy: 'The central image of our movie is the titanic Struggle of the Sculptor to release his Genius from the intractable Marble. What I need is a torso, a torso like no other, in snow-white marble.' So I store this request in my mind along with the paintings, the furniture, another twenty or more sculptures, sets, and a thousand props, every now and then giving it some attention. I search the art schools for a sculptor.

Sequence. Three weeks later, and a telephone bill as long as my arm, I discover that no one sculpts in stone any longer – fibreglass, steel, waste paper, nail clippings or teabags, any material but stone. 'Can't do it,' says the voice, and the line goes dead. It is as if I were trying to order macramé from Leonardo. Christopher, who has by now produced 'Bird Swallowing a Fish', suggests that we make the marble torso in plaster with just a hint of glitter.

Sequence. The artist's studio. Film set. 'Plaster with a dash of glitter, would that do?' The director fixes me with a steely, unforgiving eye. Improvised conversation along the lines of what the fuck's the world coming to. We're making a film about a *sculptor*. Some joker suggests why not try a monumental mason and everyone agrees, as if we're fools not to think of it.

Sequence. The monumental mason's. Kent. Rain-soaked designer stands in a graveyard of angels and forlorn blocks of Sicilian marble. Attempts to describe what he wants to ex-POW from Naples. 'I want a torso like this.' Designer fumbles in his pocket for drawing which conveys 'the artist's titanic struggle to release his genius from the intractable marble.' The response is a blank stare, misted by angels. 'Oh, you want something sexy,' this said as if the madonna had just exposed herself in St Peter's. When I leave I imagine the torso being carved in the outside privy.

Sequence. Same location. Later. It's still raining. The Neapolitan stone-carver smiles as he pats it. I try to hide my emotions: it looks like an African tourist sculpture, an etiolated plant searching desperately for the sun. I have to accept it. It's cost hundreds. With heavy hearts, we heave it into the boot and travel back to Lees.

Sequence. Artist's studio set. Directorial hysteria. 'You call yourself an *artist*, you sculpt it!! You've got forty-eight hours.' Christopher, help!! We have one block of marble left, with the texture of bullet-proof glass. Our wrists have swollen and our eyes are smarting from the lethal flying splinters. We've been carving in relays, about twenty minutes at a time, for two days, and we're still not nearly finished.

+–

A few days after the film opened I was rung up by a Russell fanatic who asked me if we had any of the props left. 'Yes, I'll ask Ken if you can have something.' Ken said, 'It's all in the empty house at Lees, take what you want.' I relayed the message. When the guy saw the storerooms he quickly ordered a lorry. Then he set up a stall in Chelsea Antique Market. The first I knew of this was a phone call from John Jesse, a dealer specializing in Art Nouveau and Deco. 'A dealer friend of mine has just bought six Omega chairs for over £1,000,' he said. 'I saw them and smelled a rat.' He then described my Junk City chairs – Gaudier would have loved that.

＋

Bankside, 1971 *(Photo: Ray Dean)*

Corfe Castle *(Camera Press)*

V
Home Movies

The 'home movie' nights of my childhood were the most exciting. To watch Grandma Mimosa cutting up the Sunday chicken in 1929 seemed no less than a miracle – in Grandfather's home movies with their title cards: 'BACK TO SCHOOL, YOU CAN IMAGINE HOW THEY FELT', and, 'BANG UP TO DATE LANDING IN GAY PAREE IN SILVER WING, LANDING LOAD OF 19'. Thirty minutes of film would cover as many years, and there was always a chance the old projector might break down. Half-way, in 1939, when my father took over the filming, everything broke out into the most brilliant colour – sequences of the World Fair in New York, of my parents driving to Scotland early in the war, Lossiemouth in a blaze of purples and oranges, mountains reflected perfectly in the lochs. . . The war: aerial shots of Wellington bombers and camouflaged RAF stations. . . And post-war Italy, orchards and picnics at Ostia. Then back to England, grey Nissen huts, coke stoves and fading camouflage.

✛

BEGINNINGS
In 1970 Marc Balet, an American architectural student, who was later to become the art editor of Andy Warhol's *Interview* magazine, arrived in London with a Super 8 camera which he brought down to the studio at Bankside. I borrowed it and made a brief three-minute record of the studio – the first of a whole series of films in this home movie gauge.

✛

July 1972, Worth Matravers: Andrew Logan is to play the silver masked god. Christopher Hobbs has constructed the mask of genius. Bente is a mermaid, a siren who lures sailors. Ian is a drowned sailor. The music will be *Daphnis et Chloe*. We've no props except for a hundred silver paper boats that Christopher has designed to float in the rock pools at Dancing Ledge.

Late one afternoon we drive down to Dorset in an old car, and the journey takes three hours under a lowering sky. Spirits rise at the first sight of Corfe Castle through the drizzle; and as we climb the hill to the Matravers the sun makes a brief appearance, and we look back at the gaunt grey castle guarding the entrance to the isle of Purbeck like a broken tooth. At Worth we unpack and, staggering under the bedding and camera equipment, take off across the damp fields down to the sea. Usually the chalk downs are alive with butterflies. Now everything is ominously still and silent except for a flock of crows which wheel away as we approach.

We have decided to spend the night in the huge smugglers' cave at Winspit, cut deep into the cliffs, and to emerge very early in the morning to film *The Siren and the Sailor* . . . even at Worth Matravers intrepid tourists invade by ten. Andrew has brought an old wind-up gramophone; we sit listening to an old version of 'Land of Hope and Glory', from a last night at the Proms, as it echoes through the cave. The mist is closing in and a rough sea sends up plumes of salt spray. We eat our cold supper miserably as the darkness descends, and then make up a large and very uncomfortable communal bed on some foam rubber. This is performed by the light of a single guttering candle, which does little to dispel the gloom of the strange surroundings. We sleep fitfully as the cold invades; and the water dripping in the cave and the storm raging outside combine to keep us awake. At one o'clock Marc Balet doles out valium. The project seems doomed.

At first light the whole world is awash. You can't even see the sea; and the seagulls, mewing and hovering about our cave, sound an agony. By ten, with the rain still pelting down, we realize it's hopeless and drag our rheumatized joints back up the hill, burdened with the soaked bedding and the gramophone. The village pub is open; and here, warming ourselves, we lay a plan to rescue the day by driving to Bridport further down the coast – where Michael Pinney, who has published my poems on his little press, has said we would be welcome for tea at his exquisite Queen Anne manor, Bettiscombe. Marc, an American, and Bente and Ernst from Denmark, would at least feel the long and fruitless journey had been worthwhile. I telephone Michael, and he invites us over.

At Bettiscombe we arrive to find Michael in the library with Iris Murdoch. Detached yet curious, she interrogates us over her sherry: 'And what do you do?' We all look the worse for wear, and Andrew is dressed with his usual sartorial abandon. We explain that we're making a film, and leave her (and ourselves) none the wiser. Then Michael takes down the family treasure, The

Screaming Skull of Bettiscombe, passing it round for us to admire while explaining that if it were ever removed Bettiscombe would fall like Usher. At four the weather has cleared a bit, and he suggests we walk up the hill above the house, where we link hands and wish on the Sarsen stone. Michael says you have to be very careful, as your wish always come true. We decide that a communal wish for good weather the following Saturday can do no harm. Late at night, exhausted, we return to London.

The next Saturday, we start at four as we'd all voted against another night in the caves. When we arrive, at eight, it is brilliant sunshine. The tourists who we feared might disrupt the place fail to turn up: the rocks are deserted, except for a middle-aged lady dressed as though she were in Torremolinos. She continues reading her Barbara Cartland novel without batting an eyelid at our antics and nudity. Bente assumes her mermaid position, naked on the rocks. Andrew dons his mask which glints in the sun, and a rainbow cloak he has made for Miss World. Ian, dressed as a sailor, drowns at the water's edge in an emerald-green rock pool, bobbing with the hundred silver boats. By ten we've finished filming, and spend the rest of the day getting sunburnt. Michael's stone did the trick, for it is one of the very few fine days of summer.

+—

In the autumn of 1972 I was in New York for the launch of *Savage Messiah* at a special screening organized by the Museum of Modern Art. The weather was still warm and sunny, and I spent the days walking through the lower East Side with Ken and Shirley Russell. We developed a passion for the hideous light and furniture shops of the lower East side, and ate at a deli that sported a sign: 'Send a salami to your boy in the army.' In the evenings I propped up the bar at the Ninth Circle with Bart Gorin and Silver Thin, the last scintilla of Andy Warhol's fading Factory, or disappeared into the steam of the Continental Baths, then in full swing. Ken was interviewed at the Factory for the magazine, and I found myself drawn to Max's of an evening, where satellites of Warhol would cluster round the bar. There were trips to the cinema with Richard Bernstein, who airbrushed the covers of *Interview*, with Sandy Daly, a film-maker. The latter pocketed Richard's tooth mug, and had a couple of bottles of vodka shoved into the pockets of her mac which she shared with the audience in the cinema queue, before we sat in the front row of the vast cinema to watch *Lady Sings the Blues*. I took the left side of the screen and exchanged information about what was happening while the vodka flowed freely in between. Sandy had made a film with Robert Mapplethorpe – 'Robert having his nipple pierced' – for which Patti Smith had spoken the soundtrack.

Robert lives with Patti and was the first person I looked up when I arrived. I gave Patti packets of Passing Clouds (in their blue and pink wrapping as perfect as Gitanes) which I told her were Virginia Woolf's favourite cigarette, which amused her. She flitted elfin-like between Robert's sculptures made of leather jackets and bicycle parts, and in return gave me her poems, which a quick-talking boy from the Bronx managed to extract from me a couple of days later.

The weather, which had been perfect, broke on the eve of my return – the night before Richard Nixon was re-elected – and a hurricane swept through the city. I arrived at Kennedy nearly two hours after my plane should have taken off, ran through the various departure procedures, and climbed on board as the door closed.

꜏

September 1972: We closed the doors for ever at Bankside this evening after a showing of *A Midsummer Night's Dream* and *The Wizard of Oz*. When the films were over I didn't turn the lights on, so we all crept out of the building in the dark. Downstairs I shut the massive padlock. The demolition men, who have been tearing down the buildings all around us, will be in next week. Before winter there will be just a hole in the ground and Horseshoe Alley will be no more.

꜏

ALICE

November 1972, St George's Terrace: At Max's I was introduced to someone who introduced me to Alice Cooper's manager. He suggested, as he spooned cocaine like rat poison, that I stage Alice on Broadway.

I joined the band a couple of months later in Copenhagen. There were thirty or more of them, resembling a gang of Davy Crockett trappers. They travelled in a private jet, took over the floor of an hotel, and played a long-running table-tennis tournament as they downed an infinite supply of Budweisers. I arrived late and missed the concert, but was whisked away to see a live show where Alice was to be photographed. The seedy basement was piled supermarket-high with mountains of Budweisers: Alice carried one around with him wherever he went. At the end of the basement was a double bed on which unattractive, sweaty men humped equally sweaty and unattractive girls. Alice, together with python and Budweiser, capered about like a praying mantis in bondage while the furry-looking band shouted obscenities to cover up their embarrassment – a gang of thirty-year-old schoolboys.

The lesbian scene with organ music completely subdued them, and this was followed by a girl who dressed herself in Alice bondage and wriggled on the bed inviting the band to join the action. After a few remarks like 'she'll give you a dose' the girl switched to the offensive. 'Are you all gay?' she asked aggressively. At that one of the band clambered on to the bed to the cheers of the rest of them, and the girl gave him a blow job – but to his increasing embarrassment nothing happened. She gave up with a shrug, and he hitched up his pants and climbed down scarlet-faced. The girl followed him down and sat on Alice's lap. Alice jumped like a jack rabbit, sprung on to the bed, and laid about him with a whip. The photographers clicked away. Somehow the girl tangled with the whip as Alice lashed out and she started to cry. I sat at the back with Ernst during this performance. He whispered in my ear, 'Isn't heterosexuality charming?' His wife, Bente, who had come with him, was sick. This was my introduction to the wonderful world of pop, with its aspirations to being taken seriously.

Having begun this way it carried on. In Frankfurt there was a Thanskgiving dinner complete with python, turkey and beer; and from there we travelled to Berlin for the main concert of the tour, then back to Copenhagen. But as the plane was chartered it had to land in East Berlin.

When the band emerged from the plane the East Germans decided that they had an emergency on their hands. The airport was cleared and the formalities completed faster than lightning; the coach was parked so close to the exit that you stepped right on to it. The light was failing, and my first sight of Berlin was one of drab dereliction. Hawks perched on the airport fences, and an old steam train, the last I ever saw, puffed past. The Wall was more unpleasant than Western propaganda had made it: electric fences with death's heads, crash-barriers across the road, tank-traps, a great ploughed minefield – which stretched as far as the eye could see – with look-out towers, and finally, a high concrete wall angled towards you to stop you climbing it. Our bus was stopped and searched inside and out; and the customs officers stared at you and your passport for at least two minutes. As we crossed into the West (guarded by a Red Cross emergency unit to give blood transfusions and help to any refugee who could cross that assault course), we cheered. We drove through the rain-lashed streets of the west, a dazzle of artificial lights; then booked into the Hilton, where the usual floor had been set aside. After a quick bath, we set off for the Deutsches Halle, a barn of a building packed with some thousands of Alice's fans. I sat on the stage among the sound equipment, and every now and then one of the roadies would ask aggressively what I was doing – in spite of the fact that I'd been on the plane with them for three days and my mission explained. We waited and waited. An hour or so after the concert was scheduled Alice's manager and the German organizers were to be found counting vast piles of marks. One for you, two for me. And until this primitive finance was sorted out, we were told that nothing was going to happen. The crowd grew restless, then bored, and still we waited. One for you, two for me. Finally, it began: Alice, python and beer can, cavorted around the stage singing 'School's Out' before hanging himself. When it was all over I walked round to the dressing-rooms. A roadie was allowing the prettiest of several hundred little lolitas with Alice T-shirts into the dressing-rooms; and when later the fifteen or so hired cars drove back to the Hilton, they were packed. The band and their fans invaded the lobby en masse, while the porters yelled and tried to stop them; but it was sixty against six, and the little girls screamed and ducked and ran for the lifts. *'Fumf! fumf!'* yelled the roadies, as the girls ran helter-skelter through a group of bloated German industrialists in dinner-jackets, who were themselves just leaving some gang-bang with their mink and diamond wives. Wave after wave piled into the lifts as telephones rang and porters shouted. On the *fumf* floor anarchy reigned – exhausted, I rang the porter a little later. 'What time does the first plane for London leave tomorrow?' – 5·30 – and I was on it without a goodbye.

I sent a letter explaining a staging for Alice, who was to arrive on a huge articulated black widow spider. It would crawl out of a steely web on to the Broadway stage with Alice at its helm holding a gold and leather harness, dressed in rubies from head to foot, like Heliogabalus entering Rome – and that was that. I never heard from them again.

+-

MISS WORLD

Friday, 2 October 1981, Olympia: Andrew Logan's 'Miss World' competitions have grown like Topsy to gargantuan proportions. this year he's taken the great hall at Olympia and filled it with a fairground for one thousand people. The Miss World has become the Chelsea Arts Ball of our time. The highlight this evening is a certain 'Miss' who appears with a whole troop of guardsmen (real ones, not transvestites) in evening-wear and swimwear. Her 'act' climaxes with a huge choir ranged around the balconies which sing her to her coronation. There were fire-eaters, and stilt-walkers, a ferris wheel, and a score of side events. There was also a life-size tyrannosaurus rex, twenty feet high and hideously lifelike, which waddled in led by

Interviewing Andrew Logan for *Interview Magazine*, 1974
(Photo: John Dewe-Matthews)

Beardsley androgynes. Every freezing minute was worth the enormous entrance fee, as was the beautiful commemoration programme. Over the years the Miss Worlds have provided many people with an immense amount of fun. Of the five to six so far, I've been to four.

+-

PEGASUS

10 January 1983: Andrew Logan is curled up in his convolvulus chair, an Edwardian picture-book fairy – Tinkerbelle. For him, everything is make believe: in a thousand smashed mirrors he has stolen all the world's bad luck. He has snatched a dream out of thin air, his cloud-capped towers and gorgeous palaces are built with everything you and I have thrown away. The jealous, who do not know the secret of making do with nothing, will never want to understand. For them it's just precious. But there is no excess in Andrew's vision. It is truly egalitarian. He would have us all be butterflies – such an easy change, and the means are there and cost nothing. He ought to be the most revered of artists, who has made no distinction between his life and art. Fly away with him on Pegasus, over the rainbow, 'Oh I can't believe it, no, over the rainbow!!' and then laughs, 'Oh, Derek, I couldn't.' But he knows he is already there.

+-

November, 1972, Kensington High Street: Derry and Toms' Ladies' Department is colour co-ordinated, and run by a dragon-like hostess. Lost in the sea of navy, pink and olive-green is a demure little stand of flowery plastic bathing-hats. When Patrik and I see them we are like Yukon explorers at a gold strike. However, before I had managed inexpertly to fit one on, for size, the scarlet dragon lady arrives: 'Get out of here!!'

'I was only trying it on to see it it fitted! I want to buy it.'

'You heard me, we don't serve your types in here. You're in the wrong department.'

It's the only swimming-hat for sale in London, it's mid-November and I'm desperate – it completes days of hard work on my costume as the Southern belle, Mrs Hippy. Whoever heard of swimwear without a floral hat? 'I want to see the manager.'

'He won't see you. Get out of here, you heard.'

On the fifth floor, we pushed past startled secretaries into the manager's office. A wicked plan had entered my head. The manager rose from his desk, 'Can I help you?'

'I've been thrown out of the Ladies' Department while trying on a bathing-hat.'

'Were you in the right department, sir?'

'Yes!' And then the killer, 'I'm designing Ken Russell's new movie, *Wagner*. We have an enormous drag ball at King Ludwig's palace. We thought Derry and Toms would be the ticket.'

I got the hat reduced while the manager fluttered around. The floor manager smouldered in a corner, reduced to a heap of ashes. I convinced him that she'd lost the store a contract worth thousands.

Shortly afterwards, Derry and Toms closed its doors for ever.

Patrik Steede, who had never intended entering, won the first Miss World as Miss Yorkshire – a last-minute decision made in the dressing-room. I came third. So much for trying.

+

Saturday 22 January 1983: On the floor of my room still stands that copy of a fragment of one of the seven wonders of the ancient world, the several times life-size head of Mausolus, which once crowned the top of his tomb at Halicarnassus. When the antique-room was dismantled at the Slade in 1965, it struck some deep chord: at that moment, the Renaissance had at last succumbed to the air-conditioned nightmare of Pop. Five centuries of the European love affair with antiquity was quietly labelled 'obsolete' by the Slade, its last guardians. In the life-room I made a final series of drawings of the nude with fragments of statuary strewn across the floor. Ever since, the dismembered marble torsos have haunted my work. In 1970 I brought what remained of the room to Pinewood, where I had it recast for the study of Urbain Grandier in *The Devils*. On the wall was a copy of Poussin's 'Triumph of Pan' which Michael Ginsborg had produced for me. Poussin had reinvented classical antiquity with meticulous care and had painted the 'Triumph' like the frieze of a sarcophagus. But when I built this room I had no foreknowledge that Ken Russell was going to have it smashed to pieces in the scene in which Grandier is led to his death. I stood looking on with complete horror as this destruction was completed, carrying with it even the Poussin. The whole action could never have been contemplated in seventeenth-century France. The annihilation of the Renaissance was complete.

During the 1970s, in several large canvases and drawings, I presented the graveyard of the old culture. In 'The Fragments of Antiquity' and 'The Pleasure of Italy' the statues are piled one on top of another like used cars in a breaker's yard. An apocalypse had overtaken the old dream. The bust of Mausolus was used again and again. In *In the Shadow of the Sun* it becomes a mighty idol consumed by flames. It's in *Jubilee* and also on the desk of Prospero in *The Tempest*. Back in 1965, when I came home from the life-room to the studio in Cunningham Place, I made designs for *Orphée:* the gates of hell are the Brooklyn Bridge. This unconsciously delineated my attitude to 'American' Popism, nicely. The Elysian Fields, on the other hand, are strewn with the perfect fragments of the classical world we were casually discarding.

+‒

JULY 1971 – THE BILLBOARD PROMISED LAND

'Their footsteps echoed in the silence, which was broken by the steady sound of dripping water and the clutter of stone chips dislodged by their feet. Huge, unseeing eyes stared up at them. Locks of stone hair, massive hands with broken fingers pointed vacantly to the sky. Two lizards scuttled in the crevices and flies warmed themselves on these stones, as the blue of the sky was as cold as ice and cast a deadly chill. Heavy frost glittered in gaping mouths and tightened its grip on marble torsos. Here was the broken statue of a great Emperor on horseback, there a great winged bull – a pathway opened ahead of them. Meandering between precipitous cliffs of marble fragments which glowed an unearthly blue in that cold light deeper and deeper they travelled into the twilight. Now they were in an avenue lined with tall obelisks which resembled the darkest recesses of a pine forest. A great space unfolded itself. A huge stadium surrounded by cascades of marble statues. John and the King walked into it.'

+‒

GARGANTUA

April 1973, Rome: Every morning I catch a taxi from Albergo d'Inghilterra to PEA, the production company which is making Russell's *Gargantua* in EUR on the outskirts of Rome. Our basement office is alongside the one from which Pasolini's *Arabian Nights* is being run. Every morning Patrik Steede and I go to dinner with Gerald Incandella, who works in a clothes shop in a street near the Piazza Navona.

Gerald lives in a tiny silver-painted basement near the walls of the Vatican. It is cluttered with objects: a treasured puppet, a large plastic apple-green ice bucket, and a small Art Nouveau table. He sits cross-legged on the bed with his friend Elizabeth. Both wear baggy white oriental trousers, are stripped to the waist, with masses of dark curly hair falling over their shoulders. They are playing in a scene from the *Satyricon*. Gerald was born in Tunis, which he refers to as 'Carrtarrhge', pronounced breathlessly. His parents now live in Nice, and he has arrived in Rome via Berlin where he spent last summer with other young drifters. When the *Gargantua* project collapses he returns with me to London.

+–

20 May 1973, Shad Thames: We've spent the week making a Tourist film with Gerald. The plot is simple: a photographer cruises a tourist and follows him to the sights of London. Huge urns of tulips in Regent's Park – the pagoda at Kew, and the worthies of the Albert memorial. Gerald, in black coat and pork-pie hat, complains of the cold and the wind which whips across Tower bridge. The photographer clicks away. They end up making love in the greenhouse. The film is shot through a piece of red gel which accentuates dramatic light and shade – particularly in the greenhouse sequence, with the light bouncing off the glass facets.

+–

THE ART OF MIRRORS

July 1973, Shad Thames: The footage for *The Art of Mirrors* came through the door this morning. It's some of the most unusual film I've ever seen. It will be impossible to edit as there is not a moment I'll want to lose – each reel is more surprising than the last. The mirrors flashing sunlight into the camera with the light meter set at automatic sends the whole film lurching into negative. Luciana Martinez and Kevin Whitney in black evening-dress are excellent. There's one shot of Luciana where the light falls through her mesh hat on to the blue triangular make–up which is wonderful. Gerald looks sinister in his paper-bag mask – the green filter takes less of the light than the heavy red, but you still need the sun to make it really sing. This is the first film we've made on Super 8 with which there is nothing to compare. The other super 8s of the last few months are still too close to 16mm work; whereas this is something which could only be done on a Super 8 camera, with its built-in meters and effects. At last we have something completely new.

+–

Gerald Incandela, 1973 *(Photo: John Dewe-Matthews)*

From *The Art of Mirrors*, 1973 – Kevin Witney and Luciana Martinez

BUTLERS WHARF

August 1973: The studio is a forest of emerald-green columns. At sunrise, the ducks float in on the driftwood over a glacial river which reflects orange and vermilion, while the sun pours in through open doors. As the river fades to blue the first barges pass and disappear downstream. Tower Bridge opens slowly and silently to let a sailing-boat through. Gerald pulls on his black silk dressing-gown and sits at the pink metal table by the open window eating his breakfast. I throw a towel over my shoulder and walk to Bermondsey Public Baths for a shave. Outside each cubicle the mongoloid attendant turns on the taps; inside you shout 'Hot, more hot' – or 'cold'. The Victorian tubs are the biggest I've ever seen, and good value for 5p. I float as the shouts of hot and cold echo in the white-tiled room.

The studio is furnished; the greenhouse is up. There's a Baby Belling to cook on, carpets from the Lots Road auction-rooms – and furniture collected from the empty offices of Butlers and Colonial Wharfs. Since there is no one else working at the wharf I close and padlock the huge iron gates: now we have our own 1,000-feet terrace on the Thames where we can film undisturbed in the sun.

—+—

IN THE SHADOW OF THE SUN

During the summer of 1973 I filmed the main sequences of a full-length Super 8 film – *In the Shadow of the Sun*, which was to wait eight years before it saw the light in 1980 at the Berlin Film Festival. The first sections were already filmed a year before, in 1972 – 'A Journey to Avebury' and 'The Magician' – and the final sections were filmed in 1974 on Fire Island before the whole thing was put together. The camera I used was a simple NIZO 480 which cost £140. Most of the sections were filmed for the price of the stock, usually about £20 – some lavish sequences, the fiery mazes for instance, had a budget: costumes £5, sawdust £4, paraffin £2, roses £10, candles £4·50, notebook £1, taxis £5. The film was structured around a series of cryptic phrases which appear briefly in the film as Penny types them with one finger – these are some of them:

SLNC

IS

GLDN

Little by little the sun has imprinted its image on earth and that image is GOLD. – Then others titled 'The Kingdom of Outre Mer' and 'Ronde de la Mort'; the work changed from day to day like a kaleidoscope. I wrote in the diary – 'I've failed to

From *In the Shadow of the Sun*, 1974 – The Kingdom over the Sea

From *The Art of Mirrors*, 1973

develop in the way that was expected.' 'Am I certain the picture I'm looking at accurately portrays the contents?' The film-makers I showed the films to were generally uncomprehending. No one took Super 8 particularly seriously – they all had technical training, could read numbers on light meters, and so worked in 16mm. I was fazed by numbers and am hopeless with machines. I have never learned to drive a car. The film-makers at the Co-op were involved in the destructuring of film; to one who had stumbled on film like a panacea this seemed a rather negative pursuit – like calling water H_2O. When I received my first film back and it was in focus, the whole thing seemed magical – an instrument to bring dreams to life, and that was good enough. I disliked the subsidized 'avant garde' cinema. There was a strong official line; but super 8, which cost next to nothing, allowed one to ignore that. The resources were small enough; so if independence were a form of purity, I had my hands on the philosopher's stone. In 1974 I bought Jung's *Alchemical Studies* and *Seven Sermons to the Dead*, and this provided the key to the imagery that I had created quite unconsciously in the preceding months; and also gave me the confidence to allow my dream-images to drift and collide at random.

+–

JANUARY 1971, BANKSIDE

From 'The Billboard Promised Land' (a short story)

Chapter 7

'Archaeology of words' . . . . . . 'and now the old poet sat by the lake watching the ripples on the water where the goldfish swam. Every now and again where the young god had cast his shadows a word or a phrase would escape in scintillating sparks. A poetry of fire which momentarily casts the place into darkness with the brightness of its reflections.

> The heaven and earth are united in gold
> he combs (his hair)
> the golden rays
> (in his hands) the roses burn
> the days are long
> the wheel turns in the circle
> cooled by breezes from the four corners
> he enters (his chamber)
> the swallow has risen (in the east)
> the doors are open

man awakes
the poets of the sulphur baths in seven crystal tiers
star shaped, with the laughter of ghosts in its water
here watch a butterfly trapped in a glass
the sand pours in
white wings flutter into stillness
6 × 3
archaeologies
burning in high winds
one last walk
one last look
then there were other poets studying a whirlwind of shadows
a picture of wind on the sea
washing their hands in the sun
or the sign which read 'walk don't walk' as the circuit had fused
stories × the sea shore

All of this happened whilst John and Amethyst walked in the city of Disc, past the great sulphur baths, the pools of saturnalia with their laughing, sighing waters, and the poets with their tape recorders mingling with the ghosts. Debating the outcome of the battle between Love and Chastity fought at the vernal equinox each year.'

+-

KINGDOM OF OUTRE MER

This is the way the Super 8s are structured from writing: the buried word–signs emphasize the fact that they convey a language. There is the image and the word, and the image of the word. The 'poetry of fire' relies on a treatment of word and object as equivalent: both are signs; both are luminous and opaque. The pleasure of Super 8s is the pleasure of seeing language put through the magic lantern.

The images of *In the Shadow of the Sun* are fused with scarlets, oranges and pinks. The degradation caused by the refilming of multiple images gives them a shimmering mystery/energy like Monet's 'Nympheas' or haystacks in the sunset. There is no narrative in the film. The first viewers wracked their brains for a meaning instead of relaxing into the ambient tapestry of *random* images. The language is there and it is conveyed – and you don't know what you have to say until you've said it. You can dream of lands far distant.

The film became divided in my mind into four sections, although it was not constructed in that way. The first section is based on a journey to the standing stones at Avebury in Wiltshire, coupled with two fire mazes. It contains a man who points, another who takes photos, a third in bondage, and animals – dogs and a sacred cow. There are burning roses which occur throughout the film. The second maze is circular – Ronde de la Mort – in which a couple dances in the flames which devour the whole landscape and the great standing stones. A third and final image of Narcissus, a mirror which flashes the sun into the camera so that the image explodes and reinvents itself in a most mysterious way. This section is brought to a close with some refilmed footage off the screen at the Elgin Cinema in NYC from *The Devils* – the final moment when Madeleine escapes from the claustrophobic city of Loudun into the world outside, over the great white walls; but now, in my version, she walks into a blizzard of ashes.

The second section is an invocation. Black and white masked figures walk through the flames. A magician finds the key to a cabinet of secrets. Now we are in the kingdom of the other sea, where an Egyptian pharaoh materializes in the surf, ushered in by a bacchante who dances in black with the herb of grace. Atlas supports the world lost in the galaxies. Dancing at the edge of time. The section ends with a figure turning in a magic circle, which burns the film out to white.

The third section contains the typewritten messages. The images are evanescent. The pyramids burn to a candlelit requiem, the people gamble and barbarians ride through the ruins.

In the final section the images fade into blank footage where the atoms dance, punctuated by explosions, and a figure listens to a message on a shell:

SLNC

IS

GLDN

August, 1973, Verzons: The designs of the old walled garden at the Verzons are finished. The wilderness will be put back to meadow grass, with cowslips and buttercups. A simple geometric topiary garden will be planted – four circular yew hedges at the four compass points, approached by an avenue of clipped yew obelisques. Christopher is to cast two of his eighteenth-century sphinxes in terracotta – perhaps there will be statues, but those will be done later.

–⊢–

GREEN FINGERS

Masks, models, puppets, painting, sculpture, costumes, watercolours, make-up – Christopher Hobbs' work is scattered through every film I've made. He can paint a

Rembrandt, fake up rococo plasterwork, sculpt you a Gaudier. We first worked together on *The Devils*, where Christopher built the body of the burning Oliver Reed out of layers of rubber and tissue paper on a plastic medical skeleton.

For the Super 8 films, Christopher made masks and suits of armour out of silver card, models of castles, pyramids, and clothes out of yards of cheap calico. When he wasn't working on the films he was building a palace for a supermarket magnate on the top of a mountain in Spain or restoring houses for the National Trust. All this work was made in a small muddled studio off Tottenham Court Road. He lived in one room of *trompe l'oeil* grandeur in a decayed terrace house in Islington, where the water splashed through the rafters and the garden was overgrown by an enormous sleeping princess rose bush. We filmed Christopher as the magician for *In the Shadow of the Sun* in this room, looking like an extra from *Ivan the Terrible* in purple velvet with gold embroidery and a bulky fur collar among his crystal cabinets and seventeenth-century hangings. Later, he put on a top hat and tails and seduced Gerald on the riverbank, while bouquets of flowers burned in slow motion, and Gerald danced in a filmy black dress covered with hand-painted orchids.

+−

BURNING FOR PROFIT

August 1973, Butlers Wharf: All through the summer the buildings burn on the river, bringing a glint to the speculators' eyes. The first to go was the beautiful regency building that John Betjeman had listed after I showed it to him last year. Then the huge ice storage warehouse at Hays went, followed by St Catherine's Dock. Some of the finest buildings in London – then Mary's Wharf opposite, and a warehouse just beyond St Saviour's Dock – Not a bad tally for one summer's speculation.

+−

Nicholas and Fiona Logsdale, who own the Lisson Gallery, were here this evening to see the fire films *In the Shadow of the Sun* and *The Art of Mirrors*. Pyromania was in the air as at about ten we heard a fire engine bell. The music was loud and the room plunged into darkness – down below a second fire engine passed. 'I wonder where the fire is,' I remarked, then walked out on the metal bridge which crosses Shad Thames at the back of my room, to find the building next door a sheet of flame. The firemen went wild when they saw that what they'd thought were deserted warehouses were in fact occupied. They shouted at us to come down at once. I put the speakers out on the balcony and played Roberta Flack's 'Sweet Bitter Love' as loud as possible over the roar of the flames – I don't think they were amused – and went back inside to save my films. Nicholas and Fiona took an armful of drawings down with them. Thankfully by midnight the fire was out, and I crept back upstairs to sleep fitfully.

SILVER APPLES

September 1973: Beryl Grey has banned *Silver Apples of the Moon* after an argument with Tim Spain the choreographer over the flesh-coloured tights the dancers wear at the end of the piece. The opening at the Coliseum has been announced and people have bought tickets – but this is ignored. It's a dictatorial decision: no one was invited in for any discussion, and several thousand pounds of the Gulbenkian Foundation's money have been thrown away for the most ridiculous prudery. 'We're not that sort of company,' she told Tim. It's destroyed Tim's career here as you can imagine the rumours, and the ballet will never be seen. I'm furious, because the ballet is simple, totally harmless, and also probably the best design work I've ever done. The front cloth is painted from a black and white photograph of a galaxy – the set is simple, consisting of several hundred half-silvered bulbs in silver holders on transparent flex which hang from the bars in rows. Behind them is a second black and white cloth painted with arcs tracked by comets with small red, yellow and blue arrows. The costumes follow this through – the men are in black dinner-jackets with red, yellow and blue gloves and shoes, and silvered spectacles – the girls are in primary coloured tutus and the mirrored glasses. The opening is a *coup de théâtre* – no stage lighting is used, the curtain rises in darkness, and the hundreds of bulbs are suddenly switched on about six inches from the floor. The dancers stand motionless against them; and as the music starts they fly upwards, a thousand glittering stars. On the first, and only, night (in Oxford), the audience burst into spontaneous applause.

VANDALS

October 1973, Sloane Square House: This month Anthony left London for NYC and gave us his flat, as heating Butlers Wharf during the winter was proving impossible. The glittering sixties' interior was no more – eighteen months before it had been stripped by the bailiffs while Anthony was in France. This was done with the connivance of Bob, the hated porter, who had a key. I arrived shortly after Anthony walked into the flat and discovered the destruction, to find him standing in the middle of the rubble. Everything had been taken except the bed, and that had been vindictively vandalized. The Bernard Leach vase and the Japanese tea bowls were inexplicably untouched. The wind-blown tree was overturned and the glass icicles lay smashed on the floor. Scattered among them were books which Jean Cocteau had dedicated with drawings; their covers were torn and stamped with heavy boot-marks. Dom Sylvestre-Houedard's Tralee Dingle laminate lay untouched. Anthony shrugged his shoulders without a flicker of emotion, ordered another typewriter and carried on in the chaos as if nothing had happened. All his treasures had been sold, including the grey mirrors on the walls. He changed the locks and refused access to the instigator of this act – a mean little glass merchant with a ritzy shop in the Fulham road, who had bought the best pieces at knockdown prices.

–⃛–

MISS SYNTHETIC

1973, Butlers Wharf, Downham Road: Gerald is entering Miss World, and I'm going to film it in fast new black and white Super 8. Like the first one, it's being crushed into Andrew's new studio at Downham Road.

Gerald has made himself a see-through polythene costume which makes him waddle like a fish. He's decorated it with some black ostrich-feathers and painted his face with dead white pancake. He's calling himself Miss Synthetic. In the dressing-room he sits like a sad little bird that has plunged into an oil slick. He chain-smokes and seems overwhelmed by the event. I've never seen him so nervous before. He's an extraordinary contrast to Karl, who's swishing around like a Phoenix Matron in a mink coat, silver, wild or something Lindy Guiness has lent him. Later, he gets jammed on the catwalk – which hardly allows two to pass by – against the wet palette of the vampish Miss St Germain des Près. This is a catastrophe for the mink. I sit in the dressing-room and film as much as I can. It's hardly possible to move. Miss Holland Walk wins; Miss Yorkshire crowns him, draped with a python.

–⃛–

CRISIS

31 January 1974, Sloane Square: My thirty-second birthday, and Gerald left in tears. I've put him in a taxi to Thilo's. The last month, aggravated by his jaundice, has been really bad. I've had all the flak, while Thilo has the good times. I rang the producer, Harry Benn, to turn down Russell's *Tommy*. Harry has tried all week to seduce me back, but I've made up my wavering mind – I've had enough of film design and the huge amount of energy and time it takes punches gaping holes in my own work. Patrik is on his way to Italy to sort out *Sebastiane*. Perhaps the jolt will get him working. We're all dead broke, but I refuse to be the soup kitchen any longer. It's very difficult to fight Harry's offers of huge sums of Stigwood money, but it's done. On Monday I'm going to sell a decade's clutter of possessions at the studio in Butlers Wharf. With Anthony paying the rent at Sloane Square it should be easy to get by until I go to NYC in early June.

–+–

CORFE

March 1974: there was always a prize of sixpence for the first one to see Corfe Castle as we drove to Swanage for our childhood holidays. I know every bend in the road after crossing the bridge at Wareham. The Purbeck hills in the distance cast a shadow across the sandy, gorse-covered heath. Corfe looms up massive on its conical mound guarding a cleft in the hills. Ahead lay the twilit England – old Harry and his wife, Peveril Point, Dancing Ledge, Tilly Whim. Rocky cliffs and smugglers' coves, limpets and seaweed (which twists through the water and by which you can tell the weather), buckets, spades, and candy floss.

At Corfe, the jackdaws circle round the grey stone keep with its towers still at the crazy angles after they were mined by Cromwell in the 1640s. The road spirals through the little stone village up to the drawbridge. Today, years later, Paul Humfress wears the silver paper armour with its faery decoration, and the mirror mask which flashes in the sunlight. The rain blows in from the west across the Purbeck hills. We shelter in the keep as the showers scurry by; this morning we have the castle to ourselves. Luciana glides along the battlements in a white calico gown, sown with pearls – her headdress a-flutter with little white birds. The wind catches her train and swirls it around. The pale-blue filters catch the rain; but at lunch the sun comes out for an hour, and we complete the Troubadour film.

Expenses for the film at Corfe: two nights in hotel – £30. Petrol £10. Costumes £15. Film stock £50.

FIRE ISLAND

10 June 1974, Fire Island: Anthony has taken a home here which he shares with some New York lawyers. On the wall above the fire is the only artwork in the house: an immaculate *boîte en valise* which the Los Angeles police department has dedicated to drug identification. As perfect as a Duchamp, it is the icon of the house. Each drug is faked in plastic. Last night, after dinner, Anthony produced an elaborate silver sweet dish – the sort you find in Indian restaurants, to serve chutney – which was passed around the table. It contained nearly every drug you could identify in the attaché case.

+--

12 June 1974, Fire Island: I'm living rough as I have been expelled from Anthony's house in a farce which could only happen here.

Yesterday, I met a lad on the beach and invited him back to swim in the pool. For half an hour we fooled around with no clothes on. This morning I came down to breakfast and was greeted by an uncomfortable silence. Tom and his friends were watching a video that they had made the night before which left nothing to the imagination. Breakfast was cooked by Tom's peroxide blonde mother, who'd arrived from Washington. After she had organized the eggs and bacon, she joined us and watched her son tying up some muscle-bound hunk on the television without batting an eyelid. After breakfast was over, and we'd washed the dishes, Tom informed me that I was no longer welcome at the house. I was completely taken aback when he said, 'How dare you bring a stranger to the house and swim in the pool with no clothes on, knowing that my mother had arrived from Washington. She saw you and was deeply shocked.'

+--

September 1974, New York City: The prettiest boys in the Continental Baths are the hustlers – not sex but drugs. They lounge around behind half-open doors with tumescent cocks and catch you with their angel dust eyes. Once lured in, you are presented with acid and mescalin and bags of grass – they fuel the dynamo which keeps the baths dancing. At $11 a night the baths are cheaper than an hotel, and some of the dealers have lived there for months. There are bars and restaurants, a hairdresser's, saunas and steam-rooms, a swimming-pool with fan-shaped fountains, games-rooms, and floor after floor of cubicles. On Fridays the stars of the subculture sing – Jackie Curtis, Bette Midler; and the socialites arrive in their Yves

St Laurent, lace their champagne with coke, and watch the boys making it in the hammocks around the pool. Forty-eight hours on acid passes in figures of eight, and Sunday morning at dawn brings a cool, sharp clarity. At six the sun sparkles down the empty avenues casting de Chirico shadows – the carefree boys of the night return home to empty apartments where the roaches can be heard clattering through a week's washing up. the boys put out notes for themselves to call the exterminator in the morning.

—⊦—

The houses in the pines are run by ad-men and lawyers in their thirties. Fire Island has a deadly, well heeled monotony. Well tanned Ambre Solaire, work-out muscles, and faces wrinkled by over-exposure to the December sun-ray lamps. At the tea-dance the music pounds away while these muscle-bound fantasists bob up and down in a thundering mass with whistles and fans, and moustaches pinned on like limp wrists. When the sun goes down there is dinner at any number of houses, barbecues from overstocked fridges and gallons of Californian wine. Then around midnight the parties begin, and carry on till dawn. Fireflies float amongst knots of men cruising along the wooden walkways. As the sun comes up it reveals a world of failing looks and crushed boutique clothes mirrored to infinity in a house where the walls, ceilings and floors are mirrored – reflecting the desperate hope of a good fuck.

—⊦—

The derelict piers stretch out into the West river, huge covered sheds with the ground under your feet sparkling with smashed glass. Moonlight falls through the broken windows in the long sequences of empty rooms, while phantom figures cruise past in silence. Young Puerto Rican pickpockets move deftly amongst the groups of men making it in odd corners – you have to put your change in your shoes. Eyes soon grow accustomed to the gloom, and your ears becomes sensitive to surrounding danger. The cop cars prowl – throughout the night, men cruise through the piers, and at midday you'll find a guy in boxer shorts being blown as he leans against his bike.

—⊦—

I've spent the last three months in NYC, most of the time at Hal's empty apartment, and now in an empty roach-infested loft with an escaped python in SoHo. Money has been a continuous problem, as Anthony's promises of accommodation faded; and he's so wrapped up in Robert he seems oblivious to my difficulties. I managed to sell some of the Diaghilev costumes I bought at the Sotheby sale, but that soon ran out. Now I'm making the odd dollar putting Robert's flat in order. This enables me to eat one meal a day at the West Side Diner, where Reggie, the peroxide waitress, plays tricks – dispensing four-leaf clovers for luck – and slips me the biggest portions of french fries to keep me going. However, there are plusses. I've filmed the final section of *In the Shadow of the Sun* out at Fire Island, more for the name than its reputation – though even that was held up when sand got into the lens as I was sleeping rough after my expulsion by the lawyers from Anthony's house.

I'm temperamentally unsuited to New York life – my journeys here seem founded in a self-destructive impulse. But I'll be back in London next week, so perhaps some friendly djinn looks over me.

+–

Anthony's dream flat is being built in the usual sea of debts – he's purloined Nina's sapphires to make it possible. Into one small room he's put a sofa by Claus Oldenberg, sewn in ultra suede; and a glass desk, with a sophisticated lighting system by Dan Flavin. The only decoration is a porcelain chess set by Malevich. The entrance is an infinity cube. What the rather dull lawyer who is getting all this makes of it I can't say. I spend the day shifting books and polishing.

+–

1 JANUARY 1974, SLOANE SQUARE

Ars Mortis The End of Tradition
The Disaster of War
Bring the Goya etching from Norwood and burn it. Film and tape the event. The ashes framed between two sheets of glass and exhibited with the film. The resulting work to be exchanged for another work of art which will be similarly processed. A legally binding document to go with the work to prevent its resale unless an exchange is made and further work processed.

+–

THIRD TIME LUCKY – MISS WORLD

March 1975, Butlers Wharf: Keith dyes my hair primrose with a black triangle at the back; it's very short, a crew cut. I've a massive wardrobe of costumes from the Super 8s, including the silver diamanté dress from *In the Shadow of the Sun*, and a troubadour dress and armour from the film we made last summer at Corfe. I have a headdress made from a green rubber frog, with pearls and lashings of ruby and diamanté drops. This time I'm going to win. On stage I act: I fall in the swimming-pool with a bottle of gin as a drunk from the *Titanic*. As Joan of Arc, I conceal Josephine Baker's *'J'ai deux amours'* on a small tape-recorder beneath my armour. Seizing the mike, I secretly switch it on. No one knows where the sound is coming from as I mime to it. I win.

Andrew has constructed the most unstable of thrones. I wait in terror as Hermine totters towards me along a tightrope, bearing the sceptre and orb high above a very anxious crowd. In a brief speech as reigning Miss World, I offer my services formally to close bankrupt British industries in the coming year, by tying them up with pink ribbon.

The Third Miss World, 1975 – official portrait (*Photo: Marc Balet*)

VI
St Sebastian

I met James Whaley, who was to become the producer of *Sebastiane*, at a Sunday lunch. He asked me what I did. Films. 'What sort?' 'Little ones.' Have you ever thought of features? No – impossible! Well I'm going to make one, he said, what ideas do you have? *The Tempest* perhaps. I've always dreamed of that; I chatted with John Gielgud for a whole evening about it. He said if he did it he would film it in Bali. I've made a script of it. Prospero's a schizophrenic locked into a madhouse – Bedlam. He plays all the parts – Miranda, Ariel and Caliban; the King of Naples, the Duke of Milan and the rest of them visit him and watch his dissolution from behind the bars. It works very well, but uses less than one third of the play. Then there is Akhenaten the heretic pharaoh. Heliogabalus! EPICS!! and St Sebastian. We should make that one, he said. Well why don't you write a treatment, I said – not really believing the project would survive the coffee. We chatted about Sebastian and the London Film School, where James had just completed the course. A few days later James arrives with a synopsis.

+

On our journey through Italy three years before, Patrik Steede, fascinated by the St Sebastians in every gallery and church, dreamed up the idea of writing a film. During the next year Patrik lived at my studio at Bankside and in Sloane Square, and the project lurked in the background. But Patrik was reticent about putting pen to paper – he had written a play which he threw over Southwark Bridge one evening. So *Sebastiane* remained firmly in the mind – he came with me to Rome on the *Gargantua* project in 1973 to write *Sebastiane*; but six weeks later, after the project collapsed, we were back in London with nothing done. Before he left Sloane Square in February he promised me that I'd have the script by summer. But when we met up in NYC the subject was evaded and nothing more was said about it; and Pat cloistered himself with a young American producer. Maybe I had misinterpreted the

James Whaley, the producer of *Sebastiane* and *Jubilee* (Photo: Jean Marc Prouveur)

situation, believing the project would be written for me. James' enthusiasm presented a problem – was *Sebastiane* to be made that summer or not? Time was the factor.

After talking to Anthony, I decided to go it alone. The lines to NYC went dead. Three years later, when the film opened in the Village, Patrik told me: 'I took my lawyer, but at the end of it he said, "It's so terrible it's not worth suing."'

–+–

Sebastian. Renaissance. Pretty boy smiles through the arrows on a thousand altar pieces – plague. Saint. Captain of Diocletian's guard. Converted, stoned, and thrown into the sewers. Rescued by a Holy Woman. Androgyne icon banned by the bishop of Paris. Danced by Ida Rubinstein. Impersonated by Mishima. In love with his martyrdom.

–+–

February 1975, Sloane Square: James wants an oil and vanilla film full of Steve Reeves muscle men working out in locker-rooms. Paul Humfress, who is to edit, wants a very serious art film, slow and ponderous. I want a poetic film full of mystery. The debate rages as I write, and the script is caught in a tug-of-war between the grey mirrors of Sloane Square.

–+–

March 1975, Sloane Square: Jack Welch, a Latin scholar from Oxford, has arrived with the translation of the script. It's brought a coherence into the work. the poems sound good:

> *Sagitta funesta acu tetigit*
> *Umbraque tegit aquas*
> *Et aura tacet*
> *Aves non canunt*
> *Deficit ab orbe color.*

> *Sebastianus de mundo discessit*
> *Ad solem modo sagittae advolat*
> *Nox non umquam eum occupabit*
> *Discessit ab horis orbis atris.*

Ecce vulnera sagittarum
Sanguis vitae fluit in harena
Calthae solis in radis folia
Explicantes surgunt.

Flores apollinis aureos
Sebastiane
Sebastiane
Da iuveni deo qui luminibus aureis est multa basia
Da amatori multa basia
Et vesperis in luce
Mundum hunc recordare.

(The fatal arrow has found its mark / A shadow has fallen across the waters / The breeze is still/ No birds sing / Colour has deserted the world. / Sebastian takes leave of the world / Like an arrow he flies to the sun / No night shall ever shroud him / He leaves the dark hours of the world. / See the arrows' wounds / His life blood drips in the sand / Marigolds spring up spreading their petals in the sun's rays, golden flowers of Apollo / Sebastian / Sebastian / Shower kisses on the young god with his golden eyes / Shower kisses on your beloved / And in the evening light / Remember this world of shadows).

+—

16 April 1975, Sloane Square: Ken Hicks, who is playing one of the soldiers, brings over a Roman strigil to show me how the boys in the bath-houses used to scrape the oil from their bodies. I filmed him as he covered himself with oil and started to scrape the excess with the bronze patinated sickle. It's a very charged object for him and he uses it quite often. He says he gets a hard-on imagining where it has been.

+—

17 April 1975, Sloane Square: *Sebastiane* has to be the first feature made without a telephone. Outgoing calls are made from the phone at the Royal Court stage door downstairs, and if anyone wants to see me I have a rule that I'm always at home for tea after five.

Later that day: We've begun to make the props and costumes, which are few but very important. The half-circular cloaks are make from unbleached oatmeal wool, hemmed and painted with natural dyes in the colours of the Etruscan wall-paintings in the mysterious tombs at Tarquinia. We are making gold strigils and gilded frisbees. Today, the black leather nose for Max arrived, like the one Christopher painted for the Super 8 film *A Garden at Luxor*.

24 April 1975, Rome: James Whaley and I have been in Rome for nearly a week at the hotel Senato. Our windows open on to the Pantheon, now besieged by flocks of nuns, Holy Year tourists, and pilgrims. We've spent most of our time in the prop- and costume-houses looking at shoes and armour, shields, spears, Roman oil lamps, wooden practice swords. It's been made easy as everyone recognizes me from the Gargantua project; and envisaging an enormous film, give us plenty of time. James, with his flashing blue eyes and easygoing love affair with Italy, speaks the language fluently and strikes bargains.

+

25 April 1975, Rome: I asked Leonardo Treviglio to play Sebastian. I hesitated all morning as he seems so melancholic, but Nando Scarfiotti, who designed *Death in Venice* for Visconti and who is an old friend of both of us, says he's the one. I remember how beautiful Leo was when he came to London with the Keralese dancers at the Roundhouse. Now he has grown a beard. James is completely thrown. He has an image of Sebastian which is out of *GQ* – sexy and muscle-bound – and he makes fun of the beard all day.

+

27 April 1975, Sardinia: Cala Domestica is a perfect location. An hour's drive over the mountains brings you to two small rocky coves with sandy beaches. An old Etruscan watch tower stands guard on the cliffs, above sharp luna rocks with bright green rock pools, and a blue sea beyond. Except for a ruined cottage – once a fisherman's house – at the top of the beach with two ancient fig trees growing in the dunes, there is no sign of habitation as far as the eye can see.

We are using the ruined fisherman's house as set and barracks. Each night a group of us stays to guard the place as it is full of indispensable props. By the light of the Roman oil lamps, we talk late into the night, eat the local rough bread and goats's cheese *peccorino*, and drink the local red wine. The sky is crystal-clear – for each star at home at least one hundred seem to shine here. The cove is bathed in soft moonlight.

At four, I wake with a start. The valley is alive with bells and barking dogs. I light an oil lamp and throw on a pair of jeans. Piero appears out of the dark, the youngest of three shepherd brothers who graze their sheep on the hillside. They provide our food and the horses for the film. Antonio, the eldest, is in love with Guy – who offended him this morning by brewing coffee and failing to hand him the first

Sebastiane, **Adrian (Ken Hicks)** *(Photo: Gerald Incandela)*

mug. Piero is the most handsome of the young men, and deep in the night he gives you the feeling that time has stopped; a blanket thrown across his shoulders resembles an antique cloak. He carries a crook.

A storm has blown up and, waves are smashing against the cliffs in a continuous roar. I grab a bottle of wine and one of our Roman cloaks against the cool of the night, before we climb the mountains together to the Etruscan tower. Meanwhile, Piero whistles at the dogs who herd the large flock each of which wears a copper bell. We climb the tower and sleep there wrapped in blankets, until the sun rises. A fine spray from the waves crashing far below falls like dew.

—+—

June 1975, Cala Domestica: Gerald Incandela insists on travelling to Sardinia by boat from Marseilles; he arrives two days late, carrying a huge old plate camera over his shoulder, and a swallow that he'd rescued from the sea. He's dressed in white bathrobes and a straw picture hat. Daniel, who's helping with the stills, follows up behind with the three enormous suitcases that contain his darkroom. This is built into a storage cupboard on the stairs of the hotel in Iglesias . . . there's a lot of musical chairs about rooms, but they finally settle together on the top floor.

While we film, Gerald weaves crowns of wild flowers by the sea shore, sings *chansons* and dances with Daniel. When he is tired he sun-bathes on the silver reflectors. Every now and then he takes a photo. In the evenings he organizes 'events', ties up local youths with sellotape and grumbles. He is always one step ahead in any rocky climb and has the stamina and stubbornness of a camel. He carries improbable souvenirs, pieces of broken greying mirror and large rocks across continents. Today he poses in a bikini too brief for Bardot, does a 'work-out', and makes up those parts the sun never reaches for our all-over camera work!

When we return to London he haggles and barters over his photos like an old carpet salesman from Shiraz; for in business Gerald is an old soul and wins his way with charm. Tick-tock and the photos are printed, upside down, sideways-on, ten of one and none of another. He arrives with them on his moped, bundled against the cold in a huge fur-lined banker's coat circa 1910 Berlin, bursting at the seams and tied together with a leather thong. Today he is complaining about the iniquities of our film company, Megalovision; his pictures are spread on the floor; when they are not the *luxe calme* of Matisse, the photos seem to chuckle perversely, like an old goat that has butted you and then frisks away before it can be caught.

—+—

Sebastiane, **Saint Sebastian (Leo Treviglio)** *(Photo: Gerald Incandela)*

VIDI VICI VENI

June 1975, Iglesias: When I told the cast, at our first meeting in the hotel, that we were really going to be filming in Latin they looked incredulous. They'd spent all day with the frisbees, getting sun-tanned. Jack Welch, our classicist, promised individual tuition, and I promised to swap the Latin around and rewrite for those who couldn't manage their lines, while Jack came up with instant translations in what he called 'silver' Latin.

+—

We are using everyone's talents – Ken Hicks plays his recorder – Leo Treviglio dances his Keralese dance – Donald Dunham organizes his Chinese shadow-boxing with Leo and Ken. Gerald spends the day weaving crowns.

+—

The hotel in Iglesias which we have taken over is straight out of a black comedy. Octavia, the huge pregnant wife of the miniscule hotel-owner, sits at her front door and every now and again starts a battle over the shower, which we are meant to use without wetting the floor. Sometimes she wins, as the shower has a habit of drying up unexpectedly.

+—

We're up at six; a quick cup of black coffee and a dry roll are provided by the hotel. This has been supplemented by boiled eggs after complaints about the meagre breakfast. Then we're off over the rock-strewn dirt track to the location, where those who've stayed the night have brewed tea on the camp fire. We are filming by about 10·30, and carry on with a short break for lunch – wine, mineral water, fruit and rolls, which Luciana buys at 5·30 in the morning at the market. Then work until six, before trekking back over the mountain to a proper meal in the hotel. It's a long day, and with temperatures soaring into the nineties, exhausting. After four weeks of this the idyllic cove and desert landscape shimmer with a subtle malevolence – trudging through the sand dunes with heavy equipment across razor-sharp rocks and through thorn bushes parallels the isolation of the group of Roman soldiers in their remote outpost, and has given the film an edge. If any of us thought we were making 'boys in the sand' when we arrived that illusion is now dispelled.

+—

Sebastiane, **Gerald Incandela** (Photo: Guy Ford)

Sebastiane, **Finale** (Photo: Gerald Incandela)

July 1975: I arrived back at Sloane Square and collapsed with withdrawal symptoms. On the last day at Cala Domestica I somehow managed to touch one of the poisonous plants that grow in the dunes, and rub my face, so that my lips and cheeks blew up like giant puff balls which was more frightening than uncomfortable. Vasily had the same experience with a vengeance when he took a pee after touching one of the fatal plants. . .

+-

July 1975, Cala Domestica: The love scene between Ken and Janush this afternoon caused the group to fragment into warring factions. The leader of the coup was Paul. He walked out, accusing me of being a pornographer as he blinked back crocodile tears.

It was scorching hot by the rock pool and Ken, desperate to get the scene together, found himself unable to get a hard-on as he's totally unattracted to Janush, who's playing his film lover. Leo, with whom he is in love, has been acting with true Latin jealousy all morning. Ken, adamant he should have a hard-on, asks me to banish the rest of the crew, including Paul, who are sitting around on the rocks watching. Paul stumps off in high dudgeon. Ken gets his hard-on; we complete the filming, pack up, and clamber over the rocks to be met by a revolution. Paul screams at me. He's got Daniel in tears and has wound Leo up. I stand silently while I'm subjected to a barrage of abuse; then he says he's going back to London and is taking the crew with him. I say great, see you in London. The first vans leave and Paul pulls out with them. I decide to stay alone in Cala Domestica that night and leave them to fight it out in the hotel in Iglesias. At about nine, as the sun's going down, Howard Malin, the co-producer, arrives back with Ritchie Warwick having done the drive both ways to see if I'm all right. The next morning there are apologies all round. We're so hot and exhausted by the pressure of filming that tempers are easily lost.

+-

Nando Scarfiotti arrived with Joe d'Allesandro at Cala Domestica this evening, and we all went swimming in the cove. James wanted me to put Joe in the film but I refused point-blank – it would completely unbalance the cast who are all equally unknown, and lead to more problems than it's worth.

+-

During the middle of one shot a local lad and two girls suddenly appeared over the rocks into the little cove where we were filming, to discover the cast romping about in the nude. By the time Howard had blown his whistle and the cast had dived for their pants it was too late.

In the evening Iglesias was alive with rumours, and James was up before the local police commissioner, who insisted that unless we were confined to the hotel we'd have to leave town. He said we were causing too much commotion among the youth of the town. With Danny shinning up lamp posts and flirting with the boys, Gerald tying them up with sellotape to photograph them, and Barney James drumming away in the garage, he was probably right.

Today we had the police commissioner and his wife out to inspect the filming – but we managed to get by with James' impeccable manners and a system in which we rehearsed with pants on. When I shouted that this was a take, James make the police commissioner duck while we quickly stripped off and filmed. Everyone had their pants on before I called all clear. I'm certain he couldn't have been fooled that easily, but nothing was said. The whole day was spent in this game of hide and seek.

+—

4 June 1975, Cala Domestica: I wanted Sebastian tied to a palm tree for his death scene, not to the bare-looking stake they've erected by the tower. James was fraught because he's been having trouble with the Iglesias police again and was worried they might discover the film was about Saint Sebastian and not a Roman romp. The town is deeply religious, and palm trees have their special place in popular myth. After immense trouble, some fronds were brought out to the location in a lorry; but it was impossible to fake up a tree with them. So in order not to waste them, we put them behind Max in a scene in which Justin is tortured. Tempers became more frayed as the day passed. The temperature was in the nineties, and a howling wind burned into Leo who was tied for hours at the stake while angles were discussed – even covered with his cloak, the burning continued. Signor Rombaldi, the special effects man, whom we flew in from Rome at huge cost and put up at the best hotel, took for ever, as though we were working on *Cleopatra*. He stood around, in a pair of Bermuda shorts, with his fat assistant, Isadoro; holding his glue pot, he complained that Leo's nudity made it impossible to fire the arrows. This brought laughter from the other actors as during the last three weeks they have been used to wandering about like naturists – and I'd given him a huge write-up at dinner the

***Sebastiane*, love sequence** (Photo: Gerald Incandela)

***Sebastiane*, Finale** (Photo: Gerald Incandela)

night before: telling them about the mechanical Gina Lollobrigida he'd made for a car-crash scene. He announces that arrows without clothes are impossible; at which Leo loses his temper, and sulks with Ken. Hell breaks loose as everyone throws in their tuppenny-worth of ideas. Fine nylon wires are stretched between posts with hollow arrows whose rubber heads are to thud into Leo. When Donald, after hours of preparation, fires the first arrow it bounces right back along the invisible thread. Other arrows fly off mark; pins are attached to them and one sticks into Leo's leg. Leo becomes even angrier.

＋

August 1975, Sloane Square: The film has grown organically out of the harsh and rocky landscape. The script, a fragile skeleton conceived in Sloane Square, barely held together in the brilliant sunlight of Cala Domestica. Some sequences, particularly those which revolved around props we made or bought in London (like the pearl shell in which Sebastian hears the voices), came to life just as they had been written.

Seashore

On a group of rocks Justin and Sebastian rest after swimming. The sunlight sparkles on the water, the scene is quiet and contemplative. Justin points to a shell which glitters in the water:

SEBASTIAN: *Quid vides?* (What can you see?)
JUSTIN: *Testam candidam. Ecce testam ostreae.* (A beautiful shell. Look! A pearl shell.)
SEBASTIAN: *Potesne eum contingere?* (Can you reach it?)
 Justin dives into the water.
JUSTIN: *Ecce Sebastiane ea est tibi.* (Here, Sebastian, it's for you.)
 He climbs back on the rock, Sebastian looks at the shell and puts it to his ear.
JUSTIN: *Quid audis?* (What can you hear?)
SEBASTIAN: *Audio deos veteris ab imis pectoribus suspirare. Et tu?* (I hear the old gods sighing . . . and you?)
JUSTIN: *Nihil.* (Nothing.) *Iterum proba!* (Wait!) *Gaviam flere et tempestatem magnam. Adio nomen tuum. Sebastiane! Sebastiane! Delectissime Sebastiane! Huc ausculta!* (A seagull crying and a great storm. I can hear your name. Sebastian! Sebastian! Much loved Sebastian! Here listen!)

＋

Other scenes, which demanded a physical prowess or a command of Latin that the actors did not possess, were abandoned, while a whole series of new sequences were hastily put together inspired by the location – such as the pig-hunt and a scene built around the big black beetles that cling to the poisonous plants which live in the sand dunes.

+–

September 1975, Butlers Wharf: During August we painted Andrew Logan's studio upstairs at the Wharf as Diocletian's palace, and we festooned the place with gold material. Christopher gilded a caryatid – everyone was invited for nine in the morning and asked to dress Roman. At the last moment Andrew painted the floor pink marble. James and I spent a day at Berman's hiring everything that was gold: copes, capes and crowns.

By eleven that following morning we had the strangest lot of Romans ever assembled. Andrew arrived in a toga with a tin-plate medallion of the Eiffel Tower. Duggie Fields got together a distinctly Miro toga. Johnny Rosza dyed himself pure gold and carried a lyre. Robert Medley (Diocletian) looked splendid in bishop's robes and a crown with turquoise and pearl drops. Christopher encased Leo in solid gold and jewelled armour. Neil Kennedy, the wicked Max, had a gold nose to replace the black one; and Jordan arrived, her hair piled up like candy floss, in black leather bondage gear.

All day it rained like thunder on the metal roof – making sound almost impossible. But as it turned out this hardly mattered: by the time everyone was assembled we had to cut the filming to the bare action. Lindsey Kemp and a gang of boys danced a lascivious dance with barber-pole cocks, and ended it with a condensed milk orgasm. Modern London winked at ancient Rome. Our original intention of a cruel cocktail party where the glitterati met Oriental Rome disappeared – even the truncated version took till nine in the evening.

+–

SEBASTIANE – SCENE 1

I was always rather sad that the first scene of the film was never developed, though Paul and others were relieved. But there was method in the 'campness', and the vicious decadence of Diocletian, the ageing, isolated and paranoid Emperor who unleashed the last great purge of the Christians, might have been brought vividly to life.

***Sebastiane*, Max (Neil Kennedy)** *(Photo: Gerald Incandela)*

***Sebastiane*, Lindsay Kemp** (Photo: Gerald Incandela)

Setting: 25 December 303. A party to celebrate the festival of the Sun and Moon. Diocletian reclines on his couch in the banqueting-hall of the golden pavilion. The camera pulls back to reveal Vigilantia, a gossip columnist, and her two secretaries, Dulcissima and Euphorio. Vigilantia is dressed *à la moderne*, very chic. She sips champagne and introduces us to the cast in hushed Dimbleby tones.

> *Music and adoratio:* Ave deus et dominus noster.
>
> *As the party hots up into an orgy of killing, the court gossips.*

VIGILANTIA: Everyone who's anyone is here tonight. There's Galerius and Maxentius, and that's Constantine, ruler of Gaul and Britain, with the Lady Imperial Valeria. . .

(*Close up*) VALERIA (*aside*): Galerius and I are so bored with Rome – all this crime. Mind you London was quite dreadful.

VIGILANTIA: . . .and those strange ones over there are the Kings of the Barbarians – Vahram of Armenia and Narses, Prince of Persia. That's Tagis the new chief augur standing with the priests of Isis from Thebes. The Imperial Mother Diocla is talking to Tagis. She really looks wonderful at seventy-five. She's wearing one of the hats she designs; who could guess that such an elegant woman started out as a slave girl in Anolinus' estate in the Pontine Marsh . . .

Close up of Diocla with extravagant hat.

DIOCLA: I made it myself for the *Circenses adiabencis victis* when my husband was made a god.

TAGIS: Exquisite.

DIOCLA (*calling a slave to powder her nose*): I have to look my best, you know, now I'm a goddess myself . . .

. . . and so forth.

＋

This sequence was researched for me by Dom Sylvestre Houedard, the concrete poet and Benedictine historian, who sent twenty pages of meticulous notes and family trees in the smallest of hands with a thousand ideas of who might have been at such a reception, with a host of scurrilous suggestions about their relationships.

＋

Sebastiane, **with Leo Treviglio** (Photo: Gerald Incandela)

ULA'S CHANDELIER

August 1975 – a wake: *Ula's Chandelier* (15 min. film in Super 8) Luciana and Andrew organized a garden party to pay for Ula's fine. Andrew auctioned clothes and bits and pieces that people had brought.

Ula had been caught liberating a chandelier from Harrods. Rumour had it that she'd worn a sort of chastity belt with a hook, and had hung the chandelier between her legs under a massive ethnic skirt. All had gone well until she arrived at the escalator, which proved extremely difficult to negotiate and caused her downfall. People stopped and stared as she jangled tortuously towards the exit, and a Harrods detective sniffed a rat. The magistrates did not find the story amusing, fining her several hundred pounds.

James brought Liliana Cavani and we paid our dues for a really pleasant afternoon on the lawn. Liliana spent her time talent-spotting for her projected film *Nietzsche*, and I made a stop-frame film of the whole afternoon. Somehow this sunny party, with its long-haired musicians, was the last ghost of the sixties. The guests smiled and sat in the sun. Duggie wore a T-shirt that said Amour Amour, while Rae Mouse and Little Nel cavorted across the makeshift stage selling the clothes they were wearing to raise the money for the fine.

—

January 1976, Sloane Square: Anthony sailed through life on unpaid bills. When he received unpleasant-looking brown envelopes through the post he put them into the kitchen cupboard unopened. Every now and then he tripped up. This month has been overshadowed by the court case over a year's unpaid rent at Sloane Square – which the landlords have refused to accept from me as they would be able to charge a fortune for his flat if they could get it back into their hands. It's £15 a week and worth over a hundred.

I put on my grey suit and sat through the afternoon in the magistrates' court. Capital and County mounted a really mean attack through Bob the porter, accusing Anthony of everything in the book short of sodomy, but that was hinted at as well. I thought there was no chance but we won. The judge asked how many bedrooms there were – 'Two' – 'Well if that's the case I see no reason for Mr Jarman not to live there and take care of the place.' The landlords brought up the lack of furniture, which Bob himself had helped to remove in the last onslaught when he let the bailiffs in. The judge smiled when I said that Mr Harwood, a writer, lived a Japanese lifestyle – 'It's better with no shoes,' he wrote, 'no shoes at all.'

January 1976: Michael Ginsborg telephoned to say that Anthony died suddenly this morning in New York – at the time I was alone, listening to Brian Eno's elegaic 'Another Green World'.

When Guy Ford arrived at tea-time I told him to ask Eno if he would do the music for *Sebastiane*. Guy was pleased as it's his dream that Eno should be involved with the film.

+−

May 1976, Sloane Square: Within a few days of Anthony's death Bob stopped me in the hall with a glint of triumph in his eye, to say how sorry he was. A couple of days later a letter came through the door starting the court case business all over again. The landlords, with Machiavellian perspicacity, had stopped my first cheque to them. At the court case today they won outright. As the first judge had given me the right to pay rent, they claimed two years' rent, reparations and all the court fees. The whole business has left me penniless as the year we have been working – putting *Sebastiane* together bit by bit – has left me with no income. This evening Anthony Redmile told me he'd buy all the grey mirrors – which will help. But I'm homeless again.

+−

COMPLETION OF SEBASTIANE

Paul Humfress started to edit *Sebastiane* in the autumn of 1975 after we had received further promises of money from the investors. Funds came through in dribs and drabs, and by the time the film was finished it had cost about £30,000. The film was edited in Paul's cutting-room in Westbourne Grove, where I would spend two or three days of the week. It was a complicated business because our four weeks' shooting had produced barely enough footage to make a film; and Paul had to cut the film as slowly as possible to make up the eighty minutes plus which was the minimum for a feature. He did a marvellous job. Our rushes were in black and white, so we had no idea how the final film would look. By April we were nearly finished.

James and I took the cutting copy to show the Cannes selectors in Paris, but met with no success. Then in June the director of the Locarno Festival arrived in London to look for British films, and took it for his festival in August. Meanwhile Eno had agreed to do the music, which he produced like a magician in a couple of nights in the studios, juggling small pieces of paper marked with cryptic hieroglyphs. Then we received our answer print for grading, and discovered that the black and white images we had grown used to in the past year had turned into the most beautiful colour. Peter Middleton's kitchen-foil reflectors, which we all held at various times, had done the trick.

+—

REMOVAL PARTY – JULY 1976

(12 min. film in Super 8 and 16mm blow-up. Music by Simon Turner). The destruction of Sloane Square is complete: the mirrors are down and the whole place is sprayed with multi-coloured graffiti, on the floor, walls and ceiling. The windows have neat little crosses engraved on them with a diamond. Last night we gave a removal party in which the guests were invited to take the wiring, taps, anything they could pocket. This morning I spread the ten years of newspaper clippings I found in the end cupboard ankle-deep across the floor; and glued one about the curse of the Hope diamond to the living-room window. Everyone who possessed this diamond came to a sticky end. Then I left for Locarno, two weeks before the court order for possession was to take effect. I left Bob a neat note saying the late Anthony Harwood and I couldn't thank him enough for his kindness during these years, and enclosed the front-door keys. I wish I was a fly with a video when the tough emerald lady who brings bad news and Bob open the door. I think I have realized all their little black lies at the court case, and visualized them to the power of ten.

+—

THE PREMIERE OF SEBASTIANE

At Locarno the film was shown to an audience who barracked and protested throughout, stamping their feet and getting up noisily. At the end a petition was raised demanding the resignation of the festival's director. Paul and I sat at a news conference in the courtyard of the festival as the left and right attacked us and then each other. On the way back to the hotel a Catholic priest came up to us and said how much he had enjoyed the film, particularly the Latin.

+—

The year 1976 was the last in which I concentrated almost exclusively on my Super 8 films. A few paintings were finished, and a set of twelve glasses engraved with alchemical texts; but the bulk of the work that year consisted of two scripts with watercolour illustrations for complicated super 8 features intended to follow up the work on *In the Shadow of the Sun*. Both the John Dee script and a second reworking of *The Tempest* would in fact become feature films in the next three years. A third script, for an epic on Akhenaten, the heretic pharaoh, remained as a gilded book with beautiful watercolours which Christopher Hobbs painted from small thumb-nail sketches.

—⊹—

August 1976, Lee Studios: Ken Russell rang and asked me if I'd do a quick job designing a set for a Nescoré coffee ad. He was rather sheepish about the whole matter, as we both shared a dislike of the duplicity – to put it mildly – of the ad world. No one, given the chance to judge for themselves would have chosen Nescoré in preference to fresh coffee – though I am aware that most British people are blind with regard to food and drink, and are hooked, as I am, on those dyed green peas that used to be the mainstay of British cafes.

So we both consoled ourselves with the spurious argument that unless you'd gone into the camp of the enemy you would never really understand. But the truth was that after two court cases I was penniless.

Part one of the ad was a Marilyn Monroe look-alike sipping the brew on a heart-shaped bed and fingering croissants. These croissants had been flown to Wembley from a particular shop in Paris solely for their luscious appearance, which flagged on the journey and had to be restored with a bottle of glycerine to give them sparkle. Meanwhile the Nescoré execs fluttered around arguing about the exact degree of gold on a series of coffee sets.

Part two was a lost-looking model boy – who had been flown over with the croissants – dressed as an Earl's Court Arab impersonating Rudolf Valentino. Ian Whittaker and I fussed around the set, installing potted plants and hookahs in a sea of Persian carpets and cushions, while the make-up lady fought to transform her wooden charge, who needed more than glycerine to make his personality sparkle.

In the middle of this, at 9.30 on a Thursday morning, a fully grown African lion arrived in a van, and was prodded into reluctant action by six or more keepers. Coaxed on to the set under the glare of the lamps he suddenly decided to take off with an ominous growl, dragging his keepers with him, and most of the set, tangled with his chains. The terrified Valentino buried himself in the cushions as the coffee set went flying and the potted palm trees toppled. Ken and the camera crew, safe on a platform high up near the lighting grid, shouted orders, while Ian and I held the front line. After a while the huge moggy was coaxed back. He flopped into his film position and we covered his shackles with cushions. Then just as the camera rolled he decided to get playful, yawned and rolled on his back with his paws in the air, sending everything flying again.

--+--

August 1976, Butlers Wharf: The Andrew Logan all-stars have dominated the social life of London since the beginning of the decade, since David Hockney went into tax exile with the other working-class heroes of the sixties. They missed the sixties, but inherited the daydream which they tried to make a reality for a second generation. But they were the flash of the Super Novae before darkness. Now the seventies have caught up, and been pulled from under their feet by a gang of King's Road fashion anarchists who call themselves punks. They have stolen the all-stars' hairstyles, taken them to an extreme, and turned them on their heads. Unlike the glitterarti these boys and girls have the music business behind them to give them a real high with its coke-rolled banknotes of international finance. They've turned our gentle ineffectual friends into Demons of Nostalgia, while claiming that they are New. The music business has conspired with them to create another working-class myth as the dole queues grow longer to fuel the flames. But in reality the instigators of punk are the same old petit bourgeois art students, who a few months ago were David Bowie and Bryan Ferry look-alikes – who've read a little art history and adopted Dadaist typography and bad manners, and are now in the business of reproducing a fake street credibility. No one will admit that in a generation brought up on the consensus values of TV there is no longer such a thing as working-class 'culture' – to have any voice puts you firmly in the middle classes whatever your background. But at sweet seventeen you can kid yourself that no one has ever made love before – or that this carefully manipulated mythology is something new.

--+--

GERALD'S FILM

October 1976, Redcliffe Gardens: Gerald's film – (12 min. film in Super 8). I spent the weekend with Gerald and Thilo in the Temple in Essex, at the end of the lake with its huge eighteenth-century sweet chestnuts, a deep golden brown in the autumn sunlight. Buried in the woods is the boathouse which has lost its roof – and is in such an advanced state of decay that it would collapse if you breathed near it. Gerald shinned up a tree, climbing through a hole in the wall and into the room upstairs, which was a mass of sunlit diamonds. The rafters threw diamond shadows on the diamond panelling, and the sun shone through the diamond-leaded window panes. Gerald tiptoed across the mossy wooden floor and sat in front of the stone fireplace which is covered with carved corn and ivy leaves. I filmed him through the diamond panes. He looked like one of the workmen who might have built the place a hundred years ago, with the green felt hat from Pasolini's *Canterbury Tales* and the white scarf wound around his neck.

-+-

SEBASTIANE OPENS

October 1976: *Sebastiane* opened at the Gate cinema in Notting Hill last night after a day of record attendances and good reviews. At the opening Barney James, who plays the centurion, sat next to my parents. At the end of the film he turned to Dad and said, 'I don't suppose forces life was ever like that.' To my surprise Dad replied, 'I was out in the Middle East before the war and it's really quite accurate.'

After its opening at the Gate, where it played for four months before moving into the West End, *Sebastiane* opened all over the world to wildly different reviews. The Germans found our Latin untuned to their ears, and the French, at least so I was told, panned it. In the States it was classed S for Sex and we were unable to advertise it – so the audiences turned up expecting hardcore and were disappointed. However in Italy and Spain it was a stunning success with lyrical reviews. In Rome, Alberto Moravia came to the first press show and praised the film in the foyer saying that it was a film that Pier Paolo would have loved.

-+-

1971 BANKSIDE

The warehouse door opens into the ruinous and deserted Horseshoe Alley and no one would realize it was inhabited unless they noticed the small plastic bell tucked in a corner. Early this morning as I pushed open the door I knocked someone off the doorstep. I was surprised to find six or seven men standing deep in conversation and for a moment thought they must be visitors. As I put the heavy padlock on the door I asked them if I could help them, and as I did so I looked again and couldn't believe my eyes, as the man I had brushed off the doorstep was instantly recognizable as Pier Paolo Pasolini, talking to Franco Citti. For a moment I thought I was hallucinating. I nervously introduced myself to him in broken Italian and asked him if he would like some coffee in the studio. Before a conversation could develop a rather officious

English location-hunter brought it to a halt. I said to him I know this area like the back of my hand, but he was quite stony. Signor Pasolini is very busy, he said. I don't think Pasolini understood this conversation. He smiled at me and I'm certain he would have been happy to climb the stairs. So I quietly retired and left them to find the locations for the *Canterbury Tales* after telling Pasolini how much I loved his films.

+-

NOVEMBER 1976

Since I returned from Locarno I've had a series of floors and rented rooms, each more cramped than the last. I've come to rest in Redcliffe Gardens in Earl's Court – this is unbearable because the narrow street is a main arterial road down which the lorries thunder day and night. To sleep I have to use wax earplugs; but at least there's my own front door, though it's broken and anyone can wander in. Last night I disturbed a burglar, whom I mistook for a friend of Rufus or Donald, my flatmates. He was very calm. He said to me, 'Hi, I'm just leaving.' Something in his speed gave him away but by then it was too late. All in all Redcliffe Gardens is better than the rooming house in Drayton Gardens, guarded by its eccentric eagle-eyed proprietress (who'd taught dance to the Egyptian royal family before the war). Breakfast was a torture as you never knew whom you were going to meet; and bleary-eyed polite conversation with jolly, healthy Australians, or dull, indigestible German students, could set you up for a bad day. Also it was impossible to invite anyone back – Madame banned visitors after eight. One night I smuggled a lad in from the Coleherne, but the bedstead creaked and the floorboards even more. And we gave up.

+-

NOVEMBER 1976. HOUSTON, TEXAS

(10 min. film in Super 8). Brian Montgomery's bicentennial art junket to Houston is under way. I've ten of my slate drawings, Keith Milow's brought his ubiquitous crosses, Mario Dubsky some drawings. On the plane this morning, which took us to Houston from Miami, a blonde hostess – modelled on Jayne Mansfield in *The Girl Can't Help It* – did a sort of reverse striptease into her Mae West, posing at the end of each carefully choreographed passage for imaginary fans and photographers. Afterwards she had the plane-load of executives undressed and reeling all over the plane while she played a game of strip with bottles of champagne for prizes. It

started innocently enough with, 'Have any of you gentlemen got a hole in your left sock?'

We spent the day on an art tour of the Exxon skyscraper. The four corners of the top floor contain the four suites of the four directors. But before we were taken on a guided tour we were lectured on Texas and oil in the manner of *Dr Strangelove*: Ruskies and European faint-hearts were pushed to the periphery of existence. The first director collected tin construction helmets – they were beaten like the brass tables that are sold in the Middle East, and would have melted a clone's heart – and intricate models in solid gold of oil rigs. The second director collected slices of redwood painted and varnished with sailing-ships and impossible romantic pre-ecological views. The third – capodimonte figurines of beggar boys. And the fourth – *moderne arte*. As a lapsed artiste I studied my fellow professionals keenly. Except for one loaded question from Mario Dubsky to Dr Strangelove, British good manners won the day.

✠

January 1977, Redcliffe Gardens: I've travelled to every provincial opening of *Sebastiane* to drum up publicity. The cinemas are wonderfully old-fashioned – no wonder they're closing so fast. The proprietors are charming but from another world. The journalists from the local newspapers tread gingerly past the subject-matter of the film, but are either polite or jovial, or else unsure of themselves. In York the manager's daughter was married to a Sardinian and there was sherry for everyone. For some reason Manchester brought a local comedian, who entertained me and the press. At Reading they were grumpy, at Bristol polite. In Hull no one turned up at all – this was after a whole night spent getting there on a freezing milk train, which moved at walking-pace and stopped at every lamp post.

✠

VII
Chelsea on Ice

Spring-Summer 1977: The Super 8 film I was planning with Jordan took off like a roller coaster after the success of *Sebastiane* at the Gate. The John Dee script was pirated and used as a framing device; Jung's *Seven Sermons to the Dead*, and the *Angelic Conversations* of the good doctor Dee were scrambled with *SNIFFin Glue* and *London's OUTRAGE*. 'See natures splendours, mans achievements' – by March, HIGH FASHION as it was called at first, a R.I.P. OFF Films production, was xeroxed like a fanzine.

Throughout the filming a debate raged about the title of both the film and the company. R.I.P. OFF Films presented ONISWAKIMALIPONCE, HIGH FASHION and JUBILEE. R.I.P. OFF became Megalovision, and eventually registered as the company which produced *Jubilee*.

As usual there was no money; but James Whaley, with true bravado, gambled everything on an air ticket to Tehran and arrived back with a cheque for £50,000, one week before we started shooting. Meanwhile, Jordan helped me with the casting, introducing the Slits and Adam Ant. I'd spotted Adam several weeks before at the end of the King's Road, in a dirty white shirt ripped to show the 'Fuck' which Jordan had carved on his back with a razor blade. I moved back to the old studio at Butlers Wharf, which we used as an HQ from which to make the film in the surrounding streets; and John Maybury, a young film student, and Kenny Morris, the drummer of the Banshees, started to build the set in the building next door with rubbish which they brought in from skips. Luciana and I snapped away at concerts, looking for extras. The cast was slowly assembled. Toyah Wilcox arrived out of the blue one afternoon in a long black dress and lopsided haircut with a scarlet bang: she was so enthusiastic it was impossible to refuse her. Jordan persuaded Adam. And James asked Ian Charleson if he would play one of the parts at his gym. With Jenny Runacre, Richard O'Brien, Orlando, Hermine and Little Nell, we were nearly complete. Neil Kennedy, Linda Spurrier and Karl Johnson made up the cast, and 'Chelsea on Ice' was under way – with a gun at our heads to finish it before the end of the year.

***Jubilee*, Amyl (Jordan)** *(Photo: Jean Marc Prouveur)*

The censor demanded five cuts in the film as he was certain it was going to have a large following. In the event he was proved wrong: the film drew smaller audiences than either *Sebastiane* or *The Tempest*. But armed with statistics of identikit muggings from *A Clockwork Orange*, he said you wouldn't want to wake up to *Jubilee*-style killings in the *Sun*. I pointed out to him that *Jubilee* was not more violent than many another film, but that the violence was unglamourized, quite real and seen negatively – not like the balletic celebration of violence in *A Clockwork Orange* at all. In the end he demanded only one cut, to keep the balance between the various factions who warred over his job. It seemed that it was more than his life was worth to let the film through uncut.

Moreover I had the management of the Gate to consider, whose new cinema *Jubilee* was opening. They were desperate for a certificate with only a few days to go till the opening. I took the scissors myself and cut seven seconds from the murder in pink polythene sheets. Sex and violence were the censors' chief bugbears; but sexual violence is almost entirely committed by men, and it seemed to me that this scene was more likely to put men off than turn them on.

+−

SIGNING UP (A SEQUENCE)

Cardinale Borgia Ginz (who owned the media): You wanna know my story, Babe, It's *easy*. This is the generation who forgot how to lead their lives. They were so busy watching my endless movie. It's power, Babe. Power. I don't create it, I own it. I sucked and sucked and sucked. The Media became their only reality, and I owned the world of flickering shadows – BBC, TUC, ATV, ABC, ITV, CIA, CBA, NFT, MGM, KGB, C of E. . . You name it – I bought them all, and rearranged the alphabet.

+−

MEGALOVISION

In *Jubilee* all the positives are negated, turned on their heads. Its dream imagery drifts uncomfortably on the edge of reality, balanced like Hermine on the tightrope. Its amazons make men uncomfortable, ridicule their male pursuits. Its men are all victims. The heroines have emblematic names – Bod, Boadicea, Anybody; Viv, Viva, Life; Mad and Amyl. Amyl (alias Jordan) is the high-flown historian of the divided culture of beef and cows, mansions and houses: 'It all began with William the Conqueror, who screwed the Anglo-Saxons into the ground, carving the land

***Jubilee*, Bod (Jenny Runacre)** (Photo: Jean Marc Prouveur)

into Theirs and Ours. *They* lived in *Mansions* and ate *Beef* at fat tables whilst the poor lived in *houses* minding the *cows* on a bowl of porridge, whilst they pushed them around with their arrogant foreign accents. There were two languages in the land, and the seeds of war were sown.' Through this war Elizabeth I, the nation's anima, wanders in virgin white; while John Dee, the magus, inventor and universal man reveals to her the shadow of her time. A bitter chill blows through the film. For an audience who expected a punk music film, full of 'anarchy' and laughs at the end of the King's Road, it was difficult to swallow. They wanted action, not analysis; and most of the music lay on the cutting-room floor. Vivienne Westwood, instigator of fashion panic at the World's End, produced one of her brilliant T-shirts to rip the film to pieces and say how boring it was. To sing of boredom is one thing, to show it quite another. At the opening of the film the audience took sides. One strong man fainted; and a flower-power lady in a long dress danced in front of the audience proclaiming love. Meanwhile the motorbike girls who had stood in for the bike scene, frightening everyone with their leathers and cans of Special Brew, got up and disappeared into the darkness, declaring they were Christians.

Afterwards, the film turned prophetic. Dr Dee's vision came true – the streets burned in Brixton and Toxteth, Adam was Top of the Pops and signed up with Margaret Thatcher to sing at the Falklands Ball. They all sign up one way or another.

+—

THE END OF ENTERTAINMENT

ANGEL: The show that made Tyburn look like a picnic – save your souls! Real nails, real hammers. Naked as nature intended. The impresario has spared no expense GOLD FRANKINCENSE MYRRH plus the Daughters of God LIVE ON STAGE. It's your last chance – the show is about to end: Cardinal Borgia Ginz is going into the car-park business.

BORGIA (*to his aides*): There's more bread in cars than people – and they don't have to be entertained. I build their houses, plan their roads, plant the trees and run the buses. They're all working for me. I call it improvement, PROGRESS, Babe. And they follow blindly. I'm their life insurance. Without progress life would be UNBEARABLE – *progress has taken the place of heaven*. It's like pornography, *better* than the real thing.

AMYL: Our school motto was *Faites vos désires réalitées*; 'make your desires reality'. Myself I preferred the song 'Don't dream it, be it'. In those days desires weren't allowed to become reality. So fantasy was substituted for them – films, books, pictures, they called it *art*. But when your desires become reality you don't need fantasy any longer, or art.

+-

LITTLE ENGLAND

At the end of *Jubilee* our heroines, fleeing from the dying cities, across the Iron Curtain to a dream England of the past: the England of stately homes, which are the indispensable prop for the English way of life. The soap operas of our lives demand them – anyway, they're big at the box-office. Any film or TV series that has one is half-way to success. Private schools are housed in them, so the children of the wealthy get a taste for them young. Everyone else is encouraged to gawp at them during bank holidays. Longleat, where we made the end of the film, is one of these. Thoroughly commercialized, a banker's cottage, it appears in the schoolbooks as possessing architectural merit. In fact, it's a square, rather ugly house, with a misproportioned façade. Without its pepper-pot roof it could be a research lab in the depressed international style of the new universities. The house is in the grip of a deadly blight. My first view through the fine Victorian planting of trees and rhododendrons was of a valley filled with a thousand caravans, in the middle of which it looked like a beached whale. Signposts directed you to 'Cream Teas' or the 'Kama Sutra Apartments' – under-eighteens discouraged, and a grave warning of the erotic nature for the rest. The cream teas were mediocre, served in a basement canteen; and the sexy paintings, by one of the sons of the house, were a last-ditch attempt to bring the place to life. The bleak Victorian panelling had been daubed in emerald and purple, with figures in heavy impasto coupling lugubriously. In one bedroom a rhino horn was glued to the bed-head of a four-poster to encourage its flagging occupants. Outside, the orientalism was echoed by a sad little ying and yang garden, with some tatty cherry trees planted haphazardly round the figure-of-eight pond.

Beyond the penicillin mould of caravans lay the Safari Park, a grid of aimless tarmac roads that meandered over the old park, between high wire fences reminiscent of Ashford Remand Centre. The centuries-old oaks, now dying, were wrapped up in barbed wire and plastic in a forlorn attempt to stop the marauding exotics from destroying them. Baboons and Siberian tigers eyed you malevolently as you drove past. Nel said, 'I've never been to the country before. It's so fascinating – and the animals – I have a passion for fur.' We filmed both outside and inside the

Jubilee, **Mad (Toyah Wilcox)** *(Photo: Jean Marc Prouveur)*

Jubilee, Luciana Martinez *(Photo: Jean Marc Prouveur)*

house. Jordan facing a rhino with her spiky hairstyle, horn to horn – and at one of the gate posts we used as the border checkpoint, with its ominous fence, a red flag is draped. Much of this ended on the cutting-room floor, particularly the last scene where our stars, in the flight from reality, had tea with the ageing Hitler and his wife. One piece that went had Hitler painting those lurid murals, talking to himself about the problem of inflation – 'We came to Dorset. It's the perfect place for retirement. Josef suggested it after we met in Berlin. The people here are much too dozy to notice me, and if they did, much too polite to say anything. We're thinking of giving it up, retiring to the sun – Eva suggested South America.'

+—

ENTERING DORSET

MAD: Daddy's quite a lunatic – I hope we don't end up fighting. He's banned most things – it's the most conservative regime in England. The place is a sort of holiday camp for retired trade unionists – he's modelled his administration on Butlin's. Everything's done to the rule book – no Deviation in Dorset, you'll get no help from anyone. Daddy always said the trouble with Rome was too few lions. There are more lions in Dorset than in Africa.

CRABS: It's not true.

MAD: Yes – it's in *The Guinness Book of Records. And tigers*, though some say there're more of those in Scotland.

+—

With *Jubilee* the progressive merging of film and my reality was complete. The source of the film was often autobiographical, the locations were the streets and warehouses in which I had lived during the previous ten years. The film was cast from among and made by friends. It was a determined and often reckless analysis of the world which surrounded us, constructed pell-mell through the early months of 1977. The shooting script is a mass of xeroxes and quick notes on scraps of paper, torn photos and messages from my collaborators, and the resulting film has something of the same quality. Just as it seems that it is settling down it's off in another direction, like a yacht in a squall. Unlike *Sebastiane* there are now no amusing stories to tell, as if they occurred they were engulfed in celluloid and quickly integrated into the finished work. Whereas in *Sebastiane* we lived in a world outside the film, in *Jubilee* our world became the film. A first note to myself makes the position quite clear –

JUBILEE

is a fantasy documentary fabricated so that documentary and fictional forms are confused and coalesce.

+—

The two middle-aged ladies who play bingo in Max the retired mercenary's dingy bingo palace in Islington set the scene:

  1: They got Maureen.

  2: I told you, she had the look, you can tell you know (*she wipes away a tear*).

  1: Don't be so sentimental Joyce.

  2: She was so young.

  1: What do you expect, she never carried a gun, not even a knife.

  2: I know she couldn't get used to it.

  1: I told her last week in Sainsbury's – '. . . at least a hat pin Maureen'.

  2: They threw the toaster in the bath and she was electrocuted.

  1: Oh my God!

  2: What can you expect with millions unemployed?

+—

Max himself is equally alienated but in a different way, as he destroys the weeds in his garden.

MAX: The army was a con. It was a way of solving the unemployment problem before they gave up entirely. You're more likely to die of red tape than a bullet in the Guards. I ran a sideline selling the boys to the local punters in the pub. The army sees more action in bed these days. Dammit, this carnation's got mildew (*he sprays it with Pledge*). We never got a chance to kill anyone so I killed the weeds in the garden of an evening.

VIV: Yes, it must have been frustrating in the army.

MAX: Yeah! Think, the world's sitting on enough megatons to blast the sunrise into the west, and no one's prepared to press the fucking button. It's a fucking waste. Think what it all cost – I've paid my taxes . . .

+—

In a world that can be incinerated at any moment the will to action fades. Boredom stands at the antechamber of the Apocalypse. Values and qualities cease to exist

***Jubilee*,** **Ian Charleson and Karl Johnson** (Photo: Jean Marc Prouveur)

when all can be reduced to ashes.

Viv, the artist, in many ways one of the most sympathetic characters of the film, pleads for action. But her reality – an empty black room – reflects something quite different.

VIV: Painting's extinct, it's just a habit. I started when I was eight copying dinosaurs from a picture book. It was prophetic.

–+–

The twin brothers, Angel and Sphinx, stand on a windswept roof. Sphinx looks at a distant highrise.

SPHINX: That's where Angel and I were born. Never lived below the fourteenth floor until I was old enough to run away. Never saw the ground until I was four. Just locked alone with the telly all day. The first time I saw flowers I freaked, I was frightened of dandelions – my gran picked one and I had hysterics. Everything was regulated in that tower block, planned by the social planners to the lowest common denominator. Sight: concrete. Sound: the telly. Taste: plastic. Touch: plastic. The seasons regulated by a thermostat.

–+–

Through the world our little gang of media heroines move socially upwards – 'they all sign up in the end one way or another'. But Borgia Ginz, who owns the media, plays a double game as he rearranges the alphabet.

BORGIA: You're signed up. Now what are we going to call you? 'SCUM' hahaha! That's it! That's it! 'SCUM', that's commercial. (*Aside*) It's all they deserve.

Outside the plush offices in Buckingham Palace, which Borgia inhabits, and from which he plays 'the Power game' – 'as long as the music's loud enough we won't hear the world falling apart' – the streets are bleak with random violence in which the police indulge their natural belligerence, no longer on the side of either law or order. As Amyl puts it succinctly:

AMYL: On my fifteenth birthday law and order were finally abolished, and all those statistics that were a substitute for reality disappeared, and the crime-rate dropped to zero.

–+–

And that, with its sanitized end in Dorset, was *Jubilee*.

BOD: After the surprises of the week we decided to go to the country. Nowadays one's days are numbered in the city. We headed west through the scattered and ruined streets with the night sky flickering with the fires that had burnt ceaselessly from our childhood. High above criss-crossed the spider's web of a technology that was dying. Telephone wires and pylons whose angry buzzing was slowly falling into silence.

+—

Jubilee opened and many of the critics dismissed it as 'Chelsea on Ice', believing 'reality' is an art-ful black and white film set in some Northern industrial town. But now *image* is everything, as a Prime Minister fused with the Saatchis invites us, like a smart hostess, on board Battleship England – set firmly on a course to OBLIVION.

MAX: My idea of a perfect garden is a remembrance poppy field.

+—

***Jubilee*, Amyl (Jordan)** (Photo: Jean Marc Prouveur)

VIII
Stormy Weather

At the end of July 1978, I went to Taormina in Sicily to help with the Italian pre-publicity for *Jubilee*. The trip proved as disastrous as I had expected. The film was shown on the last night of the festival at 2.30 a.m.; I left an hour into the film, leaving an audience of nine in the cinema, of whom at least four were asleep. The lonely and isolated days at the festival were brightened up by meeting Paul Morrissey, whose rather awful attempt at 'Carry On Sherlock Holmes' was showing. I found it difficult to equate this urbane, besuited New Yorker, who epitomized the Warhol/*Interview* 'sell-out', with that dull and silly film – the canny English gent Holmes must appeal to New York gay snobbism. A party was thrown to close the festival, on the terrace of one of the plushest hotels in the town. I felt out of it, leaning against the balustrade with a perfect view behind my back, ignored by the Italians who had bought *Jubilee* as they were courting bigger fry. Knowing no one, a mixture of boredom and social unease overwhelmed me. Suddenly Amanda Lear, 'ITALY'S NO.1 singing star', appeared at the door. She spotted me, and walked straight over, rescuing what had started out as a very dull evening.

+–

Later, in the old Roman theatre built in the hill above the town, packed with an enthusiastic and noisy Sicilian crowd of at least 5,000, Amanda took the stage with a bacchanalian relish that would have pleased the ghosts of the Caesars. In a confetti of flashlights she slithered over fallen columns and tumbled stonework on to the stage, half snake, half leopard, singing her ABC in a deep husky voice. The roar which greeted her nearly put the moon out – the paparazzi broke ranks, tumbled on to the stage, and lying on their backs took photos by flashlight up Amanda's skirt. She stepped over them, catlike. Whatever your reservations, you couldn't but be carried away with the immense gusto with which it was done. The audience went wild.

I watched a curious sideline to the event, as a subtle propaganda exercise that the Russians had undertaken was destroyed. They had brought a blonde corn goddess dressed in a lavish emerald-green evening-dress, who until Amanda appeared in her leopard-skin had been the centre of attention. This was a situation which brought obvious satisfaction to her keepers who had guarded her jealously throughout the festival. Amanda won the crowd, Capitalism's ultimate weapon triumphed. At the end of the film, Morrissey's *Sherlock Holmes*, the scatological humour of which met the approval of the arena, all 5,000 of the audience lit candles as the stage lights were lowered and sang a song in the pagan dark to end the night's entertainment.

+

Brandishing knives, forks, whatever came to hand, my mother would stand on the kitchen table and recite long passages of *Henry V* she had learned at school; Agincourt would be fought against the Germans, while we stood in amazement, staring up at this aproned amazon from a schoolgirl play . . .

At Kings the Shakespeare text was *The Tempest*; and afterwards I read it often. At first I made designs for an imaginary production at the Roundhouse, in which most of the theatre space was flooded, with the audience on a magic island of inflatable silver rocks, trampolines, and a huge, banner-like cloak. I talked with John Gielgud about these designs when we worked on the ill-starred production of *Don Giovanni*. Later, in 1975, I made my first cut-up of the text, in which a mad Prospero, rightly imprisoned by his brother, played all the parts.

+

Friday 4 August 1978 – Halton: Late in the afternoon I sat with my sister, Gaye, at my mother's deathbed. She was totally lucid the whole time. Worried about her appearance, she asked for a mirror, had the photos of my nephews and nieces moved so she could see them, and asked me about Italy, where for the last three months I had been writing the first script for *Caravaggio*. I described my visit to Capri, a place I knew she loved and which she had visited in 1947 – blue sea, sunshine, beautiful flowers. In my grandfather's home movie she blinked in the sunlight and smiled into the camera; a title appeared on the screen which introduced you to 'ever-smiling Betty'. Never once during all the years since did she cease to smile – her detachment from her illness is such that in the last weeks the hospital has employed her as a therapist among the other cancer patients. Last week, when a young priest came, she put scarlet cherries in her ears, and laughing, told him she believed in no life after death; then, troubled lest she'd hurt his feelings, entertained him to tea and made him promise there should be the shortest possible ceremony. He was shattered; as were the nurses, who through the eighteen years of her illness spent in and out of hospital have become some of her closest friends. When I left Halton she said goodbye silently, with a radiant, wistful smile which told me she knew why we were all there . . . the next morning we rushed back to find her in her death agony. My sister and I took one fragile hand each as her life fluttered away like the proverbial swallows. It was difficult to know whether to speak or not – neither Gaye nor I could believe that after all these years of attentive listening she wouldn't hear. I asked her if she was comfortable – 'Are you all right?' – and she whispered so quietly that maybe I imagined the response: 'Of course not silly, but you are.'

—

I often wonder about the effect of Ma's eighteen years of illness, borne with such serenity, on myself and my sister. This flashed across my mind as I stood in the municipal crematorium, while the parson read out the briefest of committal services. Ma had asked for no ceremony, but by law you have to have one. The young priest, whom she had joked with and chatted to over a cup of tea about life, not the after life, was visibly moved by her death. He apologized to her for having to read the committal, said he'd make it as brief as possible.

She could never bear to let us see her down – forbade too-frequent visits to the hospital. Never once during the years when her life was in the balance – she must have been in considerable pain, and confusion from the drugs – did a shadow cross her face. She was an enthusiast, and had a vibrant, vivacious manner which made our home the 'centre' – all the kids played there, confided in her, and returned long after we left to discuss their problems.

She was also severely practical. Notes were left pinned on the refrigerator announcing food and then SWITCH OFF THE LIGHTS! when we returned home late. She had learned to move quickly and leave the past behind, for little could be carried on our constant removals. And when we arrived at a new home, as we did nearly every eighteen months, she managed to brighten the place up, however ugly it was. She always cooked so that there was an extra place set and friends could stay for lunch; it was never a problem. If I quarrelled with my sister, order was instantly restored: not by reprimand but theatrically – 'You should hear yourselves' – and then she'd pick a fight with Dad over something ridiculous, till we all had to laugh. I never heard my parents quarrel: a moment's irritation at the most, usually over something we had done or failed to do.

At times she seemed to be in another world; but that, I now realize, had been the effect of the huge quantity of drugs she was forced to take. Even this could provide amusement. One night she entertained some rather 'proper' friends – the editor of one of the dreaded popular dailies and his wife. She inadvertently poured salad cream over the strawberries in the kitchen. We all dipped in at once as she'd made the moment special by announcing, 'The first strawberries of the summer'. There was an uncomfortable silence. 'Oh my God how silly of me,' she said, and whipped them back into the kitchen to wash them, laughing while we tried to keep straight, grown-up faces.

When Ma died I felt elation: she had been up and about until near the end, had always been so happy with simple and homely things, never regretting anything or envying anyone. She had managed to live her life to the full in a very modest way, and keep to that way to the end. I know she worried a little about the effect her illness was having on us, just as she always worried about our health: 'Derek, you looked peaky. You don't eat enough. You must EAT.' Or, 'Do *not* worry about seeing me. It is *quite* unnecessary. I will be well content to wait till your return from Rome. I am doing all I should and surprising everyone. Writing awful – balanced pad on wobbly book on wobbly knee.'

–+–

APOLLO

The handsomest dark-haired kid in his early twenties, American collegiate but Italian, came into the Apollo restaurant with an older, rather elegant and severe woman, with greying black hair brushed back. He had a physical confidence I've hardly ever seen.

He sprawled into the window seat; then flashed a smile that would have entranced Garbo as he caught me looking. There was no hesitation or glimmer of embarrassment, as if the admiration was his by right. 'Come on, look at me' – he put his arm around the woman's shoulders slowly and deliberately. The restaurant dissolved as he caught my eye and held it; the seconds ticked past, and I stared back flushed with a cold fear; thirty, forty, fifty of them, such dark and cruel eyes, laughing at me, and those dazzling white teeth . . . 'Come on, I fucking dare you.' Later they left. In my entire life I have never been smiled at like that. I dropped my eyes after a minute that seemed like a night of love.

–+–

FILMING SHAKESPEARE, OCTOBER 1978

The settings of Shakespeare films always clash with the language: spirit turns to icy matter and falls like hail. Shakespeare works best in Russian, where the problem of his language is circumvented. Even *Henry V*, perhaps the most successful English adaptation, is a stylistic confusion – caught between the artificiality of the medieval miniatures in the *Tres Riches Heures*, and the damp naturalism of the Irish countryside.

For *The Tempest* we needed an island of the mind, that opened mysteriously like Chinese boxes: an abstract landscape so that the delicate description in the poetry, full of sound and sweet airs, would not be destroyed by any Martini lagoons. The budget was only £150,000. Britain was the magic isle. I sailed as far away from tropical realism as possible.

The key to a film *can* be its design – too often left to designers who dress the film in a kind of wrapping, like a doily around a birthday cake. Audiences see nothing beyond the surface, are willingly dazzled by the roses and silver balls; but when design is integrated into the intentional structure, and forms part of the dialectic, the work begins to sing. *Ivan the Terrible* is the most perfect example. 'Epic' has had more than its fair share of icing, but Eisenstein reinforces the humanity and ambiguity of Ivan through *design*. This integration of design in a film is not only the preserve of 'high art'. *The Wizard of Oz* is another perfect example.

+–

SYNCHRONICITY

13 November 1978: I sat on the edge of my seat at lunch with three generations of the Leigh family in the panelled dining-room of Stoneleigh Abbey. Leighs had been having lunch here since the 1540s. The meal was served by the housekeeper Ms Leigh, who had austere silver-braided hair smelling of cloves. Lunch progressed in a strange silence which I attempted to break – but there was no communication between the generations. Afterwards, in the growing darkness of a winter afternoon, old Lord Leigh (who was to die a few months later) led me through the abbey, switching on lights which I then switched off as we left each of the rooms behind. He talked quietly to his ancestors on the walls as though they were still alive – Tudor Leighs and Stuart Leighs, with names like Augusta. One was ostracized for her implication in the Gunpowder Plot. There was Lord Byron, whose picture hung in the Library; Jane Austen, writing in the Green Room; Queen Victoria, on a visit; and then silence . . . Room followed shadowy room, until we reached the vast and

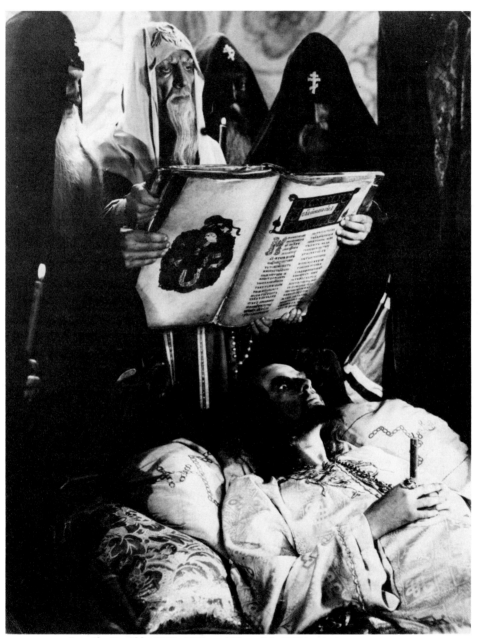

***Ivan the Terrible*, 1942–46, Sergei Eisenstein** (BFI Archive)

empty Georgian wing, where we were to film. It had phosphorescent greying mirrors, and chandeliers, which, when we later lit them with a hundred or more candles, animated the plaster ceilings in an unexpected way: the gods and goddesses, encrusted on them amongst fruit and flowers, danced in the flickering light.

As I left I noticed a portrait of a young woman in the entrance hall, and asked John Leigh who she was. 'Oh, Elizabeth, the Winter Queen', for whom *The Tempest* was performed one winter evening in 1612.

+—

November, 1978–February, 1979: During November I took out the scissors and cut up the play for the third time.

Having decided on the format of a dream film, one which enabled me to take the greatest possible freedom with the text, I cut away the dead wood (particularly the obsolete comedy) so that the great speeches were concertinaed. Then the play was rearranged and opened up: the theatrical magic had to be replaced.

The endless corridors and lost rooms of Stoneleigh suggested servants, romantic scholars with opium pipes, young girls with dresses spun from gossamer and frosted with shells and feathers. By the time filming was commenced, on 14 February, we were living in another world. The cameras began to turn with the house in darkness, its shutters closed against the blizzards outside.

+—

SPIDERS

Film is the wedding of light and matter – an alchemical conjunction. My readings in the Renaissance magi – Dee, Bruno, Paracelsus, Fludd and Cornelius Agrippa – helped to conjure the film of *The Tempest*. The magical signs that Prospero drew on the walls of his study came either from the *Occult Philosophy* of Cornelius Agrippa, or are Egyptian hieroglyphs as they were used in the seventeenth century, as the writing of 'the Adepts'. My seventeenth-century copy of the *Occult Philosophy* was open on Prospero's desk – its first English edition. On the floor the artist Simon Reade drew out the magic circles that were blueprints of the pinhole cameras he constructed in his studio next to mine at Butlers Wharf, thereby making a subtle connection. Prospero's wand was built by Christopher Hobbs in the form of John Dee's *Monas Hieroglyphica*, which symbolized the unity of spirit and matter.

Heathcote Williams (Prospero) was conversant with this pre-Scientific

A page of *The Occult Philosophy*, 1631 – Cornelius
Agrippa, Hermeticist *(Photo: Namara Features)*

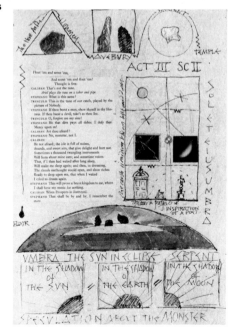

Tempest notebook for super 8 version, 1974
(Photo: Namara Features)

approach to the physical world, and so we were able to jettison the cruder theatrical magic of the stage for something more refined and developed. When Prospero calls the unwilling Ariel at the beginning of the film, the chandeliers tinkle, a glass overturns and a spider runs under the staff. Ariel is Prospero's spider and catches his enemies on gossamer threads.

The Shakespeare who spun *The Tempest* must have known John Dee; and perhaps through Philip Sidney he met Giordano Bruno in the year when he was writing the *Cena di Ceneri* – the Ash Wednesday supper in the French Ambassador's house in the Strand. Prospero's character and predicament certainly reflect these figures, each of whom in his own way fell victim to reaction. John Dee, with the greatest library in England, skrying for the angels Madimi and Uriel (so nearly Ariel) – all of which is recorded in the *Angelic Conversations* – ended up, in his old age, penniless in Manchester. Bruno was burnt for heresy.

Ten years of reading in these forgotten writers, together with a study of Jung and his disciples proved vital in my approach to both *Jubilee* and *The Tempest*. As for the black magic which David Bowie thought I dabbled in like Kenneth Anger, I've never been interested in it. I find Crowley's work dull and rather tedious. Alchemy, the approach of Marcel Duchamp, interests me much more.

— ｔ —

January 1979, London: Yolanda is designing *The Tempest*. We've known each other for twelve years, and are now working together. All she needs to do is transfer the contents of her home in Hamilton Terrace to Stoneleigh. Her house is a treasure trove, absent-mindedly cluttered over every surface. Yolanda moves around it sighing: 'Oh dear, where did I put the bamboo – Oh, here's a piece of lace, a shell, a mask.' She paints wan and ghostly figures in oils, fast, on huge canvases propped precariously in corners. Outside the window the garden is a jungle: an old cherry tree, cascading with white snowy blossom, covers it like a Victorian parasol. There are costumes and masks, mannequins from de Chirico, brushes, books, and branches hanging from the ceiling. She moves like a ballet-dancer, and dresses like one. A touch here and there – she stands forlornly like a doll in a tide of tinsel artefacts.

She works with a few deft strokes to produce collage-like costumes. Miranda's dress is created in minutes from an old silk wedding veil, feathers and shells. All the while Yolanda sighs – life is so difficult. Mournful, but endlessly resourceful, she rallies her 'students', who arrive at the oddest of hours at Butlers

Wharf, and organizes a chain-gang to make a thousand roses out of silk and satin to decorate the pergolas she has already designed for the ballroom. In the freezing cold, the studio becomes a fairyland.

+—

'ONE SONG WELSH'

24 February 1979, Stoneleigh: Elisabeth Welsh arrived in the snow to sing 'Stormy Weather'. I first heard Lis sing last December at a party with Freddy Ashton, a Ruth Etting song 'Ten Cents a Dance'. Fred told me all about her, and I decided to ask her to be in the film.

She entranced all the young sailor boys at the marriage party – her singing was an enchantment. Yolanda's bright-orange dress illuminated her like a fiery moon. In the cold ballroom she worked non-stop through the day, never missing a cue; and still had the energy to entertain everyone at the dinner-table in the refectory. Single-handed, she replaced Iris, Ceres and Juno . . . Lis told us that she hated leaving England because here the newspapers always announce the age of murderers and film stars. She picked up a copy of the *Mirror* and confirmed it. 'One song Welsh', as she called herself, had one song in *The Tempest* and true to form she stopped the show.

+—

MIRANDA

Toyah's bravado and vitality carry her through: on film she transforms like a chameleon – the dumpy Mad of *Jubilee*, in her fatigues, is hardly recognizable as the ethereal Miranda with the wicked chuckle. Her slight lisp gives her voice character. She's a born performer who plays her roles, including that of pop star, with deadly accuracy.

+—

PROSPERO

Heathcote/Prospero sleeps somewhere deep in the abbey in his shabby frock-coat and waistcoat of scarab buttons. He appears, rats in his hair, to devise new games and entertainments, his efforts fuelled by the Bulmer's Cider which Simon buys each day. We have brief discussions about his role, and he shyly produces lines he feels I should keep – 'Lest the blind mole hear a footfall'. He develops a cold which

The Tempest, **The Goddess (Elizabeth Welch)** *(Photo: Bridget Holm)*

The Tempest, **Miranda (Toyah Wilcox)** (Photo: Bridget Holm)

gives his voice a gravelly resonance. One night, at dinner, he says, 'I've been entertaining you lot far too long – if no one entertains me within one minute I'm going to piss all over you.' Then he jumps on the long refectory table and starts to pee a cider torrent. We dive for cover. Heathcote is embarrassed, and apologizes – more to himself than us. He has a wild anarchic gentleness, and is the genius of oblique strategies. He breathes fire and bends keys, not to startle, but to test divine possibility. He is an ideal Prospero, performs sympathetic magic, destroys the poetry and finds the meaning. I've rarely heard lines spoken with such clarity – 'and my Zenith doth depend upon a most auspicious star'. These words are spoken softly, not bawled across the footlights. How Shakespeare would have loved the cinema!

+—

RUSHES

The first day's rushes are disappointing; Peter Middleton, who has lit all three of my films, feels it and so do I. It's often like this, we remind ourselves, until the work settles down. We decide to let shadows invade – the lighting is too bright, too television. Gradually the rushes become more spectacular, the boundaries disappear. Each evening we eagerly watch them, and if they fail to turn up there is gloomy disappointment, as watching them is the perfect end to a hard day's work.

Without Peter there would have been no films. He has gradually encouraged me, given me confidence and helped me find my feet. A large part of me is still the reclusive painter, who breaks out with over-enthusiasm; this is tempered by Peter's technical precision, the long pauses while he lights hold me in check, and the combination produces results. The film is constructed extremely simply with masters, mid-shots, and close-ups. The camera hardly ever goes on a wander. This is deliberate, as I've noticed that if one deals with unconventional subject-matter, experimental camera work can push a film over into incoherence. What works at the Co-op and in the Super 8 films does not necessarily work within the format of the feature film, on a large scale.

In *The Tempest* we paint pictures, frame each static shot and allow the play to unfold in them as within a proscenium arch.

+—

The butterflies 'psyche' hibernate in the folds of the tattered silk curtains, a faded green washed out by a hundred summers. They were proudly hung for Queen

The Tempest, Prospero (**Heathcote Williams**) *(Photo: Bridget Holm)*

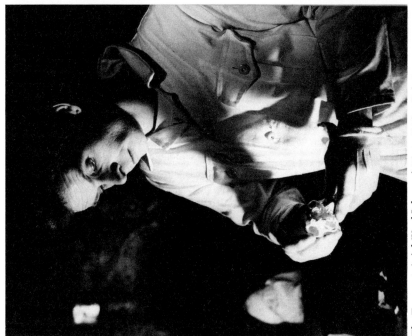

The Tempest, Ariel (**Karl Johnson**) *(Photo: Bridget Holm)*

Victoria's visit. As the lights warm up the empty rooms the peacocks and tortoiseshells wake up, thinking spring has arrived. There is a sudden brilliant flash of colour in the middle of a shot. Drowsy and easy to catch, we put them in jam-jars and ferry them to colder rooms. Today I picked the first snowdrops and put them on the mantlepiece; they are there to reflect Miranda's waking into maturity in the film.

John Leigh and one of his groundsmen bring in some of the richly gilded Venetian chairs that once furnished the house. Heathcote waylays him. 'Do you know the origin of your name?' John Leigh looks puzzled. 'STONE LEA – STONE LEY: standing stones and leylines. Very ancient, very important to know your origins.'

+—

KARL JOHNSON

. . . and who is that angel Ariel? Fettered and chained to Prospero, he flits through the air and the salt deep, flaming amazement. Our Prospero is young and healthy, the first time he has been cast that way; beside him Ariel seems wan, world-weary. It's a subtle reversal of the accepted order. Most of the lines are there: 'Do you love me master no?' – we've cut that out as with my reputation they'd expect it. Karl plays his part deadpan. He's in the most modern of our costumes, which are a chronology of the 350 years of the play's existence, like the patina on old bronze. A workman with kid gloves, he could be teasing together the parts of a computer in a dust-free factory. His voice is drained, hollow-eyed he acts with just the faint hope of a smile. When he escapes at the end – 'Merrily merrily shall I live now' – he sings with such melancholic wistfulness, and disappears to the heartbeat of swan's wings.

Karl picks his guitar in the evening, talks of his brother, and acts with a reticence that covers passion. At the end of the filming he asks Heathcote to release him. For a moment even Heathcote does not understand the request is in earnest.

+—

When you call 'Action' there is nothing more to do, everyone else is hard at work. You are the bystander, and at 'Cut' you can sense if the take has worked – the reaction of the crew and cast is usually unanimous if something has gone wrong. The first take is invariably the best; after that, each take seems a reproduction, an attempt to recapture the essence. My direction might seem slapdash, as nothing is decided beforehand – 'I flow with the glue,' as Heathcote says. In a big film you can pay to get the image in the mind on to film, a laborious process that can lose the life of the work on the way, but with small resources you allow the work to take its own course. Setting up a film like this you form a magic circle, like King Arthur. Once the circle is complete it is impossible, fatal, to attempt to break it.

When Neil Cunningham, who played Sebastian, said *The Tempest* was a party, he could not have paid me a greater compliment, as in all my work I've tried to make the working experience enjoyable. For me that is much more important than the end-product. The only audience I worry about is my collaborators on the film; everything, and everyone else, is outside the circle. Cinema audiences interest me no more than the tide of humanity that passes each day under my window in Charing Cross Road – I wish them well. Provided the cast approve of the finished result, find the experience of making the film a joy, I'm happy and wish for nothing more. This is the secret of making small films; text and idea are definitely not fixed – FLOW WITH THE GLUE. This separates my work from the British television and features industry, where the people who make the films, directors and technicians, are paid in an hierarchical order, and brought together for money, not by a community of interest. Their work is adopted and adapted; they've never put pen to paper to find out who they are, what they should be doing. Even the brightest of critics confuse the issues. For me only film/makers who initiate and write their own work are of any value. In Britain, directors who work in this way can be counted on one hand, and hardly any of them have been fortunate enough to make features. All the rest is 'veneer', reproduction which ranges from the visually ugly vacuity of *Brideshead*, to *Chariots of Fire*, a damp British *Triumph of the Will*. Their instigators are placemen with large public personae, covering a void.

It might seem obvious that work should be undertaken with spirit. In Italy or France this attitude to film neatly balances the other, but everything here is against it: the career men of the TV companies; the gold-diggers of Wardour Street; the unions with their 'left-wing' politics and reactionary attitudes to life and work, their protectionism and ill-defined and therefore corrupt systems of entry; Equity with its tedious theatre actors who destroy life on film and who view the 'film' for money before scuttling back to the National Theatre for 'Art''s sake. But having said that, who can blame them? For a tally of English film 'product' (property and product – he's bankable, 'weigh yourself in devalued fivers my boy') shows NO LIFE or vitality and NO LOVE.

-|-

The Tempest, **Prospero (Heathcote Williams) and Ariel (Karl Johnson) – Stoneleigh Abbey** (Photo: Bridget Holm)

The Tempest, Caliban (Jack Birkett) and Sycorax (Claire Davenport)
(Photo: Bridget Holm)

***The Tempest*, Caliban (Jack Birkett)** (Photo: Bridget Holm)

***The Tempest*, Prospero (Heathcote Williams) and the King of Naples (Peter Bull)**
(Photo: Bridget Holm)

***The Tempest*, Finale** (Photo: Bridget Holm)

A wild anger bubbles away like magma below the surface. I check it. Burroughs said that sometimes he was possessed by the evil spirit – I understand the feeling: a dizzy surge in the blood, the heart beats faster, the eyes turn inwards. The rarer action is in virtue than in vengeance. The concept of forgiveness in *The Tempest* attracted me; it's a rare enough quality and almost absent in our world. To know who your enemies are, but to accept them for what they are, befriend them, and plan for a happier future is something we sorely need. After the chill wind that blew through *Jubilee* came the warmth that invaded *The Tempest*; happy days rounded the cycle of three films.

+—

16 March 1979, Bamburgh: Throughout our four weeks of filming at Stoneleigh there was deep snow. During that whole time I never left the house but lived in the candlelit twilight of glistening mirrors, surrounded by people in masquerade. Neil said that the four weeks were a party given by a great eighteenth-century magnate like Beckford, our evenings occupied by Heathcote's fire-eating and Orlando's songs, performances of *The Immortalist* and Simon's guitar. We left the old house in a blizzard and travelled north through the snowdrifts to York, where we were stuck for a day as all the roads were closed by drifts and thousands of abandoned cars. At Bamburgh, which we reached by several diversions after a twelve-hour drive, the blizzard began again. That evening I went for a walk along the sands, with the snow howling in sheets off the waves, and the castle looming black through the great white plumes which vortexed around the cliffs; the foam from the surf blew through the darkness, the sea pitch-black. I walked with apprehension, for the ice seemed to be encroaching on all sides. In the days that followed we had to sweep the sand dunes free of the snow; and David Meyer (Ferdinand) had to dive into the icy sea to emerge naked from the waves.

+—

ORLANDO

Jack Birkett (who played Borgia Ginz in *Jubilee*, and now Caliban in *The Tempest*) kept up everyone's spirits: he played 'I spy' in the car, sang music-hall numbers in the evenings, and clumped around in his clogs armed with a tape-recorder from which he learned his part. We rehearsed slowly, arm in arm, often no more than twice, and he always hit the mark. His laughter echoed through Stoneleigh. 'This island's mine by Sycorax, my muvver' in his North Country brogue brought spontaneous applause from the crew. He ate the raw eggs with a wicked relish, and every so often sat in the corner in a fit of melancholy. It is seventeen years since he went blind, but during that time has turned himself into a great harlequin. Later, we went to see the film together at the NFT. When the lights came up at the end he said, 'It looks ravishing Derek.'

+-

The exterior scenes of the film were difficult, the weather atrocious. Jack had a deadline to return to his work in Italy, the sun came out fitfully, we were already delayed by a week and had five days in which to finish our work. We stared for hours, anxiously waiting for a break in the clouds. In the event we finished the shoot, but with the barest minimum of material, which made for difficulties in the editing.

The blue filters worked. I was desperately anxious that the exteriors should not look real, and chose the dunes at Bamburgh for their lack of features. Without trees or other landmarks they could have been anywhere, and we deliberately reduced the castle to a silhouette that could have been cut out of paper.

+-

The Tempest obsesses me. I would like to make it again, would be happy to make it three times. *A Midsummer Night's Dream* as well, but that will wait as the resources needed are greater. The Russians have done the *Lear* and *Hamlet*, but the *Dream* waits to be put on film; Nijinska's fairies are not to be beaten but the play was lost by Reinhardt. The masque also seems to have been lost, not only in the English theatre (Lindsay Kemp is in exile) but also in everyday life – it's such a vital element and so distrusted by chapel and Eng. Lit. *The Tempest* is a masque; what it lacks, in the theatre productions I've seen, is a sense of fun. You wouldn't subject a sixteen-year-old at her wedding to an indigestible evening. Whatever is buried in the play, the surface must glitter and entertain. If a sense of enjoyment could be restored to the work, half our problems would be resolved and the other half seem more easily dealt with.

+-

14 August 1979, Butlers Wharf: Alasdair arrived at Blitz ashen-faced at 1.30 in the morning to tell me the warehouse was burning. Within minutes we were down

there on his bike. Three floors of the building had already been gutted, down to our studio roof, and the building was surrounded by a mass of hoses pumping water on to the flames. We sat, faces drawn, on the river wall through the whole night with spectators from the neighbourhood. Jean Marc, who has lived and worked at Butlers for the last two years, was missing but the firemen assured me they had searched the building with breathing apparatus and found no one in it. He arrived at 9.30, and on the verge of tears the two of us tramped up the stairs against a cascade of oily water to find a sodden, smoke-stained ruin. By some miracle Jean Marc's polythene darkroom had collapsed over a metal cabinet in which he stored his negatives – this was all he saved of two years' work. Peter Logan lost everything . . . there was no insurance. So the ten years of warehouses along the Thames came to an abrupt end; and with it an entire style of life that had enabled me to paint, and to make the Super 8 films.

Ten years before, in August 1968, Peter Logan and I moved into the old corset factory at the end of Blackfriars bridge in Upper Ground. The rent was £2.50 a week. This was the first New York-style loft building that any of our friends had in London. That winter we froze. But when Ken Russell walked into the building I'm certain he gave me the job of designing *The Devils* as much because of that environment as for my drawings. In 1970, when Upper Ground was demolished, we moved to Bankside, which became the most beautiful living-space in London as the money pouring in from *The Devils* enabled me to convert it. At Bankside there were film shows and poetry readings and parties. For Christmas 1970 we built a table the length of the room and sat forty people down to a three-course meal cooked by Peter on improvised calor stoves. The tables were banked with scented white narcissus from Covent Garden, and a 'walky-talky' telephone connected either end. At the end of the meal, joints wrapped in the American flag were served with the coffee, and then we played charades behind a beautiful collaged curtain, a Rousseau Garden of Eden that Andrew Logan had made on transparent polythene. Fred Ashton and I kicked off as Edward VIII and Wallis Simpson.

Life in the warehouse brought fun and laughter into our lives with a thousand events. People camped out, swung or slept in the white hammock suspended across the room. Andrew kissed a thousand home-grown celebrities, and once Katy Hepburn came to tea.

+—

The Tempest, **Miranda (Toyah Wilcox) and Ferdinand (David Meyer)**
(Photo: Bridget Holm)

27 August 1979, Edinburgh: An audience of over two thousand watched the first showing of *The Tempest* at the festival. I sat at the back of the auditorium on the edge of my seat. To my relief very few people left. The sailors' dance, which Stuart Hopps had choreographed in a couple of mornings with a few dancers, brought an incredulous burst of laughter and applause, and Elisabeth's 'Stormy Weather' capped it as a show-stopper, before the film plunged back into darkness with Ariel's 'Where the bee sucks . . .'

　　The reaction to the film in America was very different. Many saw it as deliberately wilful, and the *New York Times* mounted an attack which destroyed it in the cinemas there. In such a fragmented culture messing with Will Shakespeare is not allowed. The Anglo-Saxon tradition has to be defended; and putting my scissors in was like an axe-blow to the last redwood.

+—

IX
The Oblivion Digits

After *The Tempest* it seemed a matter of months before a new project would be funded. But I miscalculated the resistance to anything that does not reflect the commercial norm. The budgeting of my films was virtually non-existent – no chance of anyone making much more than a simple wage; and the subject-matter, though acceptable to an audience once the films had been made, was wholly unacceptable in any of the legitimate channels for film-funding in this country. Not *Sebastiane, Jubilee,* nor *The Tempest* (except for a mad moment of commitment by Don Boyd) would have stood a chance of being funded by Wardour Street or the TV companies. Protected by my own substantial ignorance of all this, I had made three feature films.

Then came Channel Four, whose advent was whispered about by 'alternative' film-makers as though it were the panacea. Dutifully and optimistically I joined the queue with the others. Yet Channel Four, in spite of a much-vaunted alternative image, was to turn out all *beaujolais nouveau* and scrubbed Scandinavian, pot plants in place. It wasn't *our* alternative: independent cinema was to remain independent, disenfranchised by a channel for the slightly adventurous commuter.

Writing film scripts without a stable income is a rather uphill task. *The Tempest* finished a moderate success. I embarked on *Neutron, Caravaggio* and *Bob Up a Down* with a variety of young collaborators who wanted to learn film. Time slipped by. The execs in the TV companies who drew their monthly pay cheques had little idea of the reality of films as art (as opposed to 'art films'), and the involvement you must bring to a project as you tread an economic tightrope. Phones are liable to get cut off; and the cost of printing and binding scripts is a nightmare. Somehow you muddle by.

+—

BROKEN ENGLISH
(12 min. film in 16mm and Super 8)

September 1979, Phoenix House: Marianne Faithful is elfin, difficult to get to know. She covers herself with veils, and even in the sunshine carries the night with her. After two hours of indecision, we drive down to Blitz. Here she huddles into a corner while the kids fall over each other to talk to her. She has created a legend by steering through the Scylla and Charybdis of 'the music business' – over-exposure too young, drugs, fast living and famous friends. Underneath the frail exterior she must have a strong sense of survival. The next day she talks of revolution, of Baader-Meinhof, in a small thatched cottage in the country while her mother serves tea and we observe all the proprieties.

When we film her, the boys follow and whistle; for them she's an immortal, a flower pressed and preserved between two decades. Heathcote has written a song for her, 'Why Do You Do It?'. She is excited, has discovered her own voice.

Sequence: She walks through London late at night in black and white, from St Paul's with its haunting bells, through an arcade in Islington, around Eros in Piccadilly.

+—

Surrey Docks – Marianne's Super 8 Video: We arrived early in the morning and built a bonfire in the rubble of the old warehouses. Dark, ill-fitting dinner-jackets and old pink satin nightgowns, shimmering in the daylight, were distributed along with mirrors and masks. Michael Kostif dressed as a bishop; Gelinda wore a black soutane. Dave Baby stripped to show off his tattooed body, and improvised a love scene with 'Marilyn' on a pile of rusty anchor chains. Peter's Monroe travesty is achieved with little more than bleached hair; today he wore a workman's donkey jacket, jeans and heavy boots – but the illusion is so perfect that the locals, who arrived to see what we are up to, are completely taken in.

'Broken English' is the most successful of the three songs. We used old footage of Stalin and Hitler, cut together so that they smile and wave to each other in a ballet of destruction. There's footage of Mosley, and video material that the Oval Co-op have given me of the police at Lewisham. The film starts with the Bikini H-bomb explosion monitored on a space-invaders machine; and ends with the destruction in slow motion of the huge concrete swastika that crowned the Nuremburg stadium. The final song, 'Lucy Jordan', has Marianne contrasted with simple scenes of domestic drudgery in one long continuous superimposition.

THE ARTFUL DODGER OF CINE-HISTORY

At sixteen, Lee Drysdale arrived to guard the set of *Jubilee*. In the morning he would emerge from the mound of rubbish and graffiti that John Maybury, a film student, and Banshee Kenny had sprayed and collected. More energetic than a night at the Roxy, he would talk for hours in high-pitched Whitechapel about films, and carried on after into revolutionary politics. No one else could get a word in. He dressed like the dandy hero of a fifties' pulp thriller, hat-brim pulled over eyes, and was a master of creeping into cinemas through their exits. For much of 1980 we fought a tournament which became the script of *Neutron*.

+–

NEUTRON

There are six published manuscripts of *Neutron*, which zig-zag their anti-heroes Aeon and Topaz across the horizon of a bleak and twilit post-nuclear landscape. 'Artist' and 'activist' in their respective former lives, they are caught up in the apocalypse, where the PA systems of Oblivion crackle with the revelations of John the Divine. Their duel is fought among the rusting technology and darkened catacombs of the Fallen civilization, until they reach the pink marble bunker of Him. The reel of time is looped – angels descend with flame-throwers and crazed religious sects prowl through the undergrowth. The Book of Revelations is worked as science fiction.

Lee and I pored over every nuance of this film. We cast it with David Bowie and Steven Berkoff, set it in the huge junked-out power station at Nine Elms and in the wasteland around the Berlin Wall. Christopher Hobbs produced xeroxes of the pink marble halls of the bunker with their Speer lighting – that echo to 'the muzak of the spheres' which played even in the cannibal abattoirs, where the vampire orderlies sipped dark blood from crystal goblets.

+–

Neutron is the Sleeping Film – the shadow of the activity surrounding the *Caravaggio* project – a trailer for the End of the World based on the self-fulfilling prophecy of the Apocalypse. A dream treatment of mass-destruction, of the world's desire to be put out of its misery, the now-established place the unthinkable has in the popular imagination. *Neutron* sleeps between its covers like a Cruise or Pershing in its silo, and is overhauled every eighteen months. Jon Savage and I have resurrected its rival protagonists, Aeon, Topaz, and Sophie.

How to make a rapprochment with the financiers?

Will the film be made before the event itself?

Now we've opened the film up, and given it an ambiguous ending – allowing Aeon to transcend his death, to set out in exemplary self-chosen poverty like a Bruegel pilgrim or Langland's Conscience, complete with tall staff and wide-brimmed hat.

    ┿

14 April 1980, Geneva: Guy Ford and I flew to Geneva to meet David Bowie and talk about *Neutron*. The project hangs on his decision. We show him *The Tempest* . . . He is interested, but we have to find the money without using his name.

During the following months we met, and crept into Berkoff's *Hamlet* and *Cage Aux Folles*. He took me to hear 'Ashes to Ashes', and in September we saw him in *The Elephant Man* in New York, but by then the deadline had passed and I put *Neutron* quietly back on the shelf.

Bowie is the tuning-fork of the media humming to perfection. He is a transparency by Avedon, a xerox by Laurie Chamberlain, a voice embalmed in vinyl. He is the mirror of ambivalence and a monarch of the invisible threads of communication – touch fingers and you hear voices. The people in the streets are drawn to him, a Pied Piper who leads the dance. In repose, he is the still silence at the centre of a dust devil.

The disarray at Kendon Films, with Don Boyd absent in America, made it impossible to pull the film together in the short time that Bowie was able to give. Maybe there'd be another time. He left his sunglasses and a scrumpled pack of Marlboro on my mantelpiece. I returned the glasses but left the cigarettes. The next time he came he saw them and tore them up into pieces. I felt like a souvenir-hunter, caught with a lock of hair. Then I recalled that after seeing *Jubilee* he'd asked me if I were a black magician.

    ┿

20 JULY 1983 – THEY'RE FUCKING AROUND WITH THE OBLIVION DIGITS

Jon Savage and I are looking at the script for *Neutron* – 'The rich ones dug deep on their mortgages and emerged to laugh at the dead.' Outside, in the garden in the Chiltern hills, the sun blazes down. It's the hottest July since they started measuring.

The privet hedge is covered with a froth of white flowers which have mesmerized a host of peacock butterflies – they have spent the whole day drinking in the nectar. The yellow brimstone butterflies keep their distance and stick to the scarlet runner beans. A solitary brilliant orange comma suns itself on the pebble drive and occasionally circles the garden, hedged in by a dark beech wood, with subliminal swiftness, before returning to its chosen spot. Ken Butler sits on the garden bench and reads the life of the sixties' superstar Seedy Edgewick. Every hour or so we break our work round the circular table for a game of croquet on the uneven lawn. The gentle tap of the mallet and ball camouflages a competition as fierce and lethal as Monopoly . . . repeat – you have the name of being alive but you are dead . . . over . . . do you hear me . . . you have the name of being alive but you are dead.

Later in the afternoon we walk through the beech woods down into the valley and up back along a deep lane whose sides are strewn with flowers. Jon says, 'What do you think will remain of any of this?' Nothing much . . . It's not really our concern . . . We walk a long way in silence, which is interrupted by a good-looking boy who whistles by on a racing-bike and disappears down the lane.

WASPS

September 1980, New York City: The *New York Times* review of *The Tempest* has blighted my visit here. The audience at the British Film Week Festival (where the film is being given its American première) is incredulous. They ask if they have seen the same film as the *NYT* critic, Vincent Canby. But such is the power of print over media-sapped minds they half-believe an article like this even as they reject it. The film closed after four days. It's no consolation, but I'm told Hollywood has a lot of money tied up in the projected Masursky *Tempest*: so perhaps it's a cold, calculated job to leave the field clear for the big guys. The review was vitriolic: '*The Tempest* would be funny if it weren't very nearly unbearable. It's a fingernail scratched along a blackboard, sand in spinach – like driving a car whose windscreen is shattered' and so on for a few paragraphs that ended 'There are no poetry, no ideas, no characterizations, no narrative, no fun.'

All this has darkened my disillusionment with America, and particularly New York City – a city of glittering towers built on deep foundations of alienation and misery. I'm surrounded by the brittle indifference of Manhattan artists and their hangers-on, almost all of whom are blinded with consumption, incarcerated in their precious lofts. They take everything by right, and in this way are victims of their own propaganda, namely, that NYC is the centre of the universe. They honestly believe that these hard surfaces, which cover an abyss of paranoid insecurity, constitute the matrix of Art.

To a whole generation of young English painters, brought up in the fifties, the United States was Shangri-La. So many of them drifted to well-heeled oblivion in the cultural mid-Atlantic. I can think of none whose work benefited as a result.

The gay ones went for sex in the bath-houses and clubs of Manhattan and Fire Island. Now all this has turned into a desert of ageing lawyers and execs with hangdog moustaches and work-out muscles; brawn triumphs here after midnight, while the scrambled brains are left somewhere in the closet. Did the young men who waged the battle of Christopher Street in the sixties know where they would lead us?

Of all my friends only the photographer Gerald Incandela has had the cunning to reap any advantage – but he was always a refugee and has a gypsy's stubborn charm, which insulated him.

I stay with Gerald in his apartment, high on the fourteenth floor at Lexington at 26th. He's been living here for nearly two years, ever since he left his friend Thilo's flat in Clapham, London. The flat is light and airy, with windows from which you can see all of Manhattan.

Gerald is photographing architecture. In the spring he's planned a journey to the chateaux on the Loire. Meanwhile, young Art executives in suits call to view his work – they are paralysed by this wheeler-dealer from the *souks*. They buy what he tells them; Gerald is now himself a collector. He has photos hanging in the White House and at the Metropolitan Museum. He's making books which will cost hundreds of dollars apiece. Europe is fading – just a place to take a photo. He makes me a photo in return for a particular recording of *Don Giovanni*, a picture of the Statue of Liberty on which he has written

VOUS LA-BAS! VOUS ALLEZ SOUVENT AU CINEMA?

✛

A CLASSIC DANCE

November 1980 – the London Palladium: Lynn Seymour's solo performance this evening might have been called 'Eat Your Heart out Johnny Rotten'. In fact I think it was called 'Fuck You London' – although it certainly didn't appear as that on the menu Princess Margaret was holding in the row in front of me, at the Royal Ballet

Gala for One-Parent Families. The place was packed to capacity with the rich and the famous, come to watch the stars of classical ballet perform to classical perfection in a honeyed love-in-the-mist atmosphere, occasionally punctuated by a jokey *pas de deux* set in twenties' Henley Regatta style to sibilant strings. Lynn Seymour, back from Germany, was expected to make a triumphant return to the arms of her old company with a piece choreographed by Bill Forsythe. She appeared looking extremely dishevelled and wearing a filthy mac. To the sounds of 'Money, money, money, it's a rich man's world' at Throbbing Gristle decibels she danced, or rather crawled and rolled through a feminist suicide of lipsticks and mirrors pulled from a handbag, before ending the piece, and her career in classical dance, with a gunshot aimed at the temples. A few of us began to applaud, before the unearthly silence drowned us out.

Later, at a table with Kenneth MacMillan and various nonplussed *eminences grises* of the ballet world, Peter Logan's support for Lynn was met with icy silence and the sort of condescension usually reserved for the insane. I heard that the organizers of the event had discovered Lynn in her bedroom before the performance dressed as Jackie Kennedy in a pink blood-spattered Chanel number. They were horrified and asked her to change. She wavered and put on the mac; but even in this emasculated form the dance was a most brilliant provocation of an audience. A violent reaction was impossible due to the royal presence. The audience remained stunned for the rest of the evening, and doubtless left clutching their wallets.

‡

THE GHOSTLY GALLEON

Saturday 29 November 1980: Vanessa Redgrave collected us this morning at 4·30. Three of us, Shaun, Alasdair and myself slept uncomfortably for a few hours in my bed. Outside it was grey and freezing – powdery snow drifted across the streets while we drove around collecting people. At 7·30 we joined the bus at Kings Cross, which took us, with several stops, to Liverpool. We assembled for the march and Vanessa pushed scarlet banners into our hands. Then the sun came out, and a sharp sea breeze blew up and scattered the clouds. There were thousands of marchers from all over the country; and our contingent, the Workers' Revolutionary Party, was somewhere near the end. Three hours after the march had begun we were at last on our way, a great scarlet galleon blown through the derelict streets of this sad and beautiful city. Every now and then an old lady would hang out of a window in one of the tower blocks and shout encouragement.

At last, when dusk was gathering, we arrived in front of the Liver building cheered on by a group of burly Welsh miners. Someone behind attempted to lead a chorus of the Internationale, but it quickly died away.

I've been on several marches this year. They are oddly internal and ritualistic events – passers-by seem hardly to notice. But I expect they glimpse it later on television.

+–

PYSCHIC RALLY IN HEAVEN
(8 min. film in Super 8 and 16mm)

23 December 1980: I filmed Throbbing Gristle's Psychic Rally in Heaven with wax earplugs, because for half an hour I had to lean into the speakers to get the best possible angles. I threw the old Nizo Super 8 about in time to the music, at 'stop frame'. The band is restrained, almost static on stage. Genesis P. Orridge stands on the spot in his combat-grey; Peter Christopherson adjusts the controls, twiddling a few knobs here and there. Later I refilmed the result, cutting it together with old black and white footage from the film of Dante's *Inferno*. The result had a persistent strobe which synchronized with the music of the 2nd Annual Report. It had a powerful effect on audiences. Tony Rayns said that at Melbourne the festival audience hated it one and all, and shouted while the film was being shown. At the ICA Jenny Runacre told me she had to leave because the film was affecting her physically, although she liked it.

This work takes experiments with superimposition and refilming, begun in 1972 with *In the Shadow of the Sun*, as far as I can go.

+–

New Year's Eve, 1980: At six this evening I was surprised by Vanessa, who rang up and asked me what I was doing for New Year's Eve. She caught my indecision and announced she would be around in half an hour and we would go out selling the party's daily newspaper, *Newsline*.

We drove up to the flats in Marchmont Street, near where I had lived in 1963, and worked our way down the dimly lit corridors in the freezing cold. The building, once the pride of architectural students, is streaked with London grime and beached, like a scuttled battleship, in the remains of Bloomsbury. The reception at each flat was unexpected – a small bald man cautiously peered round one door, and when he recognized Vanessa his eyes popped. He quickly disappeared, and we heard an excited whispered conversation. Then he reappeared, with the words – 'Go away Vanessa, we don't want your type round here. We vote Conservative.' And closed the door firmly. I couldn't help smiling, and I think Vanessa caught me. Later, she abandoned me outside the Aldwych with an armful of papers and a collection bucket. While the usher boys eyed me suspiciously I made a spirited attempt to sell the cause, and got two customers.

+

THE LAST SUPPER

24 January 1981, Kensington Town Hall: Vanessa sits on the campaign chair drinking tea and chain-smoking. From her briefcase she sells tickets for lectures and film shows, subscriptions for *Newsline*. She carries on talking as she discovers more pamphlets: Trotsky on art, Trotsky on internationalism. She hovers on the edge of her seat desperate to share this vision; she shakes as she speaks of conspiracies.

On the stage of Kensington Town Hall this evening she sits at the end of a long table draped in red under a huge portrait of Lenin. The WRP celebrates Eleven Years of a Trotskyist Daily Newspaper, seated at the long table the Committee-members look like Leonardo's 'Last Supper'. Instead of bread and wine we are given words. Meanwhile, not one printing worker takes the rostrum, nobody involved in the actual production of the newspaper. I left early. Thereafter the lines went dead.

+

March 1981, Berlin: *In the Shadow of the Sun*, which the German Film Archive has rescued and blown up to 16mm, was shown late last night to a large audience on an enormous screen. I had the TG music turned up loud and sat in the front row where the film was a blaze of impressionistic colour. The fiery mazes of sawdust and paraffin in which various friends perform, the footage from Avebury, Fire Island and Castle Howard fused with fragments from *The Devils* and our riverside improvisations – I took the footage and refilmed it with two projectors, using my Nizo 480, a series of coloured gels, and a postcard as a screen. Everyone said it was impossible, that nothing would come of it – but by a miracle everything synchronized to make the film which at first was called an 'English Apocalypse'. Then it was rechristened, and shown in the mid-seventies at the ICA. At the end of that first public showing a few people remained in the cinema, including one old German lady who was incredibly enthusiastic. Last night in the festival cinema there was a large and serious audience many of whom enjoyed the film as much as she did. The Germans are much more excited by my work. The English remain suspicious; they want prose, socially committed stuff to bore their pants off so they can leave the cinema and believe they have seen 'reality'.

-+-

30 MARCH 1980. PHOENIX HOUSE

There is only one English feature director whose work is in the first rank. Michael Powell is the only director to make a clear political analysis in his films, his work is unequalled. *The Life and Death of Colonel Blimp* is the finest English feature, and *A Canterbury Tale* and *A Matter of Life and Death* are not far behind. When he made these films he was heavily criticized for his treatment of serious themes. *Blimp* was banned by Churchill and remained in a savaged version for nearly forty years, a plea for tolerance and regard for the enemy as human made at the height of the war – there is no more courageous English film. It is a tragedy he has made so few films in the last twenty years, none in the last ten, and a lasting condemnation of all those who make films. He was a major casualty of the spurious social realism of the sixties, whose practitioners have grown fat and invaded the media with their well-scrubbed minds. Their films are never seen by the communities they are made in, but transported via the colour supplements straight to a land where the consciences of the Conscious are titillated and prizes for honesty are won.

Last night I was chatting to an eighteen-year-old lad. He was drunk and distraught. I never divulged I made films and acted like a sympathetic punter. He had always dreamed of being an actor since he had played an eight-year-old in *Kes*. Ken Loach chose him, though any of us might have done the same. He came from a broken and deprived family. For a few weeks he was a film star; his own and his friends' expectations were aroused. Then the film crew departed, and he was left with ambitions that could never be fulfilled. Comparison: Visconti made Bjorn Andresen (who played Tadzio in *Death in Venice*) his ward, knowing the damage that can be wrought by this kind of exposure.

-+-

MAY 1981. CANNES

It would be hard to find a seedier-looking bunch than the British Film Industry after a week of free drinks in Cannes. This evening they are standing, so to speak, around a swimming-pool downing champagne from the Chrysalis empire. The Managing

A Matter of Life and Death, 1946, Michael Powell (*BFI Archive*)

A Matter of Life and Death, 1946, Michael Powell (*BFI Archive*)

Director announces 'Joe Orton', the British *Cage Aux Folles*: I could see Steven Frears' heart go through his boots – he is the director-in-waiting. All through this charade Jack Nicholson, or a look-alike, swam around the pool causing the maximum diversion from the business at hand. Steven, who is one of the few talents in British TV, smiled manfully through it all. At the poolside he spied Gary Glitter and decided he would make a perfect Halliwell:– I went over to Mr Glitter with one of the souvenir programmes and asked him to sign it, which he did with a wild stroke of the pen that stuck and spluttered into spots across the paper. 'Stars,' I said with a smile, and he agreed. Later, I gave it to Steven.

+–

September 1981, Phoenix House: I picked up the script of *Bob Up a Down* which Tim Sullivan rewrote for me last year in Christopher's studio. Although there are some good moments, the script has its difficulties. You need a year or so on projects as complex as this. A first draft usually reveals the lie of the land; in a rewrite you discover the terraces, and can view it from different angles. *Bob Up a Down* has been brewing longer than *Caravaggio*. It started years ago as a medieval allegory, like the Roman de la Rose but based on Julian of Norwich and Richard Rolle. It has to be retold, and the central character of the anchoress who has visions must be integrated with the everyday love affair of Prophecy for the wild man Bob Up a Down.

+–

THE STRAIGHT MEDIA

Friday 18 September 1981 – Granada TV: I came up to Manchester to talk over the script of *Bob Up a Down* with Tim. I planned to sit in the library here for a few days and map out the screenplay, as he is unable to get to London. But work of this serious nature was quite impossible. The library is noisy and its medieval section consists of a few school primers; apart from that it's mostly stocked with bound colour supplements.

The centre of this cheerless building is the bar, where the disillusioned drown their mental fatigue in subsidized alcohol. Each year Granada takes in a few young graduates from the Universities who are naïve enough to believe they will be able to express their vision of the world in these eggbox surroundings. Illusions are quickly dispelled, but by that time they are hooked on fat pay cheques; and soon they are media junkies trapped in a mediocrity that isn't even their own. Granada smells and looks like a school. On the walls of the corridors Francis Bacon replaces the map of the world. Everyone grumbles about his own work and tears his colleagues' to pieces. But woe betide any outsider who criticizes the place – then they turn like a savage pack to protect their unbearable existence.

　＋–

OVERCAST

The TV replaced the hearth in the fifties. Where the fire had nourished dreams, allowed the mind to wander like the flickering flames that danced in the coals, the TV numbed the mind. Its images had to possess you, bombard you. It reinforced the tyranny of the family as a parent usually controlled the switch. In our house the weather forecast grew like a demon god – absolute silence and concentration was demanded by my father as the announcer pushed the sun and clouds over a map of England, pronouncing weather fair or foul like an oracle of the gods. The outcome was often quite different. Like the priest praying for victory in battle you could never be quite sure the gods would favour you.

　＋–

2 APRIL 1983

With the invasion of video, the Super 8 camera is becoming a thing of the past. This saddens me as the video image is still a poor second. However, that will soon change. What worries me is that each advance in technology reinforces the grip of central control and emasculates opposition – though this can work both ways, and it is for us to ensure that technology will promote greater independence and mobility. This is the key battle in our culture, one which has hardly been joined because a thousand political diversions are flown by different vested interests to obscure it. Our centralized culture mounts a concerted attack on human expression. Organizations like the BBC and the television companies talk about responsibility to their audiences, but their conduct is irresponsible. They remove expression from the individual and flood the mind with carefully selected information which is passed through their dead, institutionalized hands. It's amazing to see how blind these monopolistic arbiters of our culture can be. By now everyone knows that the idols of popular music are the figments of their promoters' bank balances. It's extraordinary how the media men are unable to perceive that they are themselves fabricated in the same way, that their success has nothing to do with integrity or intelligence, just opportunism. The ugliest film I saw last year was *The Wall*, in which the director Alan Parker caused the maximum GBH to the human spirit, while ignoring the glaring truth that he and his allies, the Pink Floyd, were themselves the Wall that had to be torn down. In this film an ad-man assaulted older institutions – school teachers, who might just be telling their students to think for themselves, were painted as monsters of conformity in order to inject the false vision of a media junky into the young. The film had the power-mad glamour of a Nazi rally and used that imagery to effect.

+

8 MARCH 1983 CONSUMERVISION.
Ian Sproat, the Tory minister, is in the *Guardian* this morning quoted as saying that *Chariots of Fire* helped the government over the Falklands with public opinion in the USA; it confirmed all my suspicions about a film which plays a tune reactionaries like to hear. If at first you don't succeed . . . *Chariots of Fire* is a film delivering the 'conservatism' of an Andropov or a Thatcher. When the film first came out Puttnam suppressed any mention of the fact that Ian Charleson had been one of the brothers in *Jubilee*, and announced *Chariots* as his first film. Ian apologized to me in Cannes. I felt sorry for him as he's scrupulously honest and I knew he never liked *Jubilee*, but was also embarrassed by the duplicity of the publicity for his new film. All establishments rewrite history. No shadows are to be cast over the Royal Command Performance. In Mitterrand's France these dubious manipulators were careful to protest their Socialism.

+

OUR ORPHAN CINEMA
The English film world is mesmerized by Oscars, and almost any project has to pass the Hollywood test. All indigenous work has to be historic and 'quaint' – *Brideshead* or *Chariots of Fire*, a dull and overrated TV film, fit the bill. All the rest take their chances. Even the music films of recent years, *Quadrophenia* and *Breaking Glass*, have fallen on stony ground in the States. So attuned have American ears become to the English Theatrical Voice that if you step off the stage and on to the streets you have to be subtitled like *Scum*. The budgets to make these 'American' films are inflated; whereas a German or Italian film-maker has to do with £500,000. Here you must talk in millions or the investors can hardly stifle a yawn. American product is 'cheaply made' in our studios, so the price of film-making here is kept inflated till only the biggest and the worst can afford it.

31 JANUARY 1983. B2 GALLERY

The first of a season of Super 8 shows took place last night. James Mackay and David Dawson organized an evening which was like the Super 8 shows at Bankside ten years ago. There were two particularly beautiful films – a boy filmed in pink, performing a slow, narcissistic dance behind muslin veils, details of hands caressing fabric. The boy's torso was lit from above, and with his outstretched arms he looked as if he was flying. This was made by Michael Kostif, whose films are always a surprise. They are economically made, and are nearly always the best lit of Super 8 films. The second film, by Cerith Wyn Evans, was also immaculately crafted and lit like a razor blade. Michael Clarke, the dancer, was hanged while flowers burned leaving narcotic smoke trails. Later a boy stood in red, painted red, etched against a cobalt background with a vase of tulips and the light and camera in shot, while another boy lay face down on a mattress on the floor masturbating. He was lit with much greater realism. Evanescent images – sex and death. I told John Maybury that I felt like the ghost in the machine. He said that my presence gave the evening credibility! It's wonderful to see this form of film-making continuing.

+–

OTHER PEOPLE'S HOME MOVIES

28 January 1983: Last week the British Film Institute's reception to launch their archive film of Royalty was attended by HRH, who talked loudly throughout the showing. When the 1937 Coronation came up she said loudly, 'Where am I?' I was there! Why didn't they film me?' Queen Victoria was greeted by, 'She NEVER said that!' Later, she buttonholed a group of admiring archivists. 'Daddy took a lot of film in that old stock of yours. I keep looking for it but Elizabeth will never leave anything alone. You can't find anything in the Palace – Elizabeth is always moving everything around.' The Lady-in-Waiting, who was keeping an eye on the level of the whisky bottle, tactfully announced, 'Time to go.'

At the BFI some home movies have arrived in brass canisters lined with red velvet and stamped with the Royal coat of arms.

+–

Monday 2 November 1981: I took John Maybury to see Steven Berkoff's play, *Decadence*. Steven gives an extraordinary performance with Linda Marlowe. They both play two roles from different social backgrounds on a stage which is bare except for a sofa and a light. Steven's command of language is electric, East and

West; Cockney fucks the Elizabethan theatre. The result pours forth in an incandescent lava-flow. He tears manners to shreds and overacts to the point of apoplexy. His movements are mesmeric: he crosses and uncrosses his legs, ties himself in knots, swallows his words, takes great drags at invisible cigarettes, drinks, farts, and enunciates in such a way that the phrases fall like ice cubes into his gin and tonic. I have rarely seen so much energy on the stage. The next morning I ring him and we decide to turn the play into a film script.

November 1981, Devonia Road: Steven's got some new chairs for his living room – scaffolding and classic leather Rover seats. You pull the lever to tilt them back. He slumps in them in his army khaki, sipping tea from a delicate silver lustre tea-cup. He creates ideas with his hands in the air, bounding words about, 'Yes, yees, yeeees.' We talk ourselves through the scenes and every now and then he starts to act them.

At home I take out the scissors and glue and paste up the play with rough indications of the shots. By Christmas I have a draft screenplay. I feel we must sleep on it – it will improve for waiting. I detect Steven's impatience. His work allows him manoeuvrability. Having to cope with the slow, Satanic reels of cinema I am learning the waiting game.

Thursday 3 December 1981 – B2 Gallery: A month ago, David Dawson asked me to exhibit in his gallery at Metropolitan Wharf in a mixed show with Andrew Logan, John Maybury and Duggie Fields. I collected together the few landscapes that I painted with varnish glazes, pencil and metal dust last year. Apocalyptic visions of fire, with skulls and minute people lost in eternity under strange moons. Then I took up my brushes again and painted dark canvases of a different kind – Night Light, Canvases of Fire, Fire of the Soul. Icons to spark off reveries.

DARK LIGHTS
The three films take place in quite consciously different light – *Sebastiane* in the sunlight, *Jubilee* in a stormy twilight, and *The Tempest* in the night.

January 1982, Phoenix House: Christmas passed and I carried on painting into the New Year. It is therapeutic: the smell of oil paint in Phoenix House gives me an old high. The canvases are very small, as I have so little space to work. I clear everything away after I have finished each evening. There is one canvas, an erased fragment of Heraclitus like a Victorian sampler, gold and black with a hint of fire. I call it 'The archaeology of words' – 'Death is all things we see awake, all we see asleep is sleep.' I have broken the stranglehold of my landscapes. They had become tedious, a fine balancing-act that I had mastered. They were no longer an adventure.

+

Wednesday 10 March 1982: Ken Russell rings and asks me to design the Stravinsky *Rake's Progress* to open mid-May at the Pergola Theatre, Florence. Michael Annals has just told him he cannot do it. I've two weeks to complete the designs. Fortunately I've seen the opera in a rather indifferent production at the Coliseum.

I catch the train to the Lake District and spend the afternoon and evening jotting down notes. The main drift of Ken's mind is to update the work. He wants an underground station instead of a graveyard. Apart from that the designs will parallel Auden's stage instructions.

The next morning I'm back down to London on the train. I spend two days at breakneck speed collecting magazines and books that throw up ideas – punk, 'new romantic', the Royal Family, horse racing, etc. – and leave on the Monday for Florence. Exhausted, I'm pushed into one of those Italian meetings where everyone shouts at the top of their lungs – to an outsider it looks as though it will end in a fight, until everyone starts laughing. The Management asks me for the designs. I show them the books and explain that the design will be a collage. They look dubious. I explain I'm never going to be able to make finished drawings for an opera with nine separate sets and about one hundred costumes in ten days.

+

Wednesday 17 March 1982, Florence: I'm embarking on this project for three reasons: first, after a year of waiting for *Caravaggio* I'm broke; secondly, I've always enjoyed working with Ken; and thirdly, it's a kind of revenge.

+

18 April 1982, Florence: Every evening Ken and I find a different restaurant to eat in. We establish a routine. At about eight we have a drink at the bar on the Piazza

Signora. He crosses the square with his white hair and sailor suit. You can spot him a mile off, he has great physical presence. We have one strong common bond: a love-hate relationship with our art which sparks off ideas.

Ken is deeply disillusioned with the cinema, the end of a love affair. Whenever the subject comes up there is sadness, tales of betrayal and hopes dashed. Making *Altered States* was a nightmare. He had no support, only petty opposition from the film company. He tells me that when Paddy Chayevsky died his heart leapt – 'He was a truly evil, monstrous man.' Ken is a romantic who sees the world in vivid black and white. His vision of the artist is pure nineteenth-century. 'Tchaikovsky' – he has twenty-six recordings of one of his symphonies; he goes to enormous lengths to find obscure recordings, spends all his spare time in record shops. Every day dry opera critics arrive to interview him and catch him out, but his knowledge of music is enormous. Maestro Chailly, the conductor, often stops orchestral rehearsals to ask Ken's opinion and acts on it.

Ken tells me that this is the happiest project he has worked on since his early days at the Beeb.

—+—

12 May 1982, Pergola: There are more than enough scandalous moments in *The Rake* to keep the journalists happy and the myth of an ageing *enfant terrible* afloat. These are also weak spots, as they allow copy to be sold sensationally at the expense of a truly original mind. We have the brothel-keeper, Michael Aspinal, in Queen Mother drag, leading the chorus who are dressed in Falklands fatigues. The Rake wears a T-shirt depicting Mrs Thatcher as a vampire holding a skull – 'Alas, poor England, I knew her well.' He croons with a set of scarlet Mohican dancers from Milan. In the auction scene, John Dobson the auctioneer sells a sex-doll – this has driven me crazy because you can't buy the things in Italy, so it had be ordered from London, and the opera management were even more unhappy when they found it cost £70.

We have created a most novel production. If this *Rake* opened in London it would never be forgotten. There are several moments of genius – the handling of the Blind Baba is done without a fault: she is a TV star, a world Ken knows well. The 'graveyard' scene will never be bettered, set in the Angel underground station, with the Devil, a drug-dealer in a heavy black leather coat, confronting the Rake, now destitute, with his heroin death-kit. It is startling and simple. The movements

The Rake's Progress, **1982 – front drop sketch** *(Photo: Marchiori)*

The Rake's Progress, **1982 – Breakfast; Baba moves into the Rake's London home**
(Photo: Marchiori)

and actions are minimal, allowing the music to take over. The Devil's exit on the shorting rails, with flashes of magnesium powder, is a knockout; and the set is classic, simple, and fits the action to a tee. The Hogarth paintings work well as adverts in the underground. Ken wants them graffitied – I have refused.

+–

13 May 1982, Florence: Modern London is perfectly at home in the Pergola Theatre. My operatic punks and new romantics have a flamboyance which mirrors the eighteenth century. Outside, Florence is a grey, dull city, invaded by hippy drug-addicts who have crawled out of another era – *everything* is history here; these tired hippies pound away aimlessly at African drums under the graffiti-stained arches of the Uffizi, gawped at by herds of deadpan blue anorak tourists from the North. Michelangelo's fake David towers over the other statues. It reminds me of the story of the American lady who exclaimed in a loud voice in front of Leonardo's 'Last Supper' – '*C'est la originale?*' The indigent population, who presumably always were bank clerks, treat us no better than our devalued money. It rains and the granitic streets are like dead prisons. The Arno runs vomit-coloured through the middle. The Renaissance: camouflage for rapacity.

+–

19 May 1982, Pensione Elisa and Santa Croce: The window of our room in the *pensione* opens on to Giotto's bell tower – round its multi-coloured marble geometry the jackdaws circle on air currents. As you lie in bed and watch they seem almost motionless, there high above. At night the geometry fades to a chalky white, while the golden ball on the dome glows in the moonlight. On the window I've placed a rough slipware jug dappled with green glaze; it is filled with marigolds and blue cornflowers which fade to paper-white. At dawn the mason with his newspaper hat climbs the scaffolding, takes out his mallet and starts tapping . . . the jackdaws caw.

Yesterday as the service ended in Santa Croce an old dwarf lady – blind as a mole and dressed in her Sunday best, plaid kilt and furs – pulls the skirts of a pretty young girl at the holy water basin, who then scoops the water with her hands and kneels with it. The old dwarf lady dips her hand in the water and crosses herself. Suddenly the young girl gives a deep curtsy. The little old lady follows the walls as the choir sings, past the gigantic tombs of Michelangelo and Dante, feeling her way in the darkness to the door.

The Rake's Progress, **1982 – The Rake's belongings are auctioned** *(Photo: Marchiori)*

The Rake's Progress, **1982 – Nick Shadow asks the Rake to choose his Exit**
(Photo: Marchiori)

SATURDAY 25 SEPTEMBER 1982
PHOENIX HOUSE – THE FINAL ACADEMY

At 5·30 this morning Genesis P. Orridge arrived in the darkness and we drove to Heathrow to collect his guru, Mr W.S. Burroughs. I carried my camera, and took a few shy snaps as we travelled back to Chelsea where Gen had booked the party into the Arts Club. During the next week Mr B. was banqueted at the B2 Gallery, filmed and interviewed across London, and did four nights of readings at the Ritzy in Brixton and one night in Heaven. I clicked away with my Nizo at him, Brion Gysin, John Giorno and others. WSB emerges tortoise-like to greet his audience. He stoops like a cadavre in the catacombs of Palermo and talks of mummies and immortality. To speak to him is almost impossible, as he is always on the move in little erratic circles. At rest he retires into himself and puts out a signal, 'Leave me alone.' The only thing to do is to be photographed with him, and that is what everyone attempted to do. His readings are immensely funny. He drawls out his lines in a Southern monotone, punctuating it only for sips of water. What might give you the shivers on the page becomes the blackest of black comedy. Brion Gysin fights an old battle with him; but William's junk vision has won out against Brion's magic and the battle isn't joined. Brion described William fishing for inspiration in the sewers of Paris. They do not share accommodation on this trip, and their friendship now seems cemented only by the common platform that their young admirers have provided. Time has parted them: Brion the Parisian with his dream-machine and Bill in Kansas with his junk.

─┼─

18 NOVEMBER 1982. EDWARD TOTAH GALLERY

My exhibition of paintings at the Edward Totah Gallery went off like a damp squib. There isn't a more interesting show opening this week and it should have thrown up more than enough ideas for any critic to get his teeth in. Many of the misgivings I felt about painting in the early seventies resurface in the wake of this disappointment. For a start, memories are very short. No one remembers or mentions the Lisson shows. No one has paid the least attention to the films and their relation to the work. The art world exists in a vacuum, however exhilarating it may be for the artist. The results are marooned in art reference in hushed galleries. At the D'Offay Gallery you don't hear Julian Schnabel's crockery smashing – embalmed in lashings of oil paint. The end of a love affair? Wait, my friends, he'll soon have his hands on the Sèvres service; and after D'Offay's, the Tate, courtesy Saatchi and Saatchi. Britain isn't working any more.

At my private view, swilling drink, after one hour the Tate 'buyer' was asked by Norman Rosenthal of the Royal Academy whether that institution would ever buy a Derek Jarman. 'Who is Derek Jarman?' was the response. Did the Tate know they had a Schnabel exhibition? No hope for the home-grown unless of course you dye your hair or wear silly suits – but never allow eccentricity to lapse into your manners. With the aplomb of a banker, you'll end up in the most hideous living-rooms in the world. The coffee-table bears the sanitized book of your work, and the magazine next to it illustrates your patron's good taste, status and investment rule.

It's interesting that art reviews, unlike film reviews, usually start with the dead – today I'm sharing the honours with Van Dyck in *The Times*, damned on his reputation. One wouldn't expect a film review to be dedicated to a revival of *Ivan the Terrible* at the NFT and *The Tempest* compared in a paragraph at the end.

+–

20 NOVEMBER 1982. PHOENIX HOUSE

I worked on the paintings in January, stopped for *The Rake*, and worked again through September – the paintings are altering significantly. The first group drew on the fragments of Heraclitus, the technical drawings of Robert Fludd, Athanasius Kircher and seventeenth-century hermeticism. In black and scarlet they are austere, emblematic paintings. In Florence in May I gilded one of the sets for *The Rake* and came back to London with several spare books of gold leaf. The second group of paintings in September used this gold as a ground, and were based on nineteenth-century photographs of the male nude mixed with sexual and religious iconography, back-room paintings, which culminated in a large painting based on El Greco's 'Pietà'. Caravaggio deeply affected these paintings. I called the show 'After the Final Academy'.

+–

HARES AND TORTOISES

Nicholas telephoned to say that *Caravaggio* had been put in the hands of a new lawyer, who was dealing with the papers much more professionally and there should be some movement at last. It was something of a relief as for the last week, with no money to paint and just the paper and ink for the Diary, I drifted uncertainly, caught on the apron strings of 'The Tortoise' as Vera Russell unflatteringly described Nicholas . 'Why don't you get yourself one of those Indians like James Ivory, darling? I saw *Shakespeare Wallah* and it was so much better than

Ginger Rogers.' I said that perhaps Nicholas was the tortoise of fable, in spite of the fact that Barry Flanagan's hares are now the fashion in art. In any case, these two years have not wasted my time. I've done the theatre design for *The Rake* and started painting again. 'THEY WERE NO GOOD,' retorted Vera.

Later, Robert Medley and I had dinner at Jimmy's, which was completely empty. 'The recession,' said Robert, 'if Jimmy's, which must be the cheapest restaurant in Soho, is empty, it must be biting hard.' It was snowing outside. The gang of gruff waiters played cards with the lady who commands the till with a smile. Conversation drifted back to painting, and Robert said that the English were only interested in illustration. Witness Peter Blake's 'Bonjour Mr Hockney'. Peter Blake had announced in an interview that he was a better painter than David. Robert glowered. 'Beside them David's work sparkles with wit and invention.' Then he switched to hares again.

+-

Gerald Incandela sat in the cafe with his leather hat from the Ozarks casting a hillbilly shadow across his face, and lambasted the new painting in New York – particularly the set-up behind Julian Schnabel, whose success marks with a vengeance the invasion of PR and advertising into the art world. Here the Saatchis carved a great hole in the Tate to show weak paintings, remarkable only for their size – while back in NYC the backers of his gallery were also ad-men who meticulously and secretly promoted the work through the media with a very clever campaign. Money was no object and each show was sold out to these PR men, creating the illusion of success. While this comes as no surprise in the art market, the fact that this ambivalent world of half-truth has managed to invade the public institutions is a disaster. It's now the turn of painting to receive the sugary brochures of the armaments industry, who produce their weapons for peace. Gerald says that the only hope for the world is its poets, for their language cannot be corrupted, or their product so easily sold.

+-

Over dinner at Norman Rosenthal's we talk about Berlin: the Neue Zeitgeist, the Wall, and the restored museum between the two secret police HQs. Then the conversation drifts to Gilbert and George, and their various, well-publicized obsessions – evensong, rough trade, flower arranging, William De Morgan pots, all held together with an interior designer's chic. They certainly titillate the closet cases of Bond Street where their sartorial style seems like a revolution, reproduces nicely and makes money. In their film there's an image of an immaculate soldier marching on the spot. Land of hope and glory. Would they sit on the fence in their tweeds watching the firing-squads, sipping *beaujolais nouveau*?

+

If we must have troops let's have them in bed. Twenty years ago I was sitting on the seashore at Rhodes watching the ships of the Greek navy. I spotted two figures walking towards me, a young lieutenant and a tough-looking little sailor, both dressed in pristine white. The officer asked me if I would like to hear 'the real Greek music'. I was led to a small apartment where the sailor danced a Dance of the Seven Veils, with a piece of chiffon spangled with silver stars which he trailed very delicately across his bronzed and muscular body. There was bazouki music and we were served sweet coffee. I fucked with the lieutenant behind a screen and later went out dancing to a bar filled with sailors who circled round, each attempting to seduce me.

+

PADELUUN

His home is a PO box number in Berlin. He travels penniless, an artist-mendicant with hollow Kafka eyes, shaved head, and baggy grey trousers tied with string. Whatever dark thoughts he harbours behind a smile and outward serenity they are kept hidden. He believes artists should work, take simple jobs, receive no funds from state or individual beyond what is necessary for the simplest existence. His last job was refilling the contraceptive dispensers at the service areas on the *autobahn* – after he had done the job he would glue on the machine an immaculate sticker in orange, blue and silver, which announced

DIESE MACHINE IST MEIN ANTIHUMANISTISCHES KUNSTWERK

with the PO box-number Padeluun Berlin. This evening we went to see *The Tempest* late-night in Finchley, and discovered that we also had to sit through the emotional slough of *A Bigger Splash*, Jack Hazan's only too revealing film of the sybaritic demi-monde which surrounded David Hockney in the early seventies – the film is an uncomfortable reworking of the hangover after the carefree party of the sixties, at which I had been an extra. I appear for a few brief moments, fortunately disguised in drag, 'revealing all' at Andrew's first Miss World where David had been a judge. Tonight the young audience, many of whom I expect were on the dole, viewed it with a scarcely veiled fury, or laughed with disbelief at the vacuous lives it portrayed, but mixed, I'm certain (though they would never admit it) with a sneaking envy for the easy life of that self-indulgent decade. The butterfly life of the sixties has become the villain, and at the end of the film the young audience hiss. On the whole I agree with them, though the lifestyles they now so readily embrace were forged during those years along with the uncritical enthusiasm that makes the period seem so suspect – I think it will prove harder for Mrs Thatcher to put the clock back than she thinks.

+—

NIGHT LIFE

The apocalypse is fulfilled. It makes little difference now whether the end is delayed four minutes or four decades: the means are there and we live daily with this reality and all our actions are shadowed by it. And what is the proper conduct for an artist living with this enormity – we should go out and slay the dragon.

This evening at the Riverside studios Michael Clarke, a young dancer of supreme artistry, performed the dance, and as he danced raised this question – as to what he should dance. For the dance is so old and alive, and the dance he danced was new, but was dead; as dead as the fragmented universe we live in. Glue, I thought; but what glue to piece together the fragments on the blank canvas bequeathed to us by modernism? In a rush we have revived our own past, every -ism and decade. In Michael's piece the videos flickered and Cerith Wyn Evans moved them with dexterity, and all this was surely done before by Merce and the others who followed him. Then perhaps it had meaning, when with a series of large NOs the old order was hemmed in, trapped. Now surely the time has come to banish the abstract space, fill it with our daily life transfigured.

Michael dances his dance at the edge of time. And if, I thought, if only he danced his own life we should all be transported – but then this was his own life. 'Banish the blank black stage and fill it with a thousand roses,' said John Maybury, and Cerith timidly handed Michael a garland which for a brief moment strangled the artifice. He commanded not only his own body but touched out to ours – dance against the void.

+—

10 NOVEMBER 1983. A PS FOR PAUL

Paul arrives: 'Write something about the cinema you love. The chapter's pretty bleak. Anyone not knowing you might think it embittered . . .'

Michael Clarke dancing, 1983 *(Photo: D. Conway)*

I'm obsessed by the cinema, but the obsession has well-defined parameters. It's a way of analysing the world about me, the garden of earthly delights, and the dirty tricks department. This analysis could easily be undertaken with the pen or paintbrush; I'm not trapped in Film. It was never an ambition, I came to it late and by chance, that's my 'Independence'.

The absence of praise in this chapter, Paul, is due to the fact that the cinema I love hardly exists in this country, and where it exists it is fragmented and discontinuous; it's largely ignored by the mainstream and because of this it's a cinema that is often private, that uses the direct experience of the film-maker, and is more likely to be in 16mm or Super 8 than 35mm. With luck it will have 'real' people, not Equity members who will be characters, not 'ciphers', which is the mid-Atlantic way. The director will have made it without the normal funding mechanism, and he or she will certainly never have worked for a TV company.

In continental Europe this cinema is called THE CINEMA and you will have heard the names of its exponents. They are Godard, Antonioni, Pasolini, Rossi, the Tavianis, Fassbinder, Schroeter and a host of others, but here it is quite likely you may not have heard of Peter Watkins, Bill Douglas, Robina Rose, Terence Davies, Chris Petit, Ron Peck – and forgive me if I include myself – who are their counterparts. The Film establishment will have taken them so 'seriously' as to leave them isolated. It's the same philistinism that runs through our schools and universities straight into the established institutions. There are film-makers in the *Overground* of a previous generation as fine as anything from the continent. Nick Roeg's *Performance* and *Walkabout*, and the early films of Boorman are exceptional. Boorman has championed *Cinema* and enabled Neil Jordan to make *Angel*, one of those rare first features like *Radio On* or *Nighthawks*.

There is a subtle distinction between this work and the ridiculous media posturings of films like *The Ploughman's Lunch*, which could pass for cinema only in this country. Wouldn't it be great if 'they' could be disposed of with the humour of *The Lady Killers*, a really wonderful British film. However I'm afraid it will take more than that because behind 'them' are the Americans who have brought you *Cruise* and *Fame*, and squatted our film to their own profit, and the whole thing's much funnier and sadder and the 'truth' of the matter would quickly lead me into libel. For the English, locked into their institutions struggling for preference, always kill with a smile; and the critics with nothing to write about will continue to replace THE CINEMA with the cinema. That which was made with love will remain a footnote until the Oblivion Digits are finally added up and darkness envelops our world.

X
Dancing Ledge

I have a very low opinion of art and an even lower opinion of what is accepted as art, put high on a pedestal, high as it is possible to make it without rendering it totally invisible. Incarcerated in bunkers, sold, bartered, and reproduced so that even the most potent images are nullified, 'art' is eulogized into something other. Unobtainable, it has a negative function in the education process. Culture begins at school and is completed at university, by which time all aspiration to selfhood is stifled, and the mind is colonized by dead wood. How right Duchamp was to end it all by turning the bottle rack into high art, and how wrongly the message was interpreted! All art is dead, especially modern art. Only when art is demoted to the ranks again, treated as nothing remarkable, will our culture start to breathe. The spurious individualism of the Renaissance, which both engendered and was born of capital, is dying. An art which began by collaborating with the banks of the Medici ends in bankruptcy on Wall St. On the way, it destroyed the sublime anonymity of the Middle Ages and replaced it with stolen goods. Creativity in the future will be measured differently, no longer tied to commodity and worldly success. Then the civilization now vaunted in the media will be no civilization at all, its artefacts as alien as Mayan sculpture.

+-

28 JANUARY 1983 – PSYCHIC TELEVISION

Providence in the form of Genesis P. Orridge arrived today at noon. With my bank account closed and the last of the Italian lira spent I'd started selling clothes and books to raise cash to pay the rent. Hearing this Genesis immediately produced £50, which he said was towards the cost of the Super 8 film I used last September recording William Burroughs at the Final Academy.

Psychic TV has been a constant presence in my life during the last three years. Initially I was surprised by their enthusiasm for *The Tempest* and my Super 8s. I thought they would discount a film like *The Tempest* – but Gen loved it. Magic bound us together. He produced an extraordinary electronic score for *In the Shadow of the Sun*. Since then I've been videoed for the Psychic TV cassettes as the Temple Spokesperson, with the honeyed voice of their tattooist Mr Sebastian, and filmed the Psychic Rally in Heaven with music from the 2nd Annual Report.

TG was the art of communication erased. Its successor, Psychic Television, conducts an investigation into the dark side.

At the moment we connect through Caravaggio, – a painter who captured the Spirit with blood-stained hands. Caravaggio is very much a TG hero.

At the Temple Gen wishes to make available Crowley's diaries and recordings of Burroughs and Gysin; to build a room for the Dream Machine where the acolytes will be able to meditate; issue special editions of the last minutes of the Reverend Jack Jones; investigate Control, immortality, and the disruptive cut-ups which are the core of the Burroughs work-method and philosophy.

Many find the Temple disturbing. Initiation is performed at the Hackney Abaton. Genesis is the androgyne spirit guide, conducting the Divine Sickness for the initiates with their krishna haircuts and austere, grey, 'Chinese' uniforms, stamped with the triple cross.

+—

31 January 1983: Howard Bruckner invited me over to see his Burroughs film for the television 'Arena' WSB, suitably inscrutable, and looking like the mummy of Rameses II, took us on a journey through his life. 'I always had nightmares as a child and when I was told opium gave you sweet dreams I knew it was for me.' And so he spoke, witchdoctor-like, of his marriage, his boyfriends, immortality, and the forgotten art of calling up a toad with a humming noise.

+—

CONTRO I CAPELLI LUNGHI

5 February 1983: Last night at John Maybury's I watched Agnes De Mille, the choreographer, on TV. She spoke, with the slightly alcoholic voice of old people who've suffered a stroke, of the Dance and how much it has changed. The artists are now well paid. But something she described as 'religious' had been lost amid the mortgages and life policies. The girls who worked for Martha Graham gave her five hours a day for virtually nothing. They waited on tables for their money each morning; but in the evenings had the consolation that they were performing in a masterpiece. This dedication seems to have been lost in the world of dance. She added that the social injustices of the period she was talking about had to be done

away with; so there's an inevitability about this situation. Nevertheless, this sense of devotion would have to be recaptured if we were to have vital art.

In the same programme there was an extraordinary TV interview at the height of the McCarthy period with her, Simone Signoret, and Hedda Hopper. After Hopper had castigated *Blackboard Jungle*, Agnes De Mille floored her with an impassioned speech about the right to protest. Hedda Hopper was left speechless, said she had nothing to say. Agnes, sitting on her chair, tapped her stick on the floor, and spoke of her boys as 'stallions'. As I left I remarked to Alasdair, 'We could all do with a few of those.'

If you want to see beauty pick up a book of George Platt Lynes photos from the forties. Nearly every aspect of gay art is prefigured in it, including much of Hockney's work. All the models he used have such clear, strong good looks. *Physique Pictorial* is another example – the models from the forties look alert and intelligent. In the sixties a marked change comes about. Is it all in the eye of the beholder? Is it because the photos are taken in natural light rather than studio light? Or have the models themselves changed, doped out on acid and television? Anyway, they have an air of neglect.

When Pasolini wrote his piece 'Contro i Capelli Lunghi' (Against Long Hair) he probably put his finger on it. He accused the last great binge of capital and consumerism of subverting all the (peasant?) values he held so dear.

At the other end of the political spectrum, Sir Francis Rose once turned up at a gay liberation meeting early in 1970. He waved his corkscrew walking-stick at a gang of boys in 'liberated' drag, covered in diamanté and make-up – 'What we need is men, not fairies!' he declared, loudly and to their disbelief. 'I'm a Grandee of Spain, off to sign the accession papers next week. In Franco's Spain you'll find real men.' And there hangs the dilemma – the reduction of manhood to the gay macho image. Perhaps the just gods heard Sir Francis, and provided a cheap substitute in the shape of the disco clones a few years later. See them at 4 a.m. pile out of Heaven on a Saturday night, whacked out on nicotine and amyl, and you know you're still in middle-class fairyland. They've got the muscles, but their minds have been locked safely in the closet.

Howard Bruckner told me that when Burroughs received a book called *Faggots* he absolutely refused to write a jacket-cover comment. He remarked that the freedom to fist-fuck in the Hamptons was no freedom at all. 'Gay liberation,' he said, 'is no liberation.' It had resulted only in the complete takeover of the homosexual world by dead-end bourgeois values. Something that was only too noticeable, said Howard, in all the gay club circuits. What we need, said William, is a gay state with our own soldiers, who'd kill anyone who attempted to disagree.

This could be started by a guerrilla movement which would blackmail rich gays – a form of taxation, said William, and use the funds to eliminate any opposition to gay life.

WSB with his customary wisdom dreams up a dream gang of Wild Boy assassins. Deep down the dream of many of us. Outside it is snowing.

+

VISIBLE MANIFESTATIONS

The dungeon redoubts of the gay world are its clubs with names like the Asylum, the Catacombs, the Mineshaft. The gay Heaven is also deep underground; though the 9th Circle is above. *Exotique* foreign names abound – Copacabana, La Douce. Down in the dungeons the inmates shout themselves hoarse against the disco music and lasers, which furthers a delicious alienation. This world eschews the overground reality which rejects it, and seeks perfection in an ideal favoured by low lights, denim, leather and the rest. Signs are important – rings on fingers and limp wrists are replaced by running shorts and vests, work-out muscles and moustaches. These in turn fall to the Haircuts.

The next day, as I look down from my window in the sunlight on Charing X Road, I see these drained, pallid faces of the night on their way to the YMCA; the fetish for 'health' the guilty reverse of the night before. Today the gay liberation march winds past. This has an air of festival. Two immaculate pink nuns with moustaches neat as clipped box take the prize. A 'lady' in a ball-gown drops out and rests languidly on the City of Westminster salt bin in front of St Martin's . . . A pink balloon escapes and circles high in the blue sky . . .

In the Mineshaft, New York City, the microbes take a Charles Atlas course – and a famous and very old man drifts past quite in the pink and into the shadows. I make a mental note of a 'decent' retirement age – but know I won't bring myself to put myself out to grass. We all know these habits are possibly damaging, but you pays your dues and takes your chances. In Ron Peck's film *Nighthawks* I played a very creditable cruiser, so lost in myself I burnt my fingers instead of the cigarette.

Usually self-preservation prevails and I'm home by two. The disastrous late nights are wrought by the unattainable barmen whom the wicked managements spread like jam.

I know the arguments against all this and am certain they have their own fair share of the truth. But I live and work in a single room which I share with some books and large sheets of blank writing-paper; so unless I make some foray into the night I could spend twenty-four hours alone. Though that's unlikely, and an excuse. The place is usually so crowded. Hardly a day goes past without the doorbell ringing at tea-time. So perhaps it's just an escape into delicious anonymity. Particularly now when everyone I meet above ground asks me what I'm working on. The price of being a film-maker is that the most visible part of you is your work; you yourself become the shadow. If you say, 'I'm doing nothing – Oh fuck film! it's really not important and who cares about it anyway,' they look discomfited. 'Surely you must take all of this seriously?' A negative answer casts a disturbing cloud, 'You have to believe in something.'

In the dungeons pure anonymity prevails and the opening line is much more likely to be, 'Can I get you a drink?' – vodka with ice: much more comforting.

And what else? Well, dressing is Fancy Dress. Down here this COUNTS. It's the real test of a person's sexual orientation – the styles forged in the dungeon slip over into the world outside. But here they are a code – the jeans with that exact tear, the leather jacket and white T-shirt. Why not go to Heaven in a suit and tie? In the Mineshaft they turn you away for wearing aftershave. Elsewhere, a dress is OK, but the suit and tie of the real world is for punters with stuffed pockets. The HAIRCUTS buy theirs second-hand.

I consciously adopt the denim/leather look most nights. I'm assured I don't look like a clone. I have a phobia about moustaches like some people have for spiders – I couldn't conceive of touching one.

Back in 1965 La Douce opened its doors on Friday evening and closed them early on Monday. We danced through the weekend on purple hearts. Those without a bed slept in the Biograph Cinema before starting out again.

Drugs are never far from the scene. After the hearts came Acid and quaaludes; then amyl, and something called Ecstasy. Someone always managed to roll a joint in a dark corner, and dance away into the small hours. It's certain that nobody who had taken the steps towards liberation hadn't used one if not all of them. The equation was inevitable, and part of initiation.

Now, from out of the blue comes the Antidote that has thrown all of this into confusion. AIDS. Everyone has an opinion. It casts a shadow, if even for a moment, across any encounter. Some have retired; others, with uncertain bravado, refuse to change. Some say it's from Haiti, or the darkest Amazon, and some say the disease has been endemic in North America for centuries, that the Puritans called it the Wrath of God. Others advance conspiracy theories, of mad Anita Bryant, secret viral laboratories and the CIA. All this is fuelled by the Media, who sell copy and make MONEY out of disaster. But whatever the cause and whatever the ultimate outcome the immediate effect has been to clear the bath-houses and visibly thin the boys of the night. In New York, particularly, they are starting to make polite conversation again – a change is as good as a rest. I decide I'm in the firing-line and make an adjustment – prepare myself for the worst – decide on decent caution rather than celibacy, and worry a little about my friends. Times change. I refuse to moralize, as some do, about the past. That plays too easily into the hands of those who wish to eradicate freedom, the jealous and the repressed who are always with us.

+–

THE ANCIENT MARINER

16 June 1983: At the Salisbury this afternoon a group of us were discussing sleep – five hours, six or eight – when a stocky young guy in a white T-shirt and close-cropped hair, who had been listening to us, interrupted and said that you could make do with two: 'We only needed two in the Falklands.' The words were like a squall in a calm sea. 'But surely that was a special case, under duress.' A silence fell over us for half an hour while, half-boastful and half-appalled, he told us his tale, as if to confess was to eradicate the horror. He told us of his two mates who died, of the 'Argies', the atrocities, and the Gurkhas – excellent men, who wore suits, were polite and tough as hell, and who cut the throats of their victims, 'to save lives', he added. The Argie conscripts were boys with no will to fight, and in the heat of it our boys shot them even as they put their hands in the air to surrender. This was done 'to save lives', and also out of anger.

As I looked at him I thought of the picture-book heroism of war, with its rules of good conduct – invented to cover the unhinged horror. I felt immensely depressed. In any other situation I'd have picked this boy up and taken him home to bed. As it was, I slipped away with an excuse and left him propping up the bar alone, waiting to tell his appalling tale of muddled heroism to the next trick.

+–

BLOW-JOB

The guy propping up the bar said he worked for the army, interrogating the SAS who fell into his hands during exercises. There wasn't one, he claimed, who after half an hour in his hands didn't accept as reality what before had been only make-believe.

He said rather nonchalantly *à propos* of the Bulgarian regime, which is doing away with people by means of poison pellets like Beatrice Lillie in ever so modern Millie – that we'd had the stuff for years, and there was one prominent victim, Hugh Gaitskell. When I asked him who fired the dart he changed the subject. Perhaps they were just testing the stuff.

+-

JUNE 1978

Anna Piaggi told me of the hot springs at Ischia. I had visions of waterfalls and hot rock pools at the sea's edge. When Jean Marc and I arrived there yesterday morning these hopes were dashed. The Bagni are housed in a seedy municipal building where the yellow-tiled cubicles are guarded by attendants in crumpled white uniforms. They stand guard in the room with you and turn the taps on and off. Ten minutes only as the water is 'radioactiva'. This makes for an extremely uncomfortable bath.

Later in the day I passed a group of soldiers lounging outside a cafe. One of them smiled at me when he saw me admiring him, and we commenced an evening of minimal communication at coffee bars and on park benches with his friends After a couple of hours of this aimless drifting around the town I asked him if he would like to come back to my hotel. He said he couldn't possibly stay at my hotel as it was far too dangerous, but if I went and got my passport he knew of a place we could go to.

In Enneo's hotel the old desk porter copied my name into the ledger with studied disinterest. My soldier boy came from a village near Palermo, was doing his national service before returning to work as a farmer and marry his girlfriend. He was a wonderful lover – we exchanged addresses and swore eternal friendship although we both knew we would never meet again. He left to get back to the barracks. As I walked home it occurred to me that the desk porter and my young soldier had probably shared the payment for my room. If they did the whole evening had been arranged with amazing finesse.

+-

ROME, 1982

Sexuality colours my politics – I distrust all figures of authority, including the artist. Homosexuals have such a struggle to define themselves against the order of things, an equivocal process involving the desire to be both 'inside' and 'outside' – a source of that dis-ease in the work of Caravaggio and Pasolini. I distrust those with blueprints for our salvation. As a group we have suffered more than most at the hands of the ideologically 'sound'. One day my Roman driver stopped singing Puccini at the top of his voice, and began talking about modern composers. Berio, he said, was a case of *'testa di sinistra, stomacho di destra'* – he was progressive in his head but reactionary in his guts.

+—

In Italy young men live with their families, have girlfriends and get married. The idea of the family remains intact, and the power of the Church has seen to it. However, most Italian boys lead bisexual lives, particularly in the brief time they are away from their families doing national service. Soldiers give themselves for a good meal or an evening's drinking. The encounters are brief and forgotten in the morning. Sexuality has a value, and *bella figura* its price. Italy is in love with outward show. Clothes, cars, the material goods that have overwhelmed a rural society in the last thirty years are consciously exhibited. This is the world that Pasolini so detested, and so accurately mirrored. In Rome the homosexual world is furtive. There are a few clubs in which overdressed boys flaunt themselves. Apart from that there is the sex of the streets – in cinemas, outside railway stations, and in the parks where married men cruise endlessly in their cars.

+—

UNA VITA VIOLENTA

Encounters in the parks are shadowed with violence. While I was in Rome working on *The Rake* I was attacked late at night on the Capitoline hill by a gang of youths, out for the kill. I was being kicked and punched senseless on the ground for a 1,000 lira, or was this the motive? Somehow an icy calm took over. I felt nothing as the boots went in and managed to collect myself and soliloquize in broken Italian *'Amici romani . . .'* Two of the boys held off as the others rifled my pockets and one carried on the assault. I managed to get up and turn my back. Half-expecting a knife I walked away.

As with rape victims, it's almost impossible to communicate this after the event. I kept my silence. Next day, the bruises were mostly covered by my clothes. Back in Florence a day later, I told the rehearsal pianist; the next morning he quietly motioned me over and showed me the newspaper. That night a businessman from Turin had been murdered in exactly the same spot.

+—

Romans are bad lovers and good fucks – men living together in supportive relationships few.

Pier Paolo, living with his mother and hitting the streets nightly to give blow-jobs to his street boys, illustrates the situation well. Though open, his sexuality was a tortured confusion, made worse by the Communist Party's adoption of bourgeois restraint. In *Salo*, his last film, all homosexual relationships are shown as decadent, unpleasant and power-based. At the centre of the film is a significant line of betrayal. Photos of loved ones lead the inquisitors on a hunt to destroy the last vestiges of private and pure relations.

At the end of the line of betrayal Pasolini exhibits a STEREOTYPE, and surely one that was not in his heart. The young soldier and the black serving-girl are found in bed together by the Fascist 'masters'. Standing naked and defiant, the boy gives a clenched fist salute, before they are both murdered in a hail of bullets.

+

Holland Park, 1976: 11.30, summer evening, cruising. A handsome-looking guy lures me into a dark corner between two buildings and before I know it two of them jump me, flashing their cards – name and addresses, all the usual aggression. 'What are you doing here?' It seems the silliest of questions. 'It's a beautiful summer night.' Mind working overtime – 'I was coming back from my film *Sebastiane* at the Gate cinema up the road. I live in Earl's Court. Have you seen the film?' I get away with this one by the skin of my teeth. It's obviously OK if you're a published middle-class queen. On Hampstead Heath different rules apply – hide and seek. They arrive after midnight with searchlight torches and whistles. The quarry scatter and run like gazelles in one of those African wildlife films, and only the foolish are caught. One night they broke the rules and brought dogs; and on another, tried to run people down on their motorbikes. But by dawn, when Michael Foot walks his dog, all is quiet again.

Raids on gay clubs follow different patterns. The last full-scale raid that I was involved with, in the mid-seventies, closed down the Gigolo in the King's Road. Saturday night, the place is packed to capacity. In the darkness at the far end people are making out. One tall, very handsome boy wades into the throng. He seems oblivious to the attention his presence is causing. He doesn't have a hard-on. I give up and stand at the bar. Three minutes later, whistles. It's a police raid. At the back the unreceptive one is in a fist-fight with a couple of leather boys. The panic is so great that I am carried at least ten feet by the surge of the crowd. Quick thinking: I empty my pockets deftly. We wait for hours in silence while each customer is given a body-search. I remember the two ladies in Port Said – oh for a bit of the English fighting spirit! But they know they've got you, this riff-raff in uniforms. The Gigolo is closed down for ever after ten years.

The British police have degenerated rapidly in the twenty years I've been in London. They watch too many American TV series. They drive through the streets risking life and limb, are surly, rude, and by turns, aggressive when they stop you. One suspects that they lie through their teeth when giving evidence; and that most of them accept bribes and pay-offs. Dealing with them you have a certain unfair advantage with a middle-class accent. Gone for ever are the days of Dixon. 'Crime' is now fought with criminal methods. Howard Bruckner says that if an American cop behaved the way they do here he would remain alive for only a few hours: too many of his adversaries pack guns. Christian says that in Moscow you hardly ever see a policeman. Here they are everywhere, protecting the degenerate establishment. A gang of uniformed hoodlums.

+—

VISIBLE MANIFESTATIONS 2

A club, the Subway, has closed its doors after two years of sweaty nights. Neither the Metropolitan Police, nor the iron guards of the Moral Majority, nor yet the semi-detached minds of *Gay News* (that sister to the *Daily Star*) will shed a tear. London has lost quite the best gay bar that I remember. It had some of the best music in London, showed the latest videos in rooms quiet enough to have a conversation in, and had the capital's first back-rooms.

Back-room sex can be the sweetest and most transient. The imagination runs riot. Earthbound minds suddenly take on angelic bodies, and the anonymity is a treasure.

+—

At twenty-three I thought my itinerant sexuality would be over by thirty; but at forty it is even easier to meet the young men I desire than when we were the same age. The company of younger men becomes infectious. On the other hand, most of my contemporaries have been pinned out by the media, like butterflies. So few of them took evasive action. Most did the expected and died in a confetti of polaroids around swimming-pools, or lost their way in a snowstorm of drugs in rich living-rooms.

+—

His body is hard, like marble, and flawless. His face is tough, utterly nondescript, chipped like an old statue – a lip damaged from a punch. He's wearing jeans and a black vest. There is a home-made tattoo on his right shoulder. He puts his beer on

Photograph by George Platt Lynes *c.* 1942

'Sunset Boulevard', 1950s – outside
Gloria Swanson's home *(Physique Pictorial)*

Andy in his chair, 1983 – Phoenix House

the space invaders machine and plays it till two, then walks into the back-room, unzips, and produces the biggest, thickest cock I've ever seen – it is hard as rock. In the reddish gloom he fucks one figure after another, none lasting long as he brings them to orgasm swiftly and deftly. One after another without a moment's rest.

+–

Until I was in my early thirties I avoided passive sex. Inhibition and social conditioning made it a traumatic and painful experience. This was hard to overcome. But now I know that until I'd begun to enjoy it I had not reached balanced manhood. You must make the sacrifice to bury the centuries. When you overcome yourself you understand that gender is its own prison. When I meet heterosexual men I know they have experienced only half of love.

+–

PILGRIM FATHERS

Allen Ginsberg describes a family tree which starts with Walt Whitman and ends with himself, along the biblical lines – Walt slept with . . . who slept with . . . who slept with me – a chain which spanned the generations. There is nothing exceptional in this apart from the social diversity of these encounters. Subservience to Family and State remains the pattern from here to China – homosexuality can cut across this sad world – sexual encounters lead to knowledge.

+–

ANDY

27 March 1983: Andy has painted the ceiling of his flat in Wenlake House, but left the walls the faded ochre plaster he found after stripping the wallpaper. On the walls he has drawn the furniture he's been making to scale in fine pencil sketches. Apart from the furniture the room is bare. There are two armchairs, some stools and a table built from old timber, floorboards and joists. Andy's furniture is based on carpenters' tables and workbenches, and looks Victorian in its solidity – Pugin would have approved. It has a sly sense of humour: one of the chairs has two panels from an Argentine corned-beef crate let into its sides.

Andy brews up coffee and sits at the table, his black hat pulled down over his eyes. He produces various prizes for us to admire – a book of thirties' interiors, photos he took in Japan last December. Michael asks Andy how long he's lived in Wenlake House. Andy says he's had the flat since, 'as yellow as a Swan Vestas packet', he turned up daily at the Islington Housing Department at the height of his hepatitis. His presence cleared the packed waiting-room. The other occupants huddled like hamsters in a crush down one end while Andy coughed loudly in a corner.

Andy is allergic to authority. Policemen and council officials are top of the list, then politicians and ticket-collectors. In the Housing Department he threatened to spit like a deadly cobra until he was given a place to live. Worn down, they eventually threw the keys across the room.

Andy has a GBH manner which he wears under a black peaked Japanese schoolboy's cap and combat jacket, accentuating his black sunken eyes. His moth-eaten haircut, his fingernails, bitten to the bone on scarred hands, suggest menace. Screwed up with concentration, his face instils fear into officialdom – a frown that's a blow beneath the solar plexus. Aware of this, Andy plays up the aggro. But the look is a weapon and a disguise. The other Andy bubbles up with stories of his adventures related with brilliant timing, full of startling language. To a parting 'Be good!' he always responds, 'I'll be careful.'

+—

May 1978, Hanway Works: I was phoned on Friday evening by a prison visitor who asked me if I'd stand bail for 'Andy', who was in Ashford Remand Home for stealing a large American car near the Hilton and crashing it fifty yards further on. At first I wondered who Andy could be; then I remembered meeting a wild-looking boy at a club on two or three occasions, who countered my interest with belligerence; but who in spite of hs 'fuck off' attitude accepted a couple of drinks and my phone number on the silver paper from a cigarette packet. That was the last time I'd seen him, several weeks ago. I walked around to the police station in Tottenham Court Road and put up the bail with a slight degree of misgiving – but the woman who rang had said I was the only one who could help him.

On Saturday afternoon I took the train to Ashford. The Remand Centre is hidden behind neat thirties' row houses with gardens, and looks like a military installation or gulag with its twenty-feet-high concrete and wire perimeter fence, searchlights and guard posts – before you reach the drab institutional buildings. In the rain it looked very bleak and depressing. As I walked up the path boys shouted at me from the windows like caged animals. I waited in the hall until Andy was brought down shouting abuse at one of the warders – 'An' if you lay a fuckin' finger on me mate . . .' I spirited him away as quickly as possible. I could detect they were quite pleased to be rid of him as he's immensely strong and quite capable of inflicting damage when his temper's wild – most of the time he seems tensed for a fight. On the train back Andy spoke with bravado of his Robin Hood exploits, and of his enemies the pigs and the screws. It was a simple conflict between good and evil and a question of who was in control. At Ashford, when a difficult new boy arrived, one of the screws would tell him to fetch something, and then shout at the boy to run. At the end of the corridor a second screw stepped out of a door and intercepted the running boy – shouted at him to stop running, running was forbidden, and sent him back walking. The first screw would shout at him when he returned empty-handed, threaten to beat the living daylights out of him, and send him back at the double. This was repeated, the verbal violence turning into physical violence, until the boy was weeping.

Afterwards, the screws would return home to their families in the thirties' row houses and tend to the cabbages.

+−

At school Andy played truant. He would disappear on summer afternoons and no one could find him. He had a little rowing-boat, and one afternoon his father caught him in it. His secret was discovered and the boat was sold. From that point the trouble started. Andy used to row out to sea in his boat to some sandbanks at low tide; he'd beach the boat and lie in the sun until the tide came in – it was his escape from school and family. Andy's family were Jehovah's Witnesses; when he was fifteen they discovered he was gay and threw him out on the streets saying he was the devil's work and no child of theirs. They refused to communicate with him, even by telephone.

Then he lied about his age and joined a merchant ship in Rotterdam, was arrested for smuggling in New Zealand, and jailed. Back on the streets of London the battle with the authorities was engaged in earnest. His parents had forgotten him: when I contacted them they washed their hands of the whole affair and hung up. At Butlers Wharf we laid plans to break the vicious circle in which he found himself.

+−

September 1980, London: In the West End the police know Andy and use every chance to pull him over. There is one PC in particular who has marked him down. They didn't get him last time, so this time they will. Constant apprehension causes the antagonism to bubble to the surface, which is what they seem to want. If

Christopher and I hadn't seen it ourselves we wouldn't have believed it. Christopher, who has Andy working with him on his plaster casts, has been pulled over with him on two occasions now. The opposition seem determined to turn Andy into a criminal; and we are just as determined they are not going to win. I told Andy yesterday, he'll have to avoid them deftly like a bullfighter, who knows that in a head-on collision he'll lose. He steps aside and lets the beast go charging past. Win with the brain, not the fists.

+—

March 1983: Andy bowls in with a wicked grin. He makes himself some coffee and complains that I've not been to see his work. I promise to, as soon as I've finished the script rewrite of *Caravaggio* with Stephen Pickles. Meanwhile, he gives me some black and white photos of his furniture, some of which are being sent to a firm in Japan who are interested. Last week he spent the night in the cells again after a long absence. He wrenched the exit-door off its hinges at some North London club, and carried it with him on to the dance floor after the bouncers had tried to throw him out. As he danced with the door the management closed in on him and threw him out the front door. He put his shoulder to that as well, and stove it in. He said the police seemed rather amused by this act of strength – it was the sort of thing they were always up to so they understood. Also they disliked the gay club and thought he was some straight boy who had got into a fight. He put them right on that score. 'You think all gay boys are limp-wristed, don't you?' He said they treated him with respect, and he didn't seem too worried about the £150 fine either.

+—

Andy sits in a room of strangers for half an hour or so, sizing up the situation in silence. When he starts to talk he becomes the centre of attention, for he has a brilliant sense of language and his stories stop all other conversation. He rolls up, stretches out, tilting back on his chair, and he's away. Robin Hood and the Sheriff of Nottingham – Andy and the Metropolitan Police. He pushes the Japanese cap back on his head. He delivers instant judgements with clear precision, his nautical adventures having left him with a tidy, perspicacious mind. Other people mumble – he's one of the very few who have no fear. His dark moments are kept to himself, otherwise humour prevails. His physical presence, even in silence, dominates a room.

+—

XI
An Inventory

Conducting an inventory. At forty I have debts of £2,000 to the bank and a further £1,000 to friends. I have no stable income, and although Nicholas hopes to sort things out in Rome, it is always tomorrow. I'm stuck with this project like an iron lung – it's too late to go back, and in any case, impossible to think of anything until *Caravaggio* is completed. I have no car or television. There is no office except for this room, which is eighteen by fifteen feet, painted white and rented. It has a walk-in bathroom and kitchen. There are four built-in cupboards. One is full of paintings by friends. The second is filled with manuscripts for the films. The third contains props and clothes, and the fourth, my Super 8 films and equipment. I've a stereo player with about one hundred tapes, and bookcases with about six hundred books. These are mostly psychology, religious, and architectural texts, biography and art books. There is a large section on Egypt and nineteenth-century exploration, some poetry, and next to no novels. There is a fold-up bed, two chairs, a metal office desk, and some carpenters' stools from the old studio. The pictures on the walls are my own, except for the portrait photo of a young man by Angus McBean. On the mantelpiece above the fire are a folding lantern, a vase of mimosa, an African ceremonial sword carved roughly from an ivory tusk, a flint from Preston, a silvered glass candlestick, and a pewter patten with a Greek inscription. Near the stereo are several treasured objects. A gold leaf from a Greek funerary crown, Anthony's Japanese tea-bowl, and an eighteenth-century plaster cast of the Portland vase. On the window is the friendship tree that Güta Minton gave me in 1965 – beside it the silver lacquer cupboard with my clothes – finally, on the floor, is the plaster cast head of Mausolus with a pink shell balancing on its head.

There is little or no colouring in this room, and the polished wood of the carpenters' stools gives it a slightly monastic look which is reinforced by the pictures and objects, mainly black and silver grey, like the bead altar flowers from Rome which glitter in the night light and the singing saw which stands by the fire.

A year has passed and I've a new chair that Andy has made, and a video monitor which is not connected to Central Control.

XII
Epilogue

From the end of *Jubilee* – July 1977, Dancing Ledge, Dorset.

+

I love these rocks with their emerald-green pools and sea anemones – the sea roaring against the cliffs with their huge silent caves. Jenny changes into her white Elizabeth dress which Christopher has made with lace gloves and great chandelier drop jewels. Her lady-in-waiting, Helen, bustles among the rocks, and David, who plays Ariel, puts in his jet-black contact lenses. The sun comes out fitfully.

+

ELIZABETH: All my heart rejoiceth at the roar of the surf on the shingles marvellous sweet music it is to my ears – what joy there is in the embrace of water and earth.

DEE: Yea – a great elixir is the seashore. Here one can dream of lands far distant, and the earth's treasure.

ELIZABETH: The sea remindeth me of youth. Oh John Dee, do you remember the whispered secrets at Oxford like the sweet sea breeze, the codes and counter-codes, the secret language of flowers.

DEE: I signed myself with rosemary, true alexipharmic against your enemies.

ELIZABETH: And I with yellow celandine, true gold of the new spring of learning. You were my eyes then as now, with your celestial geometry. You laid a path through treachery and opened my prison so my heart flew like a swallow.

DEE: Sweet Majesty, to me you are the celandine now as then before, balm against all melancholy.

ELIZABETH: Ah but I was young then.
ARIEL: There and back there and back
　　　The waves break on the shores of England
　　　The white cliffs stand against the void
　　　We gaze seaward contemplating the night journey
　　　The sun sinks lower
　　　The moon waits to make her entrance
　　　In the south at Tilly Whim
　　　A picture of wind on the sea
　　　In the west a vision of silver dew on a sea of pure gold
　　　In the east a black hoarfrost
　　　The sun eclipsed by the phoenix
　　　In the north a howling chaos into which a black rain falls without ceasing
　　　Now is the time of departure, the last streamer that ties us to what is known –
　　　parts
　　　We drift into a sea of storms.

And now Elizabeth and Dee go along that same great highway, and the light of the air about them seemed somewhat dark, like evening or twilight, and as they walked the phoenix spoke and cried with a loud voice –

COME AWAY

1983 *(Photo: Steve Pike)*